Goodbye to Good-Time Charlie

Goodbye to Good-Time Charlie

**The American Governor
Transformed, 1950-1975**

Larry Sabato
Oxford University

Lexington Books
D. C. Heath and Company
Lexington, Massachusetts
Toronto

Library of Congress Cataloging in Publication Data

Sabato, Larry.
    Goodbye to good-time Charlie.

    Bibliography: p.
    Includes index.
    1. Governors—United States—History. I. Title.
JK 2447.S2   353.9'1'313   78-333
ISBN 0-669-02161-x

International Standard Book Number: 0-669-02161-x

Library of Congress Catalog Card Number: 78-333

To Henry Howell,
one of many
who should have been
governor,

And for B. E. W.

Contents

List of Figures

List of Tables

Preface

The study of state government and politics in the United States has always taken a back seat to an academic and journalistic concentration on the national government. This is perhaps understandable since until recently most of the significant developments and innovations in government originated in Washington, D.C. Moreover, many states were prime examples of how government should *not* be run. Their administrations were often corrupt, inefficient, and either ignorant of or unmoved by a multitude of problems. It is also considerably easier to study the institutions of a national government that are conveniently situated in a single locality. State capitals are strung out over thousands of miles, and every bit of information must be requested from fifty separate centers—an expensive and troublesome proposition.

The American state governors have been neglected as much as the governments they head. This is unfortunate since the governors, especially the more recent ones, represent a rich reservoir of political and administrative talent that can rival that of either branch of Congress, and a case can be made that as many as a dozen recent governors would have made better presidents than some of the occupants of the Oval Office. Major changes in the types of persons serving as governors, as well as the growing power wielded by state executives, have also been ignored, and it is the purpose of this study to catalogue and analyze these changes.

The reader should be cautioned at the outset that this is a *macroscopic* review, and thus it stresses the similarities among governors and states rather than the many differences. Every exception to each generalization cannot be noted in a comparative volume of this size, but the rich diversity in the fifty states should be borne in mind. The American cultures are not as homogenized as television would have us believe! (For a microscopic view of individual states and regions, the reader is referred to the bibliography.)

Not all aspects of the governorship are treated extensively here, again of necessity. Primaries and other party nominating methods, for example, are not included except for the South. An actual evaluation of specific state programs and public administrations is also beyond the scope of this study. These topics, though important, are tangential to the main thesis.

Some topics in the study are analyzed regionally, and a map of the nation's "regions" for the purposes of this work is included in Chapter 1. Scholars have differed in their assignments of regional labels, and a half-dozen states clearly have characteristics of two groupings. Texas is both a Western and a Southern state; Tennessee is a Southern and a Border state; Delaware is a Border and a Northeastern state, and so forth. Some arbitrariness is unavoidable, but an attempt has been made to group states on political, historical, and demographic bases by utilizing many of the sources listed in the bibliography. Admittedly Figure 1-1 represents but one man's opinion; it will hardly end the controversy.

There will also likely be disagreement on some of the choices for the list of "outstanding governors" in Chapter 2. Before the decision for inclusion or exclusion was made, a record of the highlights of each governor's term and career was compiled. More than a dozen governors and former governors, as well as experts in the field of state government, academics, and officials of organizations like the National Governors' Association, were consulted at length. Many of the reference sources on state politics listed in the bibliography were most helpful. The final judgments, however, were my own. While the selection process was rigorous, it did not have the characteristics of a "controlled experiment" by any means, and its subjective nature cannot be denied.

Interviewing was an important component of this study's research, and seventeen incumbent and former governors were interviewed at length. Sometimes an additional interview was conducted with a governor's press secretary or administrative assistant, and informal conversations with capitol reporters were frequently sought. All formal interviews were tape recorded, and the tapes have been preserved. Most governors and their aides permitted their remarks to be taped in full. Some, however, directed that portions were not for attribution and a few asked that the tape recorder be turned off during sensitive parts of the interviews.

Briefer and unrecorded discussions were held with several dozen additional governors on the floors of the 1976 Democratic National Convention in New York City and the Republican National Convention in Kansas City, Mo. Extensive written correspondence with another half-dozen governors was also conducted. Mayor Moon Landrieu of New Orleans, the President of the U.S. Conference of Mayors for 1975-76, gave me an interview and assistance in uncovering new developments in state-local relations. A national perspective on governors was provided by A. James Reichley, a White House consultant. Finally, several questions were asked of Vice President Nelson Rockefeller by his staff on my behalf. (See Appendix B for a complete list of interviews, correspondences, and research trips.)

There are many persons and organizations whose help I wish to acknowledge, for without them this study, which began as my doctoral dissertation, could never have been completed. My dissertation supervisor, Professor Herbert Nicholas of New College, Oxford, rescued me from disasters large and small and provided assistance far beyond the call of duty. I have now seen the truth in one humorous Anglo-American anecdote: "In America students write their professors' theses, and in England it is just the reverse!" My doctoral examiners, Philip Williams and Dr. David E. Butler (both of Nuffield College, Oxford), called my attention to several errors of fact and interpretation.

All of my interviewees, too, deserve my gratitude. Without exception they were very busy persons who freely gave of their time, talents, and rich reminiscenses. Snaring governors was not always easy, and I have Professor D.K. Adams of the University of Keele to thank for two interviews conducted during a 1976 conference on American politics at Staffordshire, England. The staff of governors' offices throughout the United States were most helpful in arranging interviews. The state boards of election responded quickly to innumerable requests as well. For the allocation of guest and floor credentials to the national party conventions (which were harder to procure than moon rocks), I wish to thank staff members of the Democratic and Republican National Committees, former Lt. Governor Henry Howell of Virginia, and officials of the Republican party of Virginia.

Several organizations were the mainstay of my research efforts, and their staffs saved me countless hours. I acknowledge in particular the staffs of the National Governors' Association and the Advisory Commission on Intergovernmental Relations, both of Washington, D.C. Mr. Brevard Crihfield, the executive director of the Council of State Governments, and John Dinsmore and his librarians insured that my stay at the Council's Kentucky headquarters was fruitful. Dr. Herbert Alexander of the Citizens' Research Foundation in Princeton, N.J., shared his voluminous collections on state campaign finance and permitted me to review the galley proofs of his book on the subject. Author Neal Peirce of the *National Journal,* who has written extensively on the governments and politics of all fifty states, opened his impressive files on state government and allowed me to rummage at will. I must also acknowledge the assistance of Paul Freeman, aide to U.S. Senator Gary Hart of Colorado, in securing materials from the Library of Congress, and that of Lillian Glasgow, librarian of Legis 50 (formerly Citizens' Conference on State Legislatures), for her help in matters related to state legislatures.

My research began successfully thanks to the efforts of F.E. Leese and the staff of Rhodes House Library, Oxford. Their assistance throughout the study's preparation was invaluable. Professor Coleman B. Ransone, Jr., of the University of Alabama, whose books on the governorship serve as standard reference works for any student of the subject, was generous with his time and guidance throughout the project. Many of his suggestions have been incorporated in the analysis that follows.

The travel to twenty-five states that was required during the course of my research would have proven prohibitively expensive but for an exceptionally generous grant by the Camp Foundation of Virginia. I gratefully acknowledge the help of Dr. James L. Camp III of the University of Virginia in securing this grant. Additional financial assistance was provided by the Danforth Foundation of St. Louis, Mo., the Rhodes Trust, and the Oxford University Graduate Student Committee. The Institute of Government of the University of Virginia contributed office space, secretarial help, technical equipment, a financial accounting of the Camp Foundation grant, and coordination of all my travels. In particular I wish to thank the Institute director, Professor H. Clifton McCleskey, and staff members Sandra Wilkinson, Angela Kelly, Susan Malone, and Dotti Slaughter.

All of my manuscript typists, Mrs. Josephine Hageman, Mrs. Theresa Bishop, Miss Mary Etta Bishop, and Mrs. Margaret Sabato (who prepared the first draft) and Mrs. Maureen Stone and Mrs. Toni Tattersall (who typed the final copy) were meticulous and professional. Their deciphering skills never failed to amaze and delight me.

Finally, the kudos would be incomplete without mentioning friends throughout the country who put me up, and put up with me. The room, board, and companionship they so freely gave sustained me during my cross-country trek.

Professor Weldon Cooper of the University of Virginia, who encouraged me throughout this endeavor, also insisted that I write a bibliographic essay that could serve as a guide for other researchers in the field. He will be happy to see that yet another of his suggestions has found its way into print.

With all the help I have received in a hundred forms, I have less excuse than most for error, but whatever errors remain are solely my responsibility.

Goodbye to Good-Time Charlie

1

The Governor in American History: An Office Transformed

The state capitols are over their heads in problems and up to their knees in midgets. [1]
—James Reston, *The New York Times,* 1962

There may have been, a decade ago, stronger individual governors in the Big Five States, but never, in this reporter's experience, a group of 50 governors—from New England to Dixie—as capable as the current crop. [2]
—David Broder, *The Washington Post,* 1976

What kinds of persons are elected to head the governments of the fifty states? Are they best described as midgets or giants? Have the changes that have occurred in governors over the last two decades been as significant as the juxtaposition of Reston and Broder's comments would seem to imply?

This study of American state governors attempts to answer these questions by examining the persons who held the office during the quarter-century beginning in 1950 and the political-administrative milieu in which they worked. The analysis herein indicates that both governors and their settings have been transformed. Once parochial officers whose concerns rarely extended beyond the boundaries of their home states and whose responsibilities were often slight within the states, governors have gained major new powers that have increased their influence in national as well as state councils. Once maligned foes of the national and local governments, governors have become skilled negotiators and, importantly, often crucial coordinators at both levels. Once ill prepared to govern and less prepared to lead, governors have welcomed a new breed of vigorous, incisive, and thoroughly trained leaders into their ranks. The implications of all these changes for the federal system, its constituent parts, and the nation as a whole are not insignificant.

The Historical Progression

The title "governor" is one of the few constants throughout American governmental history. [3] Even so, the name is the only aspect of the governorship that has been immune to basic change. The governorship in the 1970s, for example, may be powerful relative to that of two decades ago, but it cannot compare with the strength of most of the colonial governors. As an agent of the crown, the colonial governor served at the king's pleasure (except in Rhode Island and

1

Connecticut where much weaker governors were popularly elected) and exercised broad powers in his behalf.[4] These powers included command of all armed forces, the supervision of law enforcement missions, the appointment of judges and other officials, the convening and dissolution of the legislative body, a veto of legislative acts, and the granting of pardons and reprieves.[5]

As Leslie Lipson has correctly pointed out, the official powers of colonial governors can give an exaggerated impression of their actual influence since colonial sentiment mattered considerably in the enforcement of the laws. There was little patronage at the disposal of the colonial governors, and they did not appoint port and customs officials (thus permitting the colonists to outmaneuver them in the execution of laws like the Navigation Acts).[6] Most important of all, the governors depended on locally elected assemblies for their financial support—a situation that would temper almost any governor's actions.

Still, the colonial governors were powerful and visible enough to be the focal point of the antiroyalist protests leading to the Revolution. It is not surprising, then, that when the newly independent Americans set out to design their state governments, the distrust of colonial executive power led to a weakened governor and a domineering legislature. The broad veto and dissolution powers were among the first to be removed from the governor's repertoire. The governor was seen to be merely the agent who would carry out the legislature's will in a system with strict separation of legislative and executive departments. As a further limitation on executive authority, the governor was given a short, fixed term of office.

The governorship was considerably weakened, as men such as Benjamin Franklin and Thomas Paine argued it should be. At the same time, the efforts of constitution framers like John Adams kept the governorship from being rendered totally impotent in all of the states.[7] The governor was weakest in the states of Pennsylvania, Vermont, Georgia, New Hampshire, and (for a time) Massachusetts that adopted plural executive offices, in which the governor was just the presiding officer of an executive council and in some cases was appointed by the legislature as well. Only in New York under the "Jay Constitution" and later in Massachusetts under its "Adams Constitution" did a strengthened governor with extensive veto and appointment powers emerge.[8]

All but three of the original state constitutions limited the governor's term to one year.[9] John Adams' dictum prevailed: "Where annual elections end, there slavery begins." From Pennsylvania southward, all states had severe restrictions on reeligibility—Georgia, for example, permitted a man no more than a one-year term as governor in any three-year period—and appointment by the legislature was also the rule. North of Pennsylvania, however, the governor was not bound so tightly. While still a weak office in most cases, the governorship in northern states was elective, with legislative selection only when no candidate garnered a majority of the votes. There were no restrictions on reeligibility in these states, and long tenure (as well as the potential for increased influence that accompanied it) often resulted. George Clinton, for example, was governor of New York for six successive three-year terms (1777-1795), and William Livingston held the governorship in New Jersey for fourteen consecutive one-year terms (1776-1790).

The powers and functions assigned to governors in the early state constitutions were almost uniformly limited, though more wide-ranging than might be supposed at first. Every state had some type of "executive council" that variously advised, limited, or overruled the governor. (Only two such councils survive today, in the New England states of Massachusetts and New Hampshire.) While the governors usually had a considerable number of appointments to make, legislative confirmation of their choices was a prerequisite.

Most legislative powers, by contrast, had no executive check. No longer could governors dissolve the assembly and, except in Massachusetts and New York, there was no provision for a veto. Still, the governor could usually call special sessions of the legislature and in a few states actually participate in the proceedings of the legislature. Judicial powers given to the governors were no more extensive than their legislative ones. Except for their role in judicial appointments, governors were virtually powerless in the judicial field. Even the pardoning power, a traditional executive prerogative, was qualified by special prohibitions and the need for conciliar consent.

In sum there were many checks and few balances in the governorships designed by the early state constitutional conventions. One North Carolina delegate returning home from his convention was asked how much power the governor had gotten. "Just enough to sign the receipt for his salary," was his reply.[10] Only the governor's military position was a strong one, with all states designating the governor as commander-in-chief.

In most states the governors were clearly subordinated to the legislature. James Madison called the governors "in general little more than cyphers" when compared to the "omnipotent" legislatures.[11] Still, some power was given to the executive even by the mistrustful constitutional fathers—a significant admission that discretionary executive authority was necessary to some degree. That the degree granted was not great enough became apparent during the years between the end of the Revolutionary War and the start of the Constitutional Convention in 1787. One scholar, in condemning the results of Virginia's executive limitations, described the situation that existed in almost all the new-born states:

The executive apparatus which emerged from the [1776 Virginia Constitutional] Convention was weak in constitutional stature, confused in lines of authority, and wholly and irresponsibly subservient to the legislative will.[12]

The governorship in this sorry position might be likened, in at least one respect, to the vice presidency of the United States as it has existed for much of the country's history. The early enfeebled governorship sometimes served as a harmless repository for ambitious and frequently capable politicians who were out of favor with "establishment" forces—a kind of "kicking upstairs" that also gave the United States some of its vice presidents. Patrick Henry of Virginia, for one, was elected governor in 1776 by this process. As Rowland Egger sized it up, the Virginia governorship was:

... designed to provide institutional care, under properly septic [sic] conditions, for politicians at the margin of the oligarchy whose popularity could not be altogether ignored.[13]

The restricted Virginia model, however, can give a slightly distorted picture of the early governor, as Joseph Kallenbach has warned. Limited though they were, the designs of the first states served as a resource lode from which a strong presidency was later extracted:

Taking all the state constitutions into account, essentially all the major elements that were later combined in the creation of a strong national chief executive were found in one or more state plans.[14]

The New York and Massachusetts constitutions, in particular, provided models for the 1787 Constitutional Convention. Those states without strong governors served, in a sense, as negative models since they advertised the results of executive enfeeblement. Finally, most of the men who held the office of governor in the immediate post-Revolution era were distinguished and capable persons. Their temperaments and administrations provided considerable reassurance to a public very wary of executives.

From Jackson to Progressivism

The governorship, in turn, benefitted gradually from the example of the presidency, and during the robust presidency of Jackson the governor's term was lengthened, usually to four years, and appointive, veto, and pardoning powers were initiated or broadened in many states.[15] Well-publicized instances of legislative corruption and incompetence lent impetus to the movement for a strengthened governorship. Adding to the governor's basic legitimacy and representativeness was the universal institution of an elected governorship and the expansion of the suffrage.

Jacksonian democracy, however, was hardly a panacea for the governor's ills. Rather, the seeds of executive disaster were sown in this period with the adoption of the "long ballot." More and more public offices were filled by popular election, and an often ill-informed electorate decided the occupants of offices that a governor should, by all administrative logic, have been able to fill by appointment. This loss of administrative control caused a corresponding loss of coordinated action. Governors were many times hamstrung by the executive departments they were supposed to rule. The plural elective executive was democracy's excess, and governors as well as their peoples were to suffer the consequences for many decades. (Indeed, state governments still are paying a considerable price for long ballots, which persist in spite of all the evidence of their undesirability.)

The situation reached its nadir in the 1880s and 1890s as urban citizens demanded an increase in state services. Old and new agencies grew like Topsy at the behest of the legislatures. In New York, for example, there were only 10 state agencies in 1800. By 1900 the number had mushroomed to 81, and by 1925 the state bureaucracy claimed 170 constituent parts.[16]

The governors were unable to exert control over this multitude of new agencies. Instead they were the dominions of special boards and commissions (normally appointed by the legislatures at least in part) or other elected executive officials. So paltry had the governor's authority become that by 1888 James Bryce could write: "Little remains to the Governor except his veto. . . . State office carries little either of dignity or of power."[17] Nevertheless he hastened to add: "A State Governor . . . is not yet a nonentity."[18]

The wisdom of Bryce's proviso can be seen in the actions of many governors in the Progressive era. Gubernatorial leadership was a major factor in the success of Progressive legislation in many states. State executives like Robert LaFollette of Wisconsin, Hiram Johnson of California, Theodore Roosevelt of New York, and Woodrow Wilson of New Jersey channelled the revulsion felt by the populace at the revelations of corruption and squalor into successful programs of reform.

The governorship, never really strong since colonial days, became a more prestigious office as a result of the battles with industry and party bosses fought by many of its occupants. The reform impulse meant added influence for the governors, if only temporarily. Governor Woodrow Wilson claimed: "The whole country . . . is clamoring for leadership, and a new role, which to many persons seems little less than unconstitutional, is thrust upon our executives."[19]

Despite the increased prestige, though, the governorship was not empowered to break the heavy chains that bound it to a minor role in government. Governors had neither the basic constitutional and statutory authority nor the control over their own branch of government that would have been necessary for them to loom larger. Even Wilson admitted that he would not be able to accomplish his plans fully because of the development ". . . not systematically but by patchwork and mere accretion [of] the multiplication of boards and commissions."[20] At base, governors did not have authority to match their responsibility. As the acknowledged political leaders of the states, they were the focus of public attention and were expected to solve perceived problems, but a myriad of institutional handicaps kept them from fulfilling either the public's or

their own expectations for performance. The disappointment and disillusionment resulting from the governor's failure caused a demanding public to look
elsewhere for action.

The Modern Decline of the Governorship

Several developments on the national level in this century also served to relegate
states and their governors to a position of secondary importance both in fact and
in the public's eyes.[21] The Sixteenth Amendment to the U.S. Constitution,
ratified in 1913, gave the federal government a vitally important tool: the
income tax. The federal government's utilization of this tax instrument, and the
effective monopolization of revenue sources that accompanied it, gave Washington "the most powerful advantage of all" in the long run. The centralization
involved in the preparation for and participation in World War I also shifted
attention to the national level.[22]

The Great Depression was an even more crucial milestone for the states,
which had neither the resources nor in many cases the will to combat the era's
massive social problems. First, of course, the Depression's causes were national
and international in scope, and any single state was helpless to effect an overall
solution. However, the inefficient and illogical machinery of state government
was wholly unprepared to administer successfully even piecemeal remedies. The
times called for decisive action, which the governors and the states were unable
to provide. The citizenry turned instead to Washington, and President Franklin
Roosevelt captured the nation's imagination and ministered attentively to the
hopes of the country. Terry Sanford of North Carolina, a governor-turned-
academic, observed:

From the viewpoint of the efficacy of state government, the states lost their
confidence, and the people their faith in the states; the news media became
cynical, the political scientists became neglectful, and the critics became
harsh.[23]

State governments did not cease functioning after the 1930s nor did they
remain unchanged. Most observers believe that state administration became
increasingly complex.[24] Coleman Ransone asserts that "... the functions of the
states increased markedly" even during the period of their greatest eclipse, from
the New Deal forward.[25] However, the gap in authority, responsibility, and
citizen confidence between national and state governments widened considerably; as the federal government reformed and expanded at a rapid rate, the
distance between the performances on national and state levels became more
apparent.

The critics, as Sanford noted, did indeed become harsh. In 1949 Robert S.
Allen issued a severe indictment of the states:

State government is the tawdriest, most incompetent, and most stultifying unit of the nation's political structure. In state government are to be found in their most extreme and vicious forms all the worst evils of misrule in the country. . . . Further, imbedded between the municipalities at the bottom and the federal system on top, state government is the wellspring of many of the principal poisons that plague both.[26]

Allen's criticism was well-grounded and documented by the states themselves. A litany of evils is conjured up by state government researchers. Corruption existed in a thousand forms. Ignorance of social needs and the consequent crippling of cities was widespread. Outright incompetence was the standard in some states. Violation of basic constitutional rights was not unheard of. Malapportionment and unjust representation in the legislatures frustrated the popular will. Special interests, vested economic powers, and political machines dominated one or more branches of state governments.

The situation seemed to change little, for in the mid-1960s Terry Sanford could still catalogue a list of state ills not unlike those of Robert Allen:

The states are indecisive.

The states are antiquated.

The states are timid and ineffective.

The states are not willing to face their problems.

The states are not responsive.

The states are not interested in cities.

These half-dozen charges are true about all of the states some of the time and some of the states all of the time.[27]

Governors contributed to and were victimized by this state of affairs. Allen had exempted some enlightened governors from blame since they were ". . . sadly thwarted and frustrated by the stifling inadequacies and imbecilities of state government," but enlightened governors were "pathetically few in number."[28]

Harold J. Laski believed that state governments were so hopeless that the governors elected to head them were either "second rate politicians" who were merely satisfying generalized ambition for public office or future national political stars whose careers in state politics were "no more than a stage in an ascent."[29] Laski insisted that ". . . the significance of the governor is set in the framework of his federal ambitions rather than of his purposes in the state."[30] Some academics and government officials predicted, and governors feared, that the federal system would dissolve, thereby leaving the states as mere administrative regions of the national government. Governors, it was thought, would fade further into the obscurity they so richly deserved.

A Reversal of Fortunes

The converse of these predictions comes closer to the truth. Instead of obscurity, governors have achieved wide public recognition. According to a 1972 Louis Harris Survey: "Governors are easily the best known political figures in the country" with the sole exception of the president. Almost nine out of ten people could correctly identify their governors, while only about six out of ten could accurately name at least one U.S. senator from their states.[31]

In 1976 a governor was elected president of the United States. Other governors were the closest contenders for each major party's nomination. The advocacy of state prerogatives became so respectable that both presidential nominees (one an incumbent president) spent the campaign from atop "anti-Washington" soap boxes. While part of this phenomenon in 1976, of course, was the result of short-term disillusionment from the deceitful failure of the Indochina War and the breach of faith implicit in the Watergate scandals, the enhancement of the governors and their dominions, the states, is the product of much more.

A glance at the annual governors' messages to the state legislatures indicates the change in the tone and quality of governors in the last quarter-century. In 1951 the "state of the state" proposals were dominated by civil defense, highway construction, and "efficiency" measures necessary to cut "waste" in state government.[32] Governors advocated "tax relief" instead of services. Scores of social and urban needs were scarcely mentioned, if at all. The programs that were advocated by progressive governors were noteworthy precisely because they were so exceptional. By 1975 the agenda conceived by the governors was a crowded one.[33] A wide range of social, health, and education programs with devotion to urban needs in particular was evident. Mass transportation (not just highways), environmental issues (like land-use planning), penal reform, campaign finance overhaul, consumer protection measures, and no-fault auto insurance were repeatedly discussed. Of special concern was the adoption of tax reform (rather than "relief") by making broad-based individual and corporate taxes more progressive while reducing the regressive sales and property taxes. Innovations in all of these policy areas now abound in the states,[34] and the federal government has found itself outstripped in several fields.

This change has not gone undetected. Academics hailed the states' attempt to shake off their cobwebs and noted that simultaneously ". . . governors have moved from low-visibility and low-activity to positions of more positive executive leadership within the states and the nation."[35] The public also seemed to sit up, take notice, and nod approval. The Louis Harris Survey in July 1976 found that ". . . a dramatic shift in public confidence away from the federal government to state government" had taken place.[36] By a two-to-one margin, the federal government was judged to give the taxpayer less value for the tax dollar than the states, and by seven to one, the public saw the federal government as more wasteful. By a lopsided 62 to 12 percent margin, state government was seen to be "closer to the people." All of these results reversed the conclusions of similar Harris surveys taken during the 1960s.

Many of the governors who served throughout this century have been variously described as "flowery old courthouse politicians," "machine dupes," "political pipsqueaks," and "good-time Charlies." This does not fairly describe *all* past governors by any means; some governors in the early part of the twentieth century, for example, could rival any of today's number. Still, it is reasonably clear to American political observers that a greater percentage of the nation's governors are capable, creative, forward looking, and experienced. As Governor Reubin Askew of Florida, himself one of the impressive new breed, commented:

I would be hard-pressed to tell you of any governor in the country right now who I did not believe was capable. . . . I have known of some in the past. But I know every governor personally . . . and it's one of the things that intrigues me—how the country has produced a lot of good men and women as governors today.[37]

Former Governor William Scranton of Pennsylvania gave higher marks to more recent governors than to his contemporaries: "They [the new governors] have a harder job, more to do, and I think they do better at it."[38]

While the trend to better quality governors has become clear, the reasons for the movement have not. It is the purpose of this study to examine the governors over the period of change (1950 to 1975) and determine those reasons. First, the 312 persons who served as governor over the twenty-five-year period will be scrutinized, and their careers surveyed. Then the structural alterations in state governments that have taken place of late will be analyzed, and the metamorphosis in the personal powers and perquisites of the governors will be assessed. A look at the revisions in the rules of state elections and the transformation in party competition follows. The important relationship between states and the other layers of the federal system—national and local governments—will provide additional evidence of a remolded governorship. Lastly, the recent resurrection of the governorship as a route to the ultimate prize in American politics, the presidency, will be discussed. Perhaps after all of these topics are thoroughly examined, we will be able to divine why the states, by and large, have bade goodbye to good-time Charlie.

Notes

1. As quoted in Andrew M. Scott and Earl Wallace, *Politics USA: Cases on the American Democratic Process,* 4th ed. (New York: Macmillan, 1974), p. 90.
2. *The Washington Post,* June 12, 1976.

3. Only New Hampshire and Georgia ever designated the executive head differently—by calling him "president"—and this was for only a brief time after the Revolutionary War. Since 1792 the title of "governor" has been universally used in the states.

4. Joseph E. Kallenbach, *The American Chief Executive: The Presidency and the Governorship* (New York: Harper & Row, 1966), pp. 3-5. See also Evarts B. Greene, *The Provincial Governor in the English Colonies of North America,* Vol. 7, Harvard Historical Studies (New York: Longmans, Green, 1898).

5. Bennett M. Rich, *State Constitutions: The Governor,* State Constitutional Studies Project. Series 11, No. 3 (New York: National Municipal League, 1960), pp. 1-2; and Leslie Lipson, *The American Governor: From Figurehead to Leader* (Chicago: University of Chicago Press, 1949), pp. 9-11.

6. Lipson, ibid., p. 11.

7. W.F. Dodd, "The First State Constitutional Conventions, 1776-1783," *American Political Science Review* 2 (November 1908):1545-61.

8. The structure of each state's executive can be found in the original state constitutions. See Francis Newton Thorpe, *The Federal and State Constitutions, Colonial Charters, and Other Organic Laws of the States, Territories, and Colonies* (Washington D.C.: Government Printing Office, 1909), 7 vols.

9. Discussion of terms and powers of early state governors is more expansive in Kallenbach, *The American Chief Executive,* pp. 15-29.

10. Lipson, *The American Governor,* p. 14.

11. As quoted by Louis Lambert, "The Executive Article," in W. Brooke Graves (ed.), *Major Problems in Constitutional Revision* (Chicago: Public Administration Service, 1960), p. 185.

12. Rowland Egger, "The Governor of Virginia, 1776 and 1976," *University of Virginia Newsletter* 52 (August 1976):41.

13. Ibid., p. 42.

14. Kallenbach, *The American Chief Executive,* p. 25; see also pp. 30-67, and Charles C. Thach, *The Creation of the Presidency, 1775-1789,* Johns Hopkins University Studies in Historical and Political Science, Series 50, Number 4 (Baltimore: The Johns Hopkins Press, 1922).

15. Lipson, *The American Governor,* pp. 16-28, which is also the source for the discussion that follows.

16. Ibid., p. 29.

17. James Bryce, *The American Commonwealth,* Vol. II (London: Macmillan, 1888), p. 149.

18. Ibid., p. 150.

19. Address before the Commercial Club of Portland, Ore., May 18, 1911, as quoted in John M. Matthews, "The New Role of the Governor," *American Political Science Review* 6 (May 1912):224.

20. "First Annual Message of Woodrow Wilson, Governor of New Jersey, to

the Legislature of New Jersey, January 9, 1912," *N.J. Legislative Documents* 1 (1911):4.

21. A more thorough discussion of these factors can be found in Terry Sanford, *Storm Over the States* (New York: McGraw-Hill, 1967), pp. 20-24.

22. Ibid., p. 20.

23. Ibid., p. 21.

24. Charles R. Adrian, *Governing Our Fifty States and Their Communities* (New York: McGraw-Hill, 1963), p. 31.

25. Correspondence with the author, November 11, 1976.

26. Robert S. Allen (ed.), *Our Sovereign State* (New York: Vanguard Press, 1949), p. vii.

27. Sanford, *Storm Over the States,* p. 1.

28. Allen, *Our Sovereign State,* p. xi.

29. Harold J. Laski, *The American Democracy: A Commentary and an Interpretation* (London: Allen and Unwin, 1949), p. 146.

30. Ibid., p. 143.

31. As quoted in National Governors' Conference, *The State of the States* (Washington, D.C.: National Governors' Conference, 1974), p. 5.

32. Council of State Governments, "The Governors' Messages," *State Government* 24 (March 1951).

33. National Governors' Conference, "The Governors' Messages" (mimeograph), Washington, D.C., February 1975.

34. See the National Governors' Conference, *Innovations in State Government: Messages from the Governors* (Washington D.C.: National Governors' Conference, June 1974); and Council of State Governments, "Innovations from the Laboratories of Democracy," *State Government News,* August 1976, pp. 2-3.

35. J. Oliver Williams, "Changing Perspectives on the American Governor," in Williams and Thad L. Beyle (eds.), *The American Governor in Behavioral Perspective* (New York: Harper & Row, 1972), p. 1.

36. Louis Harris, "The Harris Survey; More Trust for State Government," copyright 1976 by *The Chicago Tribune,* July 5, 1976.

37. Interview with the author, September 8, 1976, Tallahassee, Fla.

38. Interview with the author, August 24, 1976, New York, N.Y.

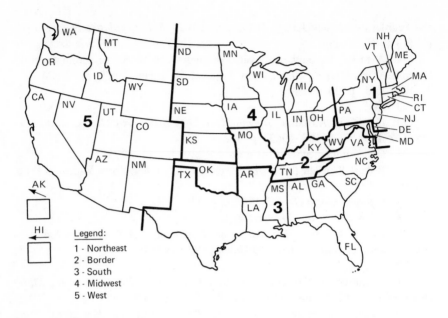

Figure 1-1. Regions of the United States

2 Career Patterns and Politics: A New Breed Emerges

The principal thing that is helpful for a governor is administrative experience— experience in persuading people to take joint cooperative actions. [1]
—Governor George Romney of Michigan

Service in the legislature is a tremendous help. It gives you a broad-gauged view of the whole spectrum of problems that state government deals with. [2]
—Governor Matthew Welsh of Indiana

Experience in public relations certainly can't hurt a governor. [3]
—Governor William Scranton of Pennsylvania

Governors must possess many skills to be successful. They are expected to be adroit administrators, dexterous executives, expert judges of people, combative yet sensitive and inspiring politicians, decorous chiefs of state, shrewd party tacticians, and polished public relations managers. No man or woman has the abilities to fill fully and balance well all of these conflicting roles simultaneously, or even singly. Yet some can do so better than others, and in this chapter we will attempt to identify those who have by examining the careers and personal characteristics of governors. The backgrounds of the outstanding governors will be compared with those of all governors over the twenty-five year period of this study. The careers of governors prior to their elections will be reviewed for different time periods to determine whether more recent governors are entering office better prepared than their predecessors. What governors do *after* they complete their terms and how this has changed is also the subject of investigation. Before these topics are discussed, a brief sketch of the contours of the study and of the basics of the electoral system for governors is given.

A Quarter-Century of Governors

Duane Lockard, upon completing a study of all New Jersey governors from colonial times to 1964, surmised: "The name 'governor' is about all that has remained constant about the position." [4] So it has been across the United States, with approximately 2,000 men (and a few women) serving as governor since the founding of the Republic. The governor has become a constitutional officer popularly elected in every state and is the only state official so established and elected universally.

During the quarter-century period surveyed in this study (1950 to 1975),

13

there has been a total of 312 governors, 182 of them Democrats (58.3 percent) and 128 Republicans (41.0 percent). Only one Independent, James Longley of Maine, has managed to win election during this period. There has also been one "Republocrat," Mills Godwin of Virginia, who was elected to his first term as a Democrat and his second term as a Republican.[5] (Apparently Godwin is in a very exclusive category, for only one other man appears to have been elected under the banners of both major parties—Joseph Brown of Georgia who served as a Democratic governor before and during the Civil War and as a Republican in Reconstruction days.[6])

It should be noted that "acting" and "interim" governors are not included in this study. Many states have provisions for the lieutenant governor and successive officers to "act" as the executive during any absence from the state by the duly elected governor. In New Jersey it even became an annual custom for the governor to leave the state for a brief time so that the president of the state senate could become acting governor. The acting governor, in turn, left the state so that the speaker of the House could enjoy the same honor. From 1947 to 1958 New Jersey had two governors and 23 acting governors![7]

Also excluded from this study are "interim" governors who held office for just a few days or weeks between a change of state administrations. In most cases the governor resigned before the expiration of his term in order to take a seat in the U.S. Senate (which organizes earlier than the end of most gubernatorial terms). The interim governors are noted at the end of Appendix B, which contains a listing of all governors by state, party, and term of office who served during the years of this study.

The average number of governors per state over the twenty-five years was 6.5.[8] There is no perceived relationship between the size of the state and the number of governors it has had. One of the least populous states, Wyoming, had the most governors (9), while two other small states, Washington and Utah, had the least (3 each). Wyoming's numerical record, incidentally, is not a recent phenomenon. Since it became a state in 1890, it has had 28 governors, thus surpassing every other state over the same time. An incomplete term was the rule in Wyoming, as one would suspect, with 20 of the 28 governors participating in a political game of musical chairs precipitated by deaths, resignations, special vacancy elections, and direct successions to the governorship.

Electoral Basics

All told, in the 1950-1975 period, there were 429 gubernatorial elections, with 247 won by Democrats, 181 won by Republicans, and 1 won by an Independent. This breakdown closely reflects the overall party figures for governors. The popular vote system that determined these elections does not, of course, date from the early Republic. The usual practice at first was for legislative selection of governors, but this gradually gave way to popular canvass in all the states, beginning with Pennsylvania (1790) and Delaware (1792).[9] Some of the original states took quite some time to make the change. Virginia narrowly refused the elective executive at her 1829-30 constitutional convention—the responsibility was considered to be too great for the people—and did not adopt popular sovereignty until 1851. South Carolina's acceptance—the last of the original thirteen states to do so—came only at the end of the Civil War. Jacksonian democracy was not the only reason for the adoption of popular election. Many states tired of the divisions, distraction from other work, and endless maneuvering that accompanied legislative appointment of the governor.[10] The newer states were less tied to traditional methods, and only two (Kentucky and Louisiana) ever had a procedure other than popular election.

Some states designed an institutional check on gubernatorial elections to guard against minority governors. All the New England states and Georgia and Mississippi as well required that a candidate secure a clear majority of the votes to be elected; a plurality was not sufficient.[11] All but one of these states used the provision at least once. (In Mississippi the Democratic candidate has never received less than a majority since the provision was added there in 1890.) In New England, the procedure called for the state senate to choose between two finalists that had been selected from among the four highest vote-getters by the lower house of the legislature. In the Georgia and Mississippi procedure, the legislature elected either the plurality winner or the runner-up. Gradually all the New England states but Vermont abolished the provision (which was used about sixty times in all), since minor independent candidates often were given crucial bargaining power by the process. Only Vermont and Mississippi still maintain their procedures. Georgia abolished its procedure after a controversial election in 1966 when the Democratic runner-up, Lester Maddox, was chosen governor over the Republican plurality winner, Howard Calloway, by a heavily Democratic legislature. The new provision requires that if no candidate polls a majority, a run-off election be held between the top two contenders three weeks after the first election. The other forty-seven states presently require only a plurality for election.

Contested Elections

With provisions like the one above and in view of the personal, party, regional, and racial passions that are often inflamed, it is hardly surprising that there have been some disputed elections among the more than 3,000 that have been held in the United States.[12] During the Civil War, rival state governments actually existed within Kentucky, Louisiana, Missouri, Tennessee, and Virginia, and a small-scale civil war was waged in Arkansas for several months in 1872 between rival Republican claimants of the governor's chair.[13]

Many legislative deadlocks have occurred. In 1832 the old slate of state officers in Rhode Island was held over for one full term since the legislature was unable to decide an election dispute, and in the same state just seven years later the senior U.S. senator served as acting governor for an entire term because of a similar situation. The Kentucky legislature sparked violence in 1900 by seating the Democratic candidate and thus overruling the finding of a state canvassing board that the Republican had been elected.[14] The Democratic governor-elect was subsequently assassinated on the steps of the state's capitol. A ruling by the Kentucky Supreme Court gave the succession right to the deceased Democrat's running mate for lieutenant governor.

The courts have been active in other election disputes as well and have either invalidated or reversed contested results of gubernatorial elections in Wisconsin (1856), Florida (1876), Arizona (1916), Rhode Island (1956), and Minnesota (1962). Of recent contested results none is more famous than the 1946 Georgia imbroglio brought on by the death of Democrat Eugene Talmadge. Without GOP opposition in the November general election, Talmadge received an overwhelming majority of the popular vote, but he died before the official returns were validated and proclaimed by the state legislature as constitutionally required. Thus, the legislature claimed it had the right to elect the successor, which it did by giving the nod to Eugene's son Herman. When the incumbent governor, Ellis Arnall, who refused to recognize the legislature's action would not vacate his office, Georgians were treated to the spectacle of his being forcibly ejected from his office by state highway patrol officers under Herman Talmadge's command. The state supreme court finally intervened and overruled the legislature by holding that the newly elected lieutenant governor, M.E. Thompson, should act as governor. The decision was accepted by all parties, albeit reluctantly. The young Talmadge had his moment, though, when he won the office handily in a special election held two years later to fill the remainder of his father's term.

A court ruling again proved decisive in 1956, when Democratic Governor Dennis J. Roberts of Rhode Island was defeated by 437 votes by Republican Christopher Del Sesto.[15] Roberts went to the state supreme court and successfully argued the invalidation of about 5,000 absentee ballots on a technicality and was then declared the winner by 711 votes. His victory was a temporary one, however. The voters reacted adversely to his ploy, and GOP shouts of "stolen election" carried Del Sesto into office by a decisive margin in a 1958 rematch.

Another court decision reversed Minnesota's 1962 election results even as the ultimate loser was serving the term in question. Incumbent Republican Elmer L. Andersen who led the official canvass narrowly retained his office when the new term began in early 1963, but three months later the state supreme court reversed the results and declared Democrat Karl F. Rolvaag the belated winner by 91 votes out of almost a million and a quarter cast. While there have been many other close elections decided by a single percentage point or less, remarkably few have been the subject of dispute. In 1839, for example, Democrat Marcus Morton of Massachusetts won by a single vote in the official canvass, but entered office absolutely unchallenged.[16]

Constitutional and Statutory Requirements
for Candidacy

Although Virginia, New York, Rhode Island, and Connecticut were conspicuous exceptions, most early state constitutions were full of restrictive clauses limiting the pool from which governors could come.[17] In Maryland, a gubernatorial candidate had to own real and personal property worth at least $5,000 of which at least $1,000 had to be in real estate. Such a requirement, which also existed in some form in South and North Carolina, Massachusetts, and New Hampshire, supposedly insured that the governor had a substantial stake in the state's economy and thus was unlikely to take frivolous or irresponsible populist financial actions.

Clauses relating to religious affiliation could be found in the first constitutions of New Hampshire, New Jersey, North Carolina, Maryland, Massachusetts, and Delaware. In New Hampshire only a Protestant could serve as governor; in Massachusetts, only a Christian. A Delaware chief executive was bound to an oath "professing belief in God the Father, in Jesus Christ, and the Holy Ghost" in addition to acknowledgment of the Holy Scriptures as divinely inspired.

The property and religious strictures have now been eliminated although they persisted for quite some time. One important ruling against a religious clause came only in 1961 with *Torcaso* v. *Watkins*,[18] when the U.S. Supreme Court ruled unconstitutional a Maryland statute entailing compulsory religious oaths for all state officers.

Not all of the early constitutional restrictions have gone by the board, however. Those stipulating age and citizenship qualifications have been retained by almost all states, as Table 2-1 shows. More than four-fifths of the states today have age requirements, with the minimum age usually being set at thirty years. A smaller number (though still about three-quarters) requires that the governor be a U.S. citizen. Few states, however, restrict the governorship to citizens of long duration, and no state any longer stipulates that the governor must be a "native born" citizen. (The last state—Maine—to abolish this restriction did so in 1955.) State residency is a nearly universal requirement, with periods of domicile prior to election varying from one month to ten years. Some states add that the governor must be a "qualified voter" as well. These same requirements also apply to the lieutenant governor in states having that office.

While normally these formal qualifications are not overly restrictive, there have been cases where duly nominated or elected candidates have been ousted

Table 2-1
Constitutional Qualifications for Election to the Governorship

Requirement		No. of States with Requirement
Minimum age	25	6
	30	34
	31	1
	None	9
U.S. citizenship	11 years +	6
	5-10 years	8
	Less than 5 years	1
	Required with no specific time	21
	No requirement	14
State citizenship or residency[a]	5-10 years	31
	Less than 5 years	12
	No requirement	7
Qualified voter	Yes	18[b]
	No	32

Source: Compiled from the state-by-state outline in the Council of State Governments, *The Book of the States, 1976-1977* (Lexington, Ky.: the Council of State Governments, 1976), Table 5, pp. 214-15.

Note: Requirements as of 1975.

[a]Maine also requires that the governor be a resident of the state during the term for which he is elected.

[b]Four states specify the number of years for which a governor must have been a qualified voter: Maryland (5 years), Michigan (4 years), Oklahoma (10 years), and Virginia (5 years).

for failure to meet one or another of the stipulations, as recently illustrated in South Carolina's 1974 gubernatorial election.[19] Charles "Pug" Ravenel, a young businessman and political unknown with South Carolina roots, entered the Democratic primary and scored a big victory over two establishment courthouse politicians. As the Democratic nominee, he was leading by a wide margin in the polls and appeared certain of election. However, Ravenel had spent considerable time out of the state on business concerns, and a law suit challenging his candidacy under the five-year residency requirement resulted in a state supreme court decision that ruled him ineligible. The Democrats substituted one of the defeated courthouse politicoes, and in November the Republicans picked up a most unexpected governorship in the "year of Watergate."

Other modern restrictions on gubernatorial office holding have found their way into state constitutions or the statute books. For example, conviction of crimes like perjury, bribery, and embezzlement normally bars a person from seeking the governorship, and Kentucky has a unique ban on dueling, which is a product of her rather violent political past. Most state constitutions also reinforce a common-law finding that no one can hold two public offices simultaneously if the duties and responsibilities are incompatible. This principle has not always been inviolable. One Tammany Hall district leader who boasted of holding four concurrent public offices—assemblyman, alderman, police magistrate, and county supervisor—and drawing salaries from three of them clearly set "a record unexampled in New York politics."[20]

Informal Requirements

Governors are an elite corps by almost any measure. The formal eligibility requirements are only a small part of the story, for more important and more restrictive are the informal norms that place severe limitations on the actual pool of gubernatorial candidates. By sex, race, occupation, education, religion, and even marital status, the number of citizens actually in a position to run for governor (as opposed to the number technically eligible) are reduced. When other political factors are added—background in public offices, support of party officials, financing, and regional location—it becomes clear that only a very few citizens really fit the unwritten prescription for a gubernatorial candidacy each election year.

As the figures in the following sections show, governors are characteristically unrepresentative of the population in many respects and in fact are a relatively homogeneous group.

Certain elites-within-elites have particular advantages in running for governor. Close relatives of governors and former governors have a leg up on the opposition because they bear well-known names that confer special status. Examples are numerous in recent history: the Battles of Virginia, Scotts of North Carolina, Browns of California, Talmadges of Georgia, Longs of Louisiana, Careys of Wyoming, McCalls of Oregon and Massachusetts, and last but not least, the Rockefellers of New York, Arkansas, and West Virginia. Wives of governors have succeeded their husbands in Wyoming, Texas, and Alabama as well. There is no recent comparable situation, though, to the Tennessee governor's race of 1886 when the Taylor brothers (Alf the Republican and Bob the Democrat) ran against each other as the major party nominees;[21] Bob won then, but Alf got the job several years later after a successful race against someone else.

Family is not the most crucial election determinant by any means. Support of party and political figures, and financial backing from business or labor, all of which are related to other factors, are supremely important. Incumbent governors, themselves members and beneficiaries of elites, often have great power to select their own successors or at least to veto candidates unacceptable to them. Quite commonly, within the party, the governor frequently will openly endorse or covertly assist one candidate for the party nomination, and many governors also select directly or indirectly the party's candidate for lieutenant governor, who is usually viewed as the "heir apparent." Outside of the party, the governor can still have an effect. In the 1962 New Hampshire election for governor, incumbent Republican Wesley Powell was defeated for renomination by a candidate repugnant to him. Powell promptly endorsed the Democratic nominee, John W. King, who became the first governor of his party in the state in thirty years.

Governor Matthew Welsh of Indiana claims that the governors, though homogeneous, ". . . are the product of the political system. They are apparently what the people want."[22] While his first statement is certainly true, the second does not necessarily follow. People are often prevented from running by factors wholly beyond their control, whether these be race, sex, or an occupation that lends itself neither financially nor operationally to a campaign. Nevertheless the gubernatorial selection among an elite is partly the fault of the voting public. As Donald Matthews convincingly argues in the similar case of U.S. senators:

As long as the system of stratification in a society is generally accepted, one must expect people to look for political leadership toward those who have met the current definition of success, and hence are considered worthy individuals. Voters seem to prefer candidates who are not like themselves but are what they would like to be.[23]

Whether or not the people approve of the current homogeneity in their governors, it is not at all clear that the situation is a healthy one in a representative system. It is inevitable in a complex society that some citizens will find themselves not in a position to run, but the pool of "legitimate" gubernatorial aspirants has been miniscule if one can fairly judge by the group of party nominees. There has been diversification—sometimes significant, sometimes barely detectable—in recent years that will be noted as the personal characteristics of race, sex, occupation, education, religion, marital status, and age are examined for governors who served between 1950 and 1975.

Racial and Sexual Mix

America's history has been one of discrimination, but also of advancing equality. At this very late date, blacks and women, two groups that have borne the lion's share of prejudice, have only begun to catch up, and though their progress is halting, it is promising. While there have been black U.S. senators, representatives, and mayors at various times in America's past, there has never been a black governor, and racism existing in both the North and the South helped produce this stark statistic. However, as the full effects of the Voting Rights Act of 1965 and its extensions are felt, and as changing attitudes begin to enforce fully the legal equality achieved by the civil rights movement in the 1960s and 1970s, blacks will hopefully begin to win a share of governorships. For example, in the 1974 elections the first two black lieutenant governors in this century, Democrats Mervyn Dymally of California and George Brown of Colorado, were elected by overwhelmingly white electorates.[24] The office of lieutenant governor has traditionally been the primary escalator to the governorship.

Some of the greatest progress for blacks has come in the South, where in 1976 Joseph Hatchett, a black Democrat, was elected to the Florida Supreme Court and became the first member of his race to win a statewide post in Florida since Reconstruction days. While the proportional underrepresentation of blacks continues, the gap is not as enormous as it was a decade ago. In Southern state legislatures, whose offices also serve as steppingstones to the governorship, blacks held 97 seats as of 1976, or 5.4 percent of the total.[25]

For women the picture is a bit brighter. As early as 1924, only five years after women were enfranchised, two women were elected state governors. Both of them, Democrats Nellie Tayloe Ross of Wyoming and Miriam "Ma" Ferguson of Texas, succeeded their husbands. Mrs. Ross was elected to fill the two years remaining in her deceased husband's term, but due to a reelection defeat, she did not serve beyond its expiration in 1927. In 1933 Mrs. Ross became the first woman director of the U.S. Mint where she served until retirement in 1953.

It was appropriate that Wyoming should have elected one of the first woman governors since the state had led the nation in granting the vote to women as a territory (in 1869) and as a state (in 1890). Wyoming also had the first woman state legislator who won a seat in 1910. Wyoming's liberal franchise, however, was not so much the product of progressivism as of desperation. It happened that men outnumbered women by a ratio of six to one in Wyoming, and the legislature—fearing zero population growth more than women's liberation—sought to attract the fairer sex to the Wild West.[26] Although the legislature later had second thoughts about its ploy and passed a repeal, the governor's veto was upheld by a single vote in a legislative override attempt. Even in modern times women have done quite well in Wyoming politics. In 1970 a woman served as speaker of the state house of representatives, and a woman was also secretary of state and thus next in line for the governorship since there is no lieutenant governor's post in Wyoming.

In Texas "Ma" Ferguson was merely the extension of her husband, James "Farmer Jim" Ferguson, the dominant figure in Texas politics from 1915 to the 1930s. A skilled stump speaker with a strong political base in rural areas, Ferguson opposed both Prohibition and the Ku Klux Klan despite their popularity. He was corrupt and caught and then convicted and impeached by the legislature in 1917. Although he was forbidden from ever holding office again, Ferguson, under the banner of "two governors for the price of one," ran his wife five times, and she was elected twice for terms of two years apiece in 1924 and 1932.

While it was almost three and a half decades before another woman was successfully elected governor, a number of women tried in the interim. Mrs. William Langer of North Dakota replaced her ineligible husband on the GOP ticket in 1934, only to lose. Anastasia Frohmiller of Arizona, after twenty-four years in the statewide elective post of auditor general, captured the Democratic gubernatorial nomination in 1950 and was defeated very narrowly by Republican Howard Pyle. In the 1962 Nebraska Democratic primary Darlene Brooks, the widow of Governor Ralph Brooks who had died in office in 1960, lost in her gubernatorial bid. Finally in 1966 another woman won a governor's chair, but it was again on her husband's coattails. Governor George Wallace of Alabama, constitutionally ineligible to succeed himself, took a cue from "Farmer Jim" Ferguson and successfully ran his wife, Lurleen Burns Wallace. She died of cancer midway through her term on May 7, 1968.

In 1974, more than a half-century after the Nineteenth Amendment gave women the vote, the first woman whose husband had not previously served in the office was elected governor with a 59 percent majority. Democrat Ella Grasso of Connecticut had served as assemblywoman, secretary of state, and congresswoman before her election and was a favorite of the party organization leaders in the state. By contrast, the second woman governor elected on her own, Democrat Dixy Lee Ray of Washington state, was not the choice of party kingpins and was nominated narrowly in a three-way 1974 primary battle with 37 percent of the vote. Ray, the former chairwoman of the Atomic Energy Commission, won the general election more handily with a 54 percent majority.

The success stories of Grasso and Ray can fairly be termed exceptional. For example, in the year Ray won, Democratic nominee Stella Hackel of Vermont, the incumbent state treasurer, was badly defeated in her gubernatorial race, as was the Republican woman candidate for lieutenant governor in Montana. In 1977 women held only 4 percent of the governorships while comprising 51 percent of the population, and women are still viewed in some party circles as "reserve" candidates who deserve to carry the banner only in hopeless elections, as did Republican gubernatorial candidates Louise Gore of Maryland and Shirley Crumpler of Nevada in 1974. Yet women are winning a good number of steppingstone offices. In 1974 Democrat Mary Anne Krupsak of New York, a state senator, was elected lieutenant governor, and the following year she was joined by Evelyn Gandy of Mississippi (the former state insurance commissioner) and Thelma Stovall of Kentucky (former secretary of state).[27] Women are also better represented in the state legislatures, where as of 1975 they held 8.1 percent of 7,563 legislative seats in the nation.[28] In New Hampshire, a remarkably large contingent of women, about 25 percent of the total, can be found in the legislature.

In sum, there is some measure of improvement for both women and blacks, as evidenced by the recent group of governors taken together with their backup officers, lieutenant governors. However, while long strides remain to achieve more than a token balance, most of the governors interviewed for this study believed that at long last a black or a woman candidate would not face a serious handicap in most states because of his or her race or sex. The governors seemed sincerely to concur with the comments of their colleague, progressive Republican Daniel J. Evans of Washington state:

I would hope we would move toward a time when two people of equal sensitivity or equal capability would have an equal opportunity to be governor in spite of the fact that one might be black and the other white, or one male and the other female. . . . I think we are moving to that point.[29]

Occupations of Governors

Woodrow Wilson saw a clear connection between his ambitions and the legal profession: "The profession I chose was politics; the profession I entered was the law. I entered one because I thought it would lead to the other."[30] There are reasonable explanations for the law-politics link.[31] Political life places a premium on the very skills in which a lawyer is trained, including verbal ability, debate, and personal relations. A legal career offers the flexibility of schedule that is both rare among professions and essential to electoral success. There are not many citizens whose job permits them to spend months on end away from the office and on the hustings. Attorneys also usually have the financial resources to wage a campaign. They are well-paid themselves and have often been in a position to establish important contacts in a community's "money circle."

To these factors must be added the public view of the lawyer's role. Lawyers are perceived by many not just as court officers and consultants but as public servants already. Law is so dominant in contemporary American government and politics that the election of lawyers to government posts seems to be a logical progression. Indeed, some public elective offices, like state attorney general and city and county attorneys, must be filled by qualified lawyers. These political toeholds give lawyers the elective experience so advantageous for promotion to higher office.

Given all of this, it would be surprising to find that lawyers did *not* monopolize the governorships. The expected, however, is the real. Lawyers have comprised more than half of all governors for most of this century,[32] and almost half (49.5 percent) of all governors who served between 1950 and 1975 were lawyers, while another 9.1 percent were combination lawyer-businessmen.[33] Businessmen alone accounted for a large portion, or about 20.2 percent of those serving from 1950 to 1975.[34] If another ten governors who held large business interests while tending a separate career are counted, businessmen and lawyers together provide the pool from which 82.5 percent of recent governors have been elected.

Other professional groups were represented, too. Over twenty-five years there were 11 educators; 5 governors who listed their profession as "public service"; 3 each of news reporters, bankers, and engineers; 2 each of accountants, publishers, medical doctors, dentists, and pharmacists; 1 chemist; and 1 architect. To complete the tally, there were 15 farmers, 7 ranchers, a florist, a chiropractor, a housewife (Mrs. George Wallace of Alabama), an actor (Ronald Reagan of California), a trucker (Harold Hughes of Iowa), and a country singer (Jimmie Davis of Louisiana, who popularized the song, "You Are My Sunshine").

Lawyers and businessmen comprised a majority of governors in every state without exception. They dominated both parties and all regions. Only two kinds of occupations were region related. Farmers were found, by and large, in their home states of the Midwest, and the ranchers similarly were found on the Western range. Two party differences did emerge from this analysis. About 39 percent of all Republican governors were businessmen compared to just over 12 percent of the Democrats. Slightly more Democratic governors were lawyers (52 percent) than were Republicans (45 percent). Despite the overall prevalence of lawyers and businessmen, only rarely was a state totally dominated by them. The political system in almost every state provided the occasion for members of other occupations to serve as governor.

The large proportion of governors with professional training indicates governorships are being filled by capable persons with some expertise. Yet, the unrepresentativeness of governors' careers becomes apparent when one considers that only 8.4 percent of the male adult population in the United States[35] is classed as professionally career based.[36] Indeed, only 40.6 percent of the total male adult population could be called "white collar" at all, and only one-half of 1 percent were lawyers over the period 1950-1975.[37]

Donald Matthews cites similar career figures for U.S. senators.[38] While the overall lack of professional diversity in governors can be regretted, there is one hopeful sidelight even though the lawyer is apt to remain a staple of politics for reasons outlined earlier. Law schools have been overwhelmed in recent years by applicants, some of whom may have recognized the wisdom of Wilson's dictum. As a result, an unprecedented number of lawyers have been graduated of late, and minority recruitment programs have greatly increased the number of blacks and women. Perhaps as the pool of attorney-politicians grows and the racial and sexual composition of the pool is altered, these changes will be reflected in the governors' corps.

Education

Governors are very well educated, and have become more so through the decades (see Table 2-2). While 64 percent of governors who served from 1915 to 1930

Table 2-2
Average Educational Level of Governors, 1950-1975

Region	1950-1959			1960-1969			1970-1975			Totals		
	D	R	All	D	R	All	D	R	All	D	R	All
South	17.7	—[a]	17.7	17.8	16.5	17.6	18.4	19.3	18.6	17.9	18.2	17.9
Border	16.9	18.5	17.1	18.5	17.8	18.2	17.4	19.5	18.0	17.3	18.3	17.6
Northeast	17.9	17.7	17.8	18.9	18.1	18.4	17.9	19.0	18.2	18.2	18.0	18.1
Midwest	16.9	17.4	17.3	17.4	17.3	17.4	16.3	19.5	17.0	17.0	17.5	17.3
West	17.4	16.6	16.9	17.0	17.5	17.4	17.4	16.0	17.2	17.3	16.9	17.1
Totals	17.4	17.2	17.4	17.9	17.6	17.7	17.6	18.8	17.8	17.6	17.5	17.6

D = Democrat; R = Republican

Sources: Marquis Who's Who, Inc., *Who's Who In America, 1950 [-1975]* (Chicago: A.N. Marquis, 1950-1975); Paul A. Theis and Edmund L. Henshaw, Jr. (eds.), *Who's Who In American Politics, 1968 [-1975]* (New York: R.R. Bowker, 1967-1975); and Michael Barone, Grant Ujifusa, and Douglas Matthews, *The Almanac of American Politics, 1972 [1974, 1976]* (New York: E.P. Dutton, 1972, 1973, 1975).

Note: The educational levels of 7 governors (out of 312 total) could not be determined from biographies listed in standard reference works. Figures presented in the table are averages of the educational levels attained by governors in each indicated grouping. In the scale used in this table, high school = 12 years, a college four-year degree = 16 years, a law degree (J.D. or LL.B) = 19 years, and so forth, depending solely on the number of years normally spent to secure a particular degree. (Years spent in undergraduate or graduate college that did not result in a degree are also counted.) All governors who served between the years 1950 and 1975 are included in the data, including those governors who succeeded to the office. Honorary degrees, frequently bestowed upon governors, are not counted in the tabulation.

[a]There were no Republican governors in the Southern states from 1950 to 1959.

had attended college and 88 percent of those from 1940 to 1950, virtually all the most recent governors have had at least some college training.[39] In addition, more governors had actually completed a higher degree before their elections than ever before. Correlating well with their professions, governors had a 1950-1975 average of 17.6 years of education (or 1.6 years of postgraduate school in addition to the college undergraduate degree). The population as a whole, by contrast, averaged only 11.1 years over the same period.[40] Governors, like the general population, showed an increase in educational levels with each decade.

Regionally, the Northeast produced the best-educated governors (18.1 years), followed closely by the South. Considering the latter region's bottom-rung educational ranking nationally, the findings may be a bit surprising. Interestingly, in the 1970s the South elected the most highly schooled governors in the country, thereby lending credence to the political perception of an able "New South" generation of governors there. Educational levels decline as one goes further west.

In a reversal of popular conceptions, Democrats were slightly better educated than Republicans overall. The slight difference, however, is easily accounted for by the disproportionate presence of lawyers in Democratic ranks (requiring 19 years of school) and of businessmen in Republican circles (most of whom received only a bachelor's degree or its equivalent). In the 1970s the Republicans overtake the Democrats educationally because 11 of the 13 first-time GOP governors are either in the legal or medical professions. Republicans also have higher averages in the Midwestern, Southern, and Border states. In the latter two regions, the educational pattern is due to the type of candidates— young professionals generally recruited by the GOP to breathe new electoral life into a moribund party.

Religion

A governor is far more likely to have an expressed religious preference and church affiliation than the average American. For governors who served from 1950-1975, almost nine in ten belonged to a religious denomination, while four in ten Americans in the same period did not.[41] Some religions are considerably overrepresented among governors as well. Among state chief executives who indicated a religious preference, Protestants have an overwhelming edge of 80.6 percent to only 15.6 percent for Roman Catholics and 1.8 percent for Jews (see Table 2-3). The breakdown is significantly different for Americans who listed a church membership: 55.2 percent Protestant, 35.7 percent Roman Catholic, 4.8 percent Jewish.[42] Through the decades, however, there is an increase in religious representativeness. Whereas in the 1950s only 13.3 percent of governors were Roman Catholic, almost a third of all governors in the 1970s are Catholic, which is very close to the percentage in the religious population overall. There were a few more Jewish governors too in the later decades, although they are still underrepresented. (It was only in 1930 that Oregon and New Mexico elected the country's first Jewish governors.[43])

Regionally, the contrast reflects the varying religious composition of various parts of the United States. Governors are almost wholly Protestant in the Southern and Border states, where the fundamentalist sects have their broadest followings. The figures might also suggest an underlying and persistent prejudice among many fundamentalists against Catholics and Jews to a degree that might deter parties from nominating members of these denominations. The Midwest has shown the greatest change. Formerly a Protestant bastion, the region elected Catholics to almost a third of its governorships by 1975. The West is perhaps the most tolerant or diversified area throughout the quarter-century studied. More than four in ten Western governors elected in the 1970s were Catholics, and even in the 1950s Catholics comprised almost a quarter of the total. These figures lend credence to the individualistic and egalitarian picture often drawn of

Table 2-3
Religion of Governors, by Region, 1950-1975

Region	1950-1959				1960-1969				1970-1975				Totals			
	Prot. (%)	Cath. (%)	Jew. (%)	Other (%)	Prot. (%)	Cath. (%)	Jew. (%)	Other (%)	Prot. (%)	Cath. (%)	Jew. (%)	Other (%)	Prot. (%)	Cath. (%)	Jew. (%)	Other (%)
South	96.2	0.0	0.0	3.8	100.0	0.0	0.0	0.0	90.9	9.1	0.0	0.0	96.6	1.7	0.0	1.7
Border	100.0	0.0	0.0	0.0	81.8	9.1	9.1	0.0	100.0	0.0	0.0	0.0	94.4	2.8	2.8	0.0
Northeast	64.0	32.0	4.0	0.0	70.0	25.0	5.0	0.0	20.0	70.0	10.0	0.0	58.2	36.4	5.4	0.0
Midwest	93.3	6.7	0.0	0.0	92.3	0.0	3.8	3.8	70.0	30.0	0.0	0.0	89.4	7.6	1.5	1.5
West	69.0	24.1	0.0	6.9	73.7	21.0	0.0	5.3	58.3	41.7	0.0	0.0	68.3	26.7	0.0	5.0
Totals	83.6	13.3	0.8	2.3	84.7	10.2	3.1	2.0	66.0	32.0	2.0	0.0	80.8	15.6	1.8	1.8

Prot. = Protestant (includes all denominations)
Cath. = Roman Catholic
Jew. = Jewish
Other = Other religions (Mormon, Syrian Orthodox, etc.)

Sources: Marquis Who's Who, Inc., *Who's Who In America, 1950 [-1975]* (Chicago: A.N. Marquis, 1950-1975); Paul A. Theis and Edmund L. Henshaw, Jr. (eds.), *Who's Who In American Politics, 1968 [-1975]* (New York: R.R. Bowker, 1967-1975); and Michael Barone, Grant Ujifusa, and Douglas Matthews, *The Almanac of American Politics, 1972 [1974, 1976]* (New York: E.P. Dutton, 1972, 1973, 1975).

Note: For the period 1950-1975, 273 of 312 governors indicated a religious preference in biographies listed in standard reference works. Figures in the table are percentages of those governors who did indicate their religious affiliations. All governors who served between the years 1950 and 1975 are included in the data, including those governors who succeeded to the office.

Western electorates. Most Roman Catholic and Jewish governors are found in the Northeast, thereby mirroring its polyglot ethnic and religious character. In fact, the only time in any region when Protestants were not predominant occurs in the 1970s, when Protestant governors were outnumbered there four to one, with seven in ten governors being of the Roman Catholic faith and another one of every ten Jewish.

The vast majority of both Republican and Democratic governors have been Protestant, but many more Republicans (90.3 percent) than Democrats (74 percent) have been so (see Table 2-4). Even though the largest number of Catholic governors by far were Democrats, the GOP has been steadily increasing its percentage of Catholic governors so that by the 1970s, 16.7 percent of Republican governors were Catholics compared to only 3.7 percent two decades earlier. The changing religious affiliations of GOP governors may indicate the altered Republican constituency. On national and state levels a greater number of Catholics than ever before has been straying from the house of their fathers. Whereas John Kennedy garnered 78 percent of the Catholic votes in 1960 and Lyndon Johnson 76 percent four years later, Jimmy Carter could muster but 57 percent in 1976.[44] Even Hubert Humphrey in 1968, who pulled only 42 percent of the total votes nationwide, won a larger Catholic mandate (59 percent).[45] No

Table 2-4
Religion of Governors, by Party, 1950-1975

Religion	1950-1959		1960-1969		1970-1975		Totals	
	D (%)	R (%)	D (%)	R (%)	D (%)	R (%)	D (%)	R (%)
Protestant	77.0	92.6	79.2	89.4	61.1	83.3	74.0	90.3
Catholic	20.2	3.7	12.5	8.5	36.1	16.7	21.5	7.1
Jewish	1.4	0.0	6.2	0.0	2.8	0.0	3.2	0.0
Other	1.4	3.7	2.1	2.1	0.0	0.0	1.3	2.6

D = Democrat; R = Republican

Sources: Marquis Who's Who, Inc., *Who's Who In America, 1950 [-1975]* (Chicago: A.N. Marquis, 1950-1975); Paul A. Theis and Edmund L. Henshaw, Jr. (eds.), *Who's Who In American Politics, 1968 [-1975]* (New York: R.R. Bowker, 1967-1975); and Michael Barone, Grant Ujifusa, and Douglas Matthews, *The Almanac of American Politics, 1972 [1974, 1976]* (New York: E.P. Dutton, 1972, 1973, 1975).

Note: For the period 1950-1975, 158 of 181 Democratic governors and 113 of 128 Republican governors indicated a religious preference in biographies listed in standard reference works. Figures in the table are percentages (e.g., in the first column are percents of all Democratic governors who served from 1950 to 1959 and indicated a religious preference).

aThe "Protestant" category includes all denominations. "Catholic" refers specifically to Roman Catholic. The "Other" category consists of the Church of Latter-Day Saints (Mormons) and the Syrian Orthodox Church. Three Republicans and one Democrat were Mormons, and one Democrat was Syrian Orthodox.

such party change is noted for Jewish governors; they have been uniformly Democratic since 1950, even though Jewish voters, like Catholics, have drifted in greater numbers from their traditional Democratic moorings.[46]

A numerical accounting of Protestant denominations by region is given in Table 2-5. Four groupings contribute exactly half of all Protestant governors: Methodist, Presbyterian, Baptist, and Episcopalian. The Methodists alone comprise almost one-fifth of these governors. As one would expect, that certain denominations dominate the governorships in most regions again reflects the proportion of the population claiming membership in the individual sects. The South has a heavy load of Methodists and Baptists, and the Border states, Methodists and Presbyterians. The Lutherans find virtually all their national quota of governorships in the Midwest. The Northeast and especially the West show a much less clustered pattern. Any single religious grouping has less political weight in these regions than in the rest of the country.

Generally, it is clear that religious constraints in politics are loosening. The number of Roman Catholic governors has reached its zenith in modern times. It would be naive to suggest that religious orientation and denominational preference do not still determine some votes for governor; yet the figures presented in this section indicate that there is greater religious equality of opportunity now in gubernatorial elections. Certainly, John F. Kennedy's victory in 1960 and his succeeding term dissolved some of the Catholic bias; Jimmy Carter's triumph in 1976 may help to eliminate bias about and within his fellow Southern Baptists. Other, less-publicized elections of governors whose religious preferences differed from the majority in their states have helped the situation. The apparent long-term decline of both church membership and church-going in the population-at-large should also not be ignored as a contributing factor.

Marital Status

Governors are the marrying kind, in part perhaps because they have sensed as did Governor G. Mennen Williams of Michigan that ". . . having a wife, children, and a good family life does have a positive political effect."[47] Only eight of the governors first elected from 1950 to 1975 were single and previously unmarried at the time of their initial elections. During the same period a little more than a quarter of all adult males in the country were single.[48] Almost all of the married governors had children as well.

At least until recently, there may have been some prejudice directed at single politicians, if not by the electorate as a whole then by the parties who sought "wholesome" candidates with an attractive family image. Even as late as 1974, Democratic gubernatorial candidate Edmund G. Brown, Jr., of California, previously unmarried, was harassed by vicious rumors about his sexual orienta-

Table 2-5
Church Affiliations of Protestant Governors, by Region, 1950-1975

Region	No. of Governors in Protestant Denominations									
	Methodist	Presbyterian	Baptist[a]	Episcopal	Lutheran	Congregational	Christian Church	Unitarian	Disciples of Christ	General Protestant[b]
South	23	11	21	3	2	0	1	0	0	1
Border	9	9	4	4	0	0	2	0	1	0
Northeast	5	1	2	10	0	5	0	3	0	6
Midwest	14	9	2	3	21	3	1	0	1	4
West	9	5	3	10	2	3	1	1	0	5
Totals	60	35	32	30	25	11	5	4	2	16

Sources: Marquis Who's Who, Inc., *Who's Who In America, 1950 [-1975]* (Chicago: A.N. Marquis, 1950-1975); Paul A. Theis and Edmund L. Henshaw, Jr. (eds.), *Who's Who In American Politics, 1968 [-1975]* (New York: R.R. Bowker, 1967-1975); and Michael Barone, Grant Ujifusa, and Douglas Matthews, *The Almanac of American Politics, 1972 [1974, 1976]* (New York: E.P. Dutton, 1972, 1973, 1975).

Note: For the period 1950-1975, 220 governors indicated their Protestant affiliations in biographies listed in standard reference works. Of the 312 governors who served during this twenty-five year period, religious affiliations could not be determined for 39 of them. No governors were affiliated with Protestant denominations not listed in this table.

[a]This category includes all divisions of Baptists.

[b]These governors listed a Protestant religious preference, but did not specify a denomination.

tion. His election staff was forced to have him photographed on "dates" and to discuss his love life to defuse the issue. Again, however, the atmosphere is changing, for Brown overcame whatever prejudice existed to win both the party nomination and the election.

Nationally, the proportion of single people of both sexes has been growing, and those who choose marriage appear to be deferring it later than ever before. Thus, most of the governors interviewed for this study believed that politically a candidate's single status "wouldn't mean a thing today," as New Jersey Governor Richard Hughes put it.[49] Governor Thomas Salmon of Vermont thought it might even be "a slight plus."[50] (The tales of congressional cavorting in 1975-76 may have convinced the electorate that they prefer their playboys unmarried!)

If the "single issue" is less important, so too is divorce, which was once considered to be political self-immolation. In all, 12 governors (7 Republicans and 5 Democrats) who were elected initially between 1950 and 1975 were divorced. Five of the governors were divorced during their terms after their first elections, so that only during a reelection campaign could the divorce have been an issue. However, divorce has seldom if ever influenced the outcome of the election. The extended public divorce proceedings of Governor Marvin Mandel of Maryland, for example, had little effect on his 1974 reelection effort that was overwhelmingly successful. In earlier years such an event could have proven very distracting for a candidate, as it did for Governors Adlai Stevenson of Illinois and Nelson Rockefeller of New York as they were making unsuccessful presidential bids.[51] In 1976 discussion of Ronald Reagan's divorce and remarriage did not occur. The Republican vice presidential candidate that year, Senator Robert Dole of Kansas, also received no undue scrutiny concerning his recent divorce and remarriage, and President Ford clearly considered it no detriment to his campaign when he selected Dole.

Changing public attitudes are again responsible. Divorce in society is becoming both more acceptable and more commonplace. Although governors and other politicians will probably be subjected, as always, to a more stringent moral code than the electorate allows for itself, most of the stigma of divorce and remarriage for public officials has already been removed. This change has the effect not only of allowing present officeholders greater latitude in their family affairs but also of permitting previously "ineligible" persons (by reason of divorce) to seek the governorship. The pool of potential governors may thus be slightly expanded.

Age

Governors have been elected at younger ages in recent years. The average age for all governors from 1950 to 1975 at the time of their first elections was 47.3

years (see Table 2-6). This age compares to about 51 years in the decade 1940-1950.[52] The governors of the 1970s are the youngest of all, with an average age of only 45.9 years. Fully 70 percent of governors who served from 1950 to 1975 were between ages 40 and 54 when first elected. Of the 7 governors who were elected at 65 years of age or older in the last quarter-century, 6 of them were elected in the first half of that time period, with the oldest being Arthur G. Crane (R-Wyoming) and James F. Byrnes (D-South Carolina), both 71. While 8 governors under the age of 35 were elected from 1950 to 1975, no one surpassed the mark of Harold Stassen, Republican of Minnesota, first inaugurated in 1938 at age 31.

The recent trend towards youth in gubernatorial elections has edged governors to a position more representative of their constituencies. The average gubernatorial age of 47.3 does not contrast too sharply with the voting population's median age of 42.4 over the same period, especially when constitutional age restrictions for governors are taken into account.[53]

The party and regional age balance presents a revealing political picture. Republican governors tend to be somewhat older than their Democratic contemporaries (48.1 to 46.7 overall), but this varies throughout the country. The Southern and Border states have had the youngest governors (especially the Democratic ones) of any region. In both the "New South" and the increasingly two-party competitive Border states, the Democratic party has inclined toward

Table 2-6
Average Age of Governors at Election, 1950-1975

Region	1950-1959			1960-1969			1970-1975			Totals		
	D	R	All	D	R	All	D	R	All	D	R	All
South	42.4	a	42.4	47.9	44.7	47.4	45.2	42.5	44.8	44.9	44.4	44.9
Border	48.1	42.5	47.4	47.2	44.6	46.0	41.2	38.0	40.3	46.5	42.7	45.5
Northeast	47.2	48.4	47.9	47.1	48.7	48.0	48.3	53.3	49.8	47.4	48.9	48.2
Midwest	47.3	46.3	46.6	48.0	50.8	49.6	47.6	48.0	47.7	47.6	48.0	47.9
West	51.6	50.7	51.0	50.0	46.6	47.7	44.7	50.5	45.6	48.6	49.1	48.9
Totals	46.2	48.2	47.1	48.3	48.1	48.2	45.5	47.2	45.9	46.7	48.1	47.3

D = Democrat; R = Republican

Sources: Marquis Who's Who, Inc., *Who's Who In America, 1950 [-1975]* (Chicago: A.N. Marquis, 1950-1975); Paul A. Theis and Edmund L. Henshaw, Jr. (eds.), *Who's Who In American Politics, 1968 [-1975]* (New York: R.R. Bowker, 1967-1975); and Michael Barone, Grant Ujifusa, and Douglas Matthews, *The Almanac of American Politics, 1972 [1974, 1976]* (New York: E.P. Dutton, 1972, 1973, 1975).

Note: The ages of 7 governors (of 303 total) could not be determined. Only those governors who were serving their first terms between 1950 and 1975 are counted in this table. Governors who succeeded to the office are counted; their ages at succession, rather than election, are used in the table.

aThere were no Republican governors in the Southern states from 1950 to 1959.

fresh and vigorous leadership, and its nominations have often gone to the moderate and better-educated young people in its midst. Simultaneously, a weak, disorganized Republican party in the South and Border states looked to a younger generation of well-educated professionals to catapult it to a position of regional political prominence. Given these twin developments, it is not surprising to find that in the 1970s the neighboring Southern and Border states together had the youngest Democrats and the youngest Republicans of any region.

By contrast, the Northeastern and Midwestern governors were generally older, and Republican governors were almost always older than Democrats. In fact, the oldest governors of any region and time period were the Republican chief executives of the Northeast in the 1970s. The West, however, elected the most senior governors when the entire period is considered. Republican governors in this region were likely to be younger than their Democratic counterparts until the 1970s when the wave of youthful Democrats who won office were more than six years younger on the average than the Western Republicans of the same time period.

This cyclical movement parallels the political upheavals in the migrant-heavy West over the past few decades. Much of the southern West, for example, had been heavily Democratic (of conservative stripe) in the pre-World War II years, but after the war, a GOP surge was powered by an influx of new young homesteaders (many of them war veterans). The Republican gubernatorial nominees were often drawn from this group and consequently were younger, while the Democratic candidates reflected the conservative traditions of earlier residents. Two decades later the positions had been somewhat reversed. The GOP had become the entrenched establishment party with a much older membership base. The Democrats had adjusted to the altered electoral climate and were able to seek effectively the support of new waves of Western migrants (younger voters concerned about environmental issues). The result can be seen in the type of governors elected in the 1970s, such as Jerry Apodaca of New Mexico, Edmund Brown, Jr., of California, and Richard Lamm of Colorado, all of whom are Democrats.

Prior Office Careers

During the interviewing done for this study, governors were asked what they believed would be the "ideal background" for a state chief executive. The wide variance of the responses indicated that there probably is no particular set of political offices or occupations that ideally prepares a person for the governorship. As Governor Thomas Salmon of Vermont claimed, the ideal preparation is more one of temperament than of career:

If a man or woman has brains, character, enduring patience, a hide as tough as a walrus, a capacity to work regularly 18 hours a day and to run the risk of almost certain political unpopularity before he or she is through, these are the essential ingredients.[54]

Despite the lack of unanimity on every point, almost all governors agreed that experience in the state legislature just prior to election as governor is invaluable, since it affords the governor a broad view of current problems faced by the state, a comprehension of the governmental structure and operation, expertise in a few specific areas, and the opportunity to develop personal relationships with legislative and administrative officials who will be serving concurrently. Governor Reubin Askew of Florida added:

A person with a legislative background is in a better position to take an early leadership stand as governor. . . . A governor will feel much more confident early on in his administration if he understands the legislative process and knows the key leadership involved.[55]

The only prime gubernatorial element missing in such a career is the executive one, but the governorship itself is a training ground for the development of that skill. Unlike the situation prevailing on the national level, there really is no "feeder channel" of well-rounded executives for the statehouses. Mayoral office and most specialized statewide elective offices below the governorship do not afford experience with the intricate array of state problems (as does the legislature), and appointive administrative office is insulated from elective politics. By contrast, the national parties, in selecting their presidential nominees, are able to draw upon an executive (the governor) who has both political and administrative skills, not just a legislator (the U.S. senator) who, while well-versed substantively and politically, lacks executive training. Since the presidency is no place to begin to develop executive talents, the executive careerist is clearly preferable to the legislator.[56] But, again, no such well-delineated choice is available on the state level, and the person with a legislative background is probably the best available alternative.

If experience in the state legislature just prior to election as governor can be used as a yardstick to measure the adequacy of preparation for the governorship, then recent governors have been demonstrably better trained than their predecessors, as is indicated in Figures 2-1 and 2-2, which are "frequency trees" summarizing the career backgrounds of several hundred governors.[57] Figure 2-1 depicts the public office careers *prior* to election as governor of the 501 governors elected from 1900 to 1949, and Figure 2-2 does the same for governors first elected from 1950 to 1975.

The trees in these figures should be read from right to left. For example, in Figure 2-1, we find that 17.8 percent of all governors (N) were members of the state legislature as the last office prior to election to the governorship. (This percentage appears under the "penultimate office" column.) Moving to the left to the column headed "office experience," we find that 100 percent of those in the state legislative category had, by definition, had experience in the state legislature and that 18 percent had also had law enforcement experience, none had held statewide office, 1.1 percent had also served in Congress, 16.8 percent held some type of administrative public office, and 15.7 percent had been elected to local office in addition to a legislative position.

One further step to the left takes us to the "first office" column, which contains the percentage of governors who, having had experience in one office or another, also began their public careers in that same office. Of all those who had held a state legislative seat, 69.9 percent started their political climb from that seat; 62.5 percent of those in a law enforcement position at some time during their pregubernatorial careers began public life in that same position, and so forth. Lastly, the column furthest to the left reveals the percentages of all governors who followed each particular office path to the governorship. Thus, 11.2 percent of the 501 governors held a legislative seat as the first public office and also held a legislative seat as the last public office before the election as governor; 2.0 percent initiated public life in law enforcement and then advanced through the legislature to the governorship; and so on through the six categories of "penultimate office."

While all past office experiences are important in shaping a person's perspectives and preparations for running for governor, none is probably more important than the last office held before the governorship. Usually it is in the penultimate office that prospective governors make a firm decision to run, start to gear toward both the campaign and the issues that will have to be addressed, and become more aware of the state's needs as a whole. The last office is also the one chosen by ambitious politicians to place themselves in the position to run. This office must fill both their own preparatory needs and the expectations of the electorate as to what constitutes proper preparation for the governorship. Consequently, most of the analysis here will center on the penultimate office. Table 2-7 contains data on the penultimate office for various periods, all regions, and both major parties.

In comparing the first half of this century with the third quarter, the most striking difference in career patterns seems to be the significant increase in state legislative posts as launching pads for the governorships. Whereas 17.8 percent of all governors held state legislative seats as the penultimate office before 1950, 24.9 percent did so after 1950, and, as we shall shortly see, the percentage has increased greatly in the last decade.

The state legislature has also gradually come to dominate more and more careers of future governors. While about 37 percent of earlier governors who had the state legislature as the penultimate office had started in another office, only about 27 percent of recent governors had done so. Thus, about three-quarters of the recent governors who were elected to the governorship from a legislative office had never held any other post. This fact suggests that there may be less

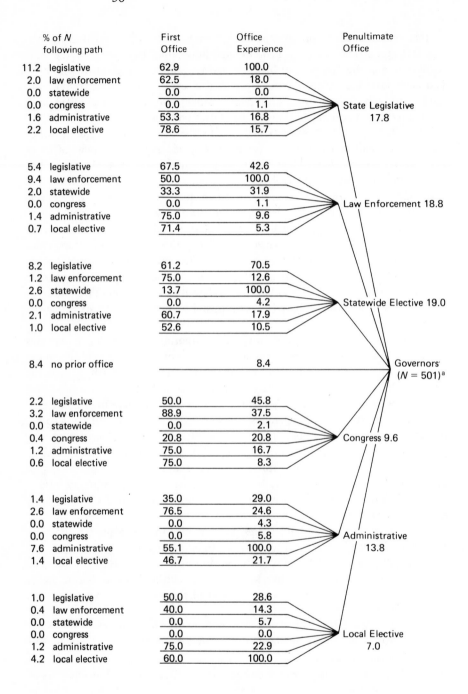

% of N following path		First Office	Office Experience	Penultimate Office
11.2	legislative	62.9	100.0	
2.0	law enforcement	62.5	18.0	
0.0	statewide	0.0	0.0	
0.0	congress	0.0	1.1	State Legislative
1.6	administrative	53.3	16.8	17.8
2.2	local elective	78.6	15.7	
5.4	legislative	67.5	42.6	
9.4	law enforcement	50.0	100.0	
2.0	statewide	33.3	31.9	
0.0	congress	0.0	1.1	Law Enforcement 18.8
1.4	administrative	75.0	9.6	
0.7	local elective	71.4	5.3	
8.2	legislative	61.2	70.5	
1.2	law enforcement	75.0	12.6	
2.6	statewide	13.7	100.0	
0.0	congress	0.0	4.2	Statewide Elective 19.0
2.1	administrative	60.7	17.9	
1.0	local elective	52.6	10.5	
8.4	no prior office		8.4	Governors (N = 501)[a]
2.2	legislative	50.0	45.8	
3.2	law enforcement	88.9	37.5	
0.0	statewide	0.0	2.1	
0.4	congress	20.8	20.8	Congress 9.6
1.2	administrative	75.0	16.7	
0.6	local elective	75.0	8.3	
1.4	legislative	35.0	29.0	
2.6	law enforcement	76.5	24.6	
0.0	statewide	0.0	4.3	
0.0	congress	0.0	5.8	Administrative
7.6	administrative	55.1	100.0	13.8
1.4	local elective	46.7	21.7	
1.0	legislative	50.0	28.6	
0.4	law enforcement	40.0	14.3	
0.0	statewide	0.0	5.7	
0.0	congress	0.0	0.0	Local Elective
1.2	administrative	75.0	22.9	7.0
4.2	local elective	60.0	100.0	

Figure 2-1. Prior Office Careers of Governors, 1900-1949

Sources: The design of this "office frequency tree" is taken from Joseph Schlesinger, *Ambition and Politics: Political Careers in the United States* (Chicago: Rand-McNally, 1966), p. 91, Figure VI-I. The calculations in this figure have been modified to include only those governors who served between 1900 and 1949. The sources used to do this are as follows: Marquis Who's Who, Inc., *Who's Who in America, 1950 [-1975]* (Chicago: A.N. Marquis, 1950-1975); Paul A. Theis and Edmund L. Henshaw, Jr. (eds.), *Who's Who in American Politics, 1968 [-1975]* (New York: R.R. Bowker, 1967-1975); and Michael Barone, Grant Ujifusa, and Douglas Matthews, *The Almanac of American Politics, 1972 [1974, 1976]* (New York: E.P. Dutton, 1972, 1973, 1975).

Note: Definition of terms used in this figure are as follows:

First Office: The first public office in a politician's career.
Office Experience: An office held at some time in a politician's career.
Penultimate Office: The office held just prior to election as governor.
State Legislative Offices: Seats in the lower or upper house of the state legislature, including leadership positions with the exception of the president of the senate whenever the lieutenant governor holds that post.
Law Enforcement Offices: County and city attorneys, district attorneys, U.S. attorneys, judges on all levels, CIA and FBI personnel, and the state attorney general (even if the latter is elected by statewide vote).
Statewide Elective Offices: All offices elected statewide by the voters with the exception of attorney general (included in the "Law Enforcement" category). The number and kind of statewide offices differs from state to state. Some "short ballot" states elect only a governor, lieutenant governor, and attorney general, with all other posts appointive. "Long ballot" states, in contrast, fill such positions as state auditor and state treasurer by vote of the populace.
Congressional Offices: Seats in the U.S. House of Representatives or the U.S. Senate.
Administrative Office: All public offices on local, statewide, and federal levels that are not elective. These are sometimes appointive offices and other times are career positions. (No law enforcement offices are included in this category.) At the local level, a director of a city's public health department would be classified "administrative", for example, as would a state department director or a bureau chief of the federal Department of HEW. At the state level, offices that are elective in some states (like state auditor) would be classified "administrative" in others. Service on part-time local boards and commissions are not included.
No Prior Offices: The politician never held any office—as defined by the categories listed above—before election as governor.

For a further explanation of the figure's methodology, see the text.

aThose who succeed to the office of governor are not included in the tabulations unless they were elected to one or more terms in their own right. The column on the extreme left (as well as the "penultimate office" column), does not total vertically to 100 percent. This is due to rounding error but especially because an "other office" category is not included. Such offices as presidential elector would fall in such a category.

Figure 2-1 (cont.)

"office hopping" and more concentration on developing expertise in one particular office. Some evidence is also found in the number of governors who held a leadership office in one or both houses of the legislature.[58] Almost 44 percent (61 of 139 who served in the legislature) were elected to one or more posts that normally are won only by long-time legislative veterans. Indeed, fully a third of these legislative leaders had devoted their entire pregubernatorial public careers to the legislature. The prominence of legislatively trained governors is apparent throughout the period 1950 to 1975, but it is especially noticeable since 1970. Four out of every ten governors elected for the first time

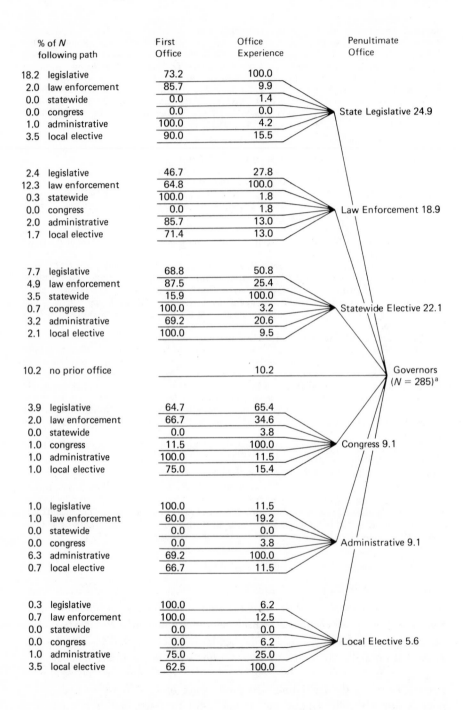

% of N following path		First Office	Office Experience	Penultimate Office
18.2	legislative	73.2	100.0	
2.0	law enforcement	85.7	9.9	
0.0	statewide	0.0	1.4	
0.0	congress	0.0	0.0	State Legislative 24.9
1.0	administrative	100.0	4.2	
3.5	local elective	90.0	15.5	
2.4	legislative	46.7	27.8	
12.3	law enforcement	64.8	100.0	
0.3	statewide	100.0	1.8	
0.0	congress	0.0	1.8	Law Enforcement 18.9
2.0	administrative	85.7	13.0	
1.7	local elective	71.4	13.0	
7.7	legislative	68.8	50.8	
4.9	law enforcement	87.5	25.4	
3.5	statewide	15.9	100.0	
0.7	congress	100.0	3.2	Statewide Elective 22.1
3.2	administrative	69.2	20.6	
2.1	local elective	100.0	9.5	
10.2	no prior office		10.2	Governors (N = 285)[a]
3.9	legislative	64.7	65.4	
2.0	law enforcement	66.7	34.6	
0.0	statewide	0.0	3.8	
1.0	congress	11.5	100.0	Congress 9.1
1.0	administrative	100.0	11.5	
1.0	local elective	75.0	15.4	
1.0	legislative	100.0	11.5	
1.0	law enforcement	60.0	19.2	
0.0	statewide	0.0	0.0	
0.0	congress	0.0	3.8	Administrative 9.1
6.3	administrative	69.2	100.0	
0.7	local elective	66.7	11.5	
0.3	legislative	100.0	6.2	
0.7	law enforcement	100.0	12.5	
0.0	statewide	0.0	0.0	
0.0	congress	0.0	6.2	Local Elective 5.6
1.0	administrative	75.0	25.0	
3.5	local elective	62.5	100.0	

Figure 2-2. Prior Office Careers of Governors, 1950-1975

Sources: Marquis Who's Who, Inc., *Who's Who in America, 1950 [-1975]* (Chicago: A.N. Marquis, 1950-1975); Paul A. Theis and Edmund L. Henshaw, Jr. (eds.), *Who's Who in American Politics, 1968 [-1975]* (New York: R.R. Bowker, 1967-1975); and Michael Barone, Grant Ujifusa, and Douglas Matthews, *The Almanac of American Politics, 1972 [1974, 1976]* (New York: E.P. Dutton, 1972, 1973, 1975). The design of this figure is taken from Joseph Schlesinger, *Ambition and Politics: Political Careers in The United States* (Chicago: Rand-McNally, 1966), p. 91, Figure VI-I.

Note: See Figure 2-1 for definitions of terms used in this figure. For a further explanation of the figure's methodology, see the accompanying text.

aThose who succeeded to the office of governor are not included in the tabulations unless they were elected to one or more terms in their own right. Governors who served a nonconsecutive term before the year 1950 are not included. (Rather, their careers are summarized in Figure 2-1 which presents data for 1914-1949.) The column on the extreme left (as well as the "penultimate office" column) does not quite total vertically to 100 percent. This is because an "other office" category is not included, since all public offices do not fall under the six broad categories listed.

Figure 2-2 (cont.)

in the 1970s have had the state legislature as their penultimate office, compared to less than two of every ten in the first half of the century.

Law enforcement positions as penultimate offices have shown a precipitous decline even as the legislature was increasing in gubernatorial stature. While 18.8 percent of all governors from 1900-1949 last held a law enforcement post before the governorship, only 8 percent of governors since 1970 have. Some notable judges have been included in this number over the years. James F. Byrnes, Democrat of South Carolina, was a U.S. Supreme Court justice. Three governors, Lee Knous (D-Colorado), Charles Terry (D-Delaware), and Thomas Mabry (D-New Mexico), had been chief justices of their states' supreme courts. Three more governors, Edward Arn (R-Kansas), Robert Kennon (D-Louisiana), and Luther Youngdahl (R-Minnesota), were members of their states' supreme courts before winning the governorship. But with the possible exception of these high judicial offices, it cannot be said that most law enforcement positions afford exceptionally good training for a future chief executive. The decrease in the category's governor-producing potential in recent years, then, might well be salutary.

Statewide offices are second in importance only to the legislature as a pool of future governors, and in the last quarter-century there has been a slight increase in the percentage of governors with statewide penultimate offices. About 22 percent of governors between 1950 and 1975 used statewide office as a steppingstone directly to the governorship, and another 11 percent held at least one statewide office sometime during their pregubernatorial careers, although not as the penultimate office. The lieutenant governorship pool accounted for the largest part of the total by far and comprised slightly more than half of the 102 men who held statewide office before the governorship. Another quarter held the attorney generalship, and an eighth served as secretary of state. The remaining eighth had won posts like state treasurer, auditor, secretary of agriculture, and member of the state public service commission.

Table 2-7
The Penultimate Office, by Time Period, Party, and Region

| | Percent of Governors Holding Penultimate Office | | | | | | | | | | | |
| Penultimate Office | Time Periods | | | | | Party (1950-1975) | | Region (1950-1975) | | | | |
	1900-49	1950-75	1950-59	1960-69	1970-75	Democrats D	Republicans R	Northeast	Midwest	South	Border	West
Legislature	17.8	24.9	22.1	21.0	40.0	22.1	28.7	22.6	22.9	26.9	17.1	33.3
Law enforcement	18.8	18.9	21.4	21.0	8.0	20.9	16.4	12.9	20.0	13.5	29.3	21.7
Statewide	19.0	22.1	22.1	25.3	16.0	23.9	19.7	21.0	22.9	26.9	19.5	20.0
Congress	9.6	9.1	9.3	6.3	14.0	8.6	9.8	16.1	4.3	11.5	9.8	5.0
Administrative	13.8	9.1	11.4	8.4	4.0	10.4	7.4	12.9	8.6	7.7	9.8	6.7
Local elective	7.0	5.6	6.4	5.3	4.0	6.1	4.9	8.1	8.6	0.0	7.3	3.3
No prior office	8.4	10.2	7.1	12.6	14.0	8.0	13.1	6.4	12.9	13.5	7.3	10.0

Source: Compiled from statistics in Figures 2-1 and 2-2, as well as ten additional frequency trees which were constructed by the author but which, because of space limitations, are not reproduced in this volume.

Note: The penultimate office is the last office held before election to the governorship. See Figure 2-1 for definitions of the offices listed in this table.

A clue to the general prestige and attractiveness of governorships can be found in the number of congressmen who risk their usually safe Washington seats for a chance to return to their home states as governors. Overall, in the first half and the third quarter of this century, about 9 percent of all governors held congressional posts as their last pregubernatorial offices. In the 1960s, however, when governors were bearing the brunt of taxpayers' revolts while trying to satisfy demands for more and better services, the congressional percentage dwindled to 6.3. By the 1970s governorships were again enticing more congressmen away from federal careers, and fully 14 percent of governors won the state office by using a congressional springboard.

Not all the congressional candidates for governor were members of the lower house. Four incumbent or former U.S. senators sought and won governorships over the last twenty-five years: Ernest McFarland (D-Arizona), William Umstead (D-North Carolina), James F. Byrnes (D-South Carolina), and Price Daniel (D-Texas). Five other U.S. senators made unsuccessful bids for the office of governor: William R. Knowland (R-California), Irving Ives (R-New York), Hugh Mitchell (D-Washington), Rush Holt (R-West Virginia), and Fred Seaton (R-Nebraska). Knowland was minority leader of the U.S. Senate at the time he ran for governor. No list would be complete without the name of one other former U.S. senator and unsuccessful California gubernatorial candidate, Richard Nixon, who had also served eight years as vice president.

Some states have an abnormally large number of congressmen running for governor, partially due to a system of nomination in which congressmen needn't abandon their seats unless they actually win the party gubernatorial nod. Connecticut, one of these states, has had the largest number (four) of "congressional governors" of all states in the past twenty-five years. Off-year gubernatorial elections (held in five states) also attract congressional candidates. Edwin Edwards (D-Louisiana) and William Cahill (R-New Jersey) are two recent examples of congressmen who ran for (and won) governorships in off-year elections. Since they would have retained their House seats even if they had lost, their candidacies were low-risk political ventures.

Twenty-five states have had at least one governor come from Congress since 1950, which is a surprisingly broad-based total. Paul L. Hain and Terry B. Smith have attributed the recent rise in congressional candidates for the governorship to two factors.[59] First, they cite the "increased attractiveness of the office of governor," which can be attributed to such factors as the lengthening of the governor's term in many states to four years and the allowance of reelection. (Additional reasons for the governorship's new allure are presented in subsequent chapters.) Secondly, the growth in the "functional relationship" between the office of governor and congressman has played a role:

An increase in the importance to the States of federal programs of various sorts and a corresponding increase in the value of the Governor's understanding of the intricacies of federal programs, bureaucratic procedures, and funding mechanisms should increase the extent to which congressmen are perceived (and perceive themselves to be) as among the best-qualified candidates for Governor.[60]

Both unelected administrative posts and local elective offices have been steadily declining as gubernatorial sources. In the first half of the century these two categories together provided as penultimate offices 21 percent of the nation's governors. By the 1970s, this figure had shrunk to just 8 percent. Apparently, experience in elective offices at levels higher than local government is more necessary for advancement to the governorship in recent times. Nevertheless some of the best-qualified gubernatorial candidates over the last quarter-century were drawn from the ranks of unelected administrators. (A distinction should be drawn between "best-qualified" and "successful," though. Some of those with the most far-ranging administrative backgrounds were not particularly successful as governors.)

Over the period 1950 to 1975, sixteen governors served in major federal administrative posts prior to their elections. Several were members of the presidential cabinet: Secretary of Commerce Averell Harriman (D-New York), Secretary of State James F. Byrnes, and Navy Secretary John B. Connally (D-Texas). Harriman and Byrnes both served in numerous other administrative posts as well. The Department of State produced several governors: Adlai Stevenson (D-Illinois), Christian Herter (R-Massachusetts), Nelson Rockefeller (R-New York), William Scranton (R-Pennsylvania), and Donald S. Russell (D-South Carolina). Chester Bowles (D-Connecticut) and Michael DiSalle (D-Ohio) were both directors of the Office of Price Stabilization.

State administration had occupied the talents of seven men before their governorships. Directors or commissioners of major state departments and boards included Winthrop Rockefeller (R-Arkansas), S. Ernest Vandiver (D-Georgia), Francis W. Sargent (R-Massachusetts), Mike O'Callaghan (D-Nevada), Christopher Del Sesto (R-Rhode Island), Buford Ellington (D-Tennessee), and George Clyde (R-Utah). A dozen governors learned their political ABC's under the tutelage of successful officeholders. There were seven former executive or administrative assistants to governors who eventually wound up heading governor's offices themselves, and five key aides to U.S. senators and representatives who became state chief executives. Finally, the administrative post of university president furnished three governors: Democrat Donald Russell of the University of South Carolina and Republicans Arthur Crane and Clifford Hansen of the University of Wyoming.

The six penultimate categories that have been discussed here do not exhaust all the office possibilities. In addition to formal elective and administrative posts, thirty-eight (or 12.4 percent) of the governors who served between 1950 and 1975 held a major party office before their elections. This office was the only one of any kind held by nine governors—a situation which arose primarily in states where one party was weak and did not have a wide variety of elected officers from which to choose at nomination time. The nominations of Linwood Holton (R-Virginia), Winfield Dunn (R-Tennessee), and J.J. Exon (D-Nebraska) seem to fall in this category.

Many governors ran for office unsuccessfully before winning governorships. Counting both primaries (in Southern states only) and general elections, twenty-eight eventually victorious governors had made previously losing gubernatorial bids; sixteen had failed in congressional races; and at least eight had lost elections for other posts. Unsuccessful though the campaigns were, they often helped to establish the candidate's identity among voters and build party and financial contacts that proved invaluable in due time.

Other offices and positions also do not fit in any particular penultimate category. Lurleen Wallace (D-Alabama) was first lady of her state just prior to assuming the governorship. William Egan (D-Alaska) staked his political claim as president of the Alaska Constitutional Convention and as head of Alaska's statehood mission to the U.S. Congress. Many other governors held no prior offices at all, and the percentage of these "citizen politicians" has been steadily increasing in the last few decades. (In the 1970s those with no prior offices comprised 14 percent of all governors compared to 7.1 percent in the 1950s.) Some of these governors—such as George Romney (R-Michigan), Russell Peterson (R-Delaware), Milton Shapp (D-Pennsylvania), and Scott Matheson (D-Utah)—came directly from lucrative businesses or law practices apparently motivated by a desire to contribute to the common weal. Others have maintained interest and participation in a wide variety of volunteer, humanitarian, and business organizations and associations that are out of the political mainstream. Still others have gained access to the governor's office by the fame attending other careers, such as acting as was the case for Ronald Reagan of California, or public controversies as was the case with Lester Maddox of Georgia and his battle against racial integration.

There are some party differences in career patterns. As Table 2-7 shows, Republican governors tend to come from the legislature or are elected without an office background more frequently than Democrats. On the other hand, more Democratic governors come from the law enforcement, statewide, administrative, and local elective offices. Regionally, the differences are sometimes greater than the party divergence. The legislature as penultimate office is a large proportion in all regions, but highest by far in the West (where exactly a third of all governors in the last twenty-five years held a legislative office just prior to election as governor) and lowest in the Border States (with 17.1 percent). Law enforcement offices as a gubernatorial source is at a peak in the Border states (20.3 percent) while waning to 13.5 percent in the South and 12.9 percent in the Northeast. Statewide offices provide large numbers of governors in all regions, especially the South. More congressmen go on to become governor in the Northeast than anywhere else, while few succeed in the Midwest or West. The Northeast also elects more administrators proportionally than any other region; the figure is about double the West's 6.7 percent, which is the nadir for unelected administrative offices. Not many persons go directly from local office to the governor's mansion in any region, but a few more do so in the Midwest and Northeast. This route is nonexistent in the South (at least recently) and very low in the West. Finally, about double the Northeastern proportion of governors with no prior offices are elected in the South and Midwest.

Only the careers of successful gubernatorial candidates have been discussed here, but of course the losing candidates—some of whom missed governorships by only an electoral whisper—have office histories almost as varied as the victors, although more of the defeated nominees appear to have had no prior public offices. Complete information is unfortunately not available in standard reference works for the 283 major party candidates defeated for governorships from 1950 to 1975. A partial compilation, however, indicates that at least a quarter had been state legislators, some of whom held leadership positions, and a number had been jurists, such as former U.S. Supreme Court Justice Arthur J. Goldberg (D-New York). At least forty-eight statewide elective officers have run unsuccessfully; slightly more than half of these were lieutenant governors and a little under a third were attorneys general. Seventeen members of the House of Representatives and six U.S. senators have also lost gubernatorial bids in the last twenty-five years, as have many major federal administrators, including Secretary of the Interior Fred Seaton (R-Nebraska) and Secretary of Labor James P. Mitchell (R-New Jersey). Mayors of major cities like Democrats Robert King High of Miami, Kevin White of Boston, and Earl J. Glade of Salt Lake City were unable to win Promotions to the statehouse. The son of FDR (James Roosevelt of New York) and a former vice president of the U.S. (Richard Nixon of California) were also rejected by their states' electorates for chief executive.

After the Governorship

What governors do after their terms is as important a barometer of the office's prestige as what paths governors followed to the statehouse. If more former governors have been elected or appointed to high office in recent years, then some additional weight would be lent to the theory of an increasingly prestigious governorship. Table 2-8 demonstrates that this is indeed the case. In general, while only about 38 percent of governors who held office between 1900 and 1909 went on to serve in some other public capacity, almost half of the governors in the last quarter-century did so.

The largest percentage of publicly active former governors graduated to federal administrative posts (18.5 percent, which is an increase of several percent over the century's first decade). The 45 governors in this category held 59

Table 2-8
Postgubernatorial Office, 1900-1909 and 1950-1975

Office	No. of Governors (% of Governors) Holding Office[a]	
	1950-1975[b]	1900-1909
U.S. senator	31 (12.8)	(12.6)
U.S. representative	4 (1.6)	(2.6)
Judicial office[c]	17 (7.0)	(2.6)
Federal administrative	45 (18.5)	(14.3)
State administrative	3 (1.2)	(8.9)
Statewide elective (except governor)	3 (1.2)	(0.0)
State legislative	3 (1.2)	(1.9)
Local elective-mayor	2 (0.8)	
Governor again[d]	10 (4.1)	(1.9)[f]
Major party presidential or vice presidential nominee[e]	7 (2.9)	
No postgubernatorial office	131 (53.9)[g]	(61.7)
	N=243	N= 154

Sources: Statistics for 1950-1975 are taken from Marquis Who's Who, Inc., *Who's Who In America, 1950 [-1975]* (Chicago: A.N. Marquis, 1950-1975); Paul A. Theis and Edmund L. Henshaw, Jr. (eds.), *Who's Who In American Politics, 1968 [-1975]* (New York: R.R. Bowker, 1967-1975); and Michael Barone, Grant Ujifusa, and Douglas Matthews, *The Almanac of American Politics, 1972 [-1974, 1976]* (New York: E.P. Dutton, 1972, 1973, 1975). Statistics for 1900-1909 are taken from Joseph A. Schlesinger, "The Politics of the Executive," in Herbert Jacobs and Kenneth Vines (eds.), *Politics in the American States: A Comparative Analysis* (Boston: Little, Brown, 1971), p. 213.

[a]Percentages total more than 100 since some ex-governors held two or more of these offices.

[b]Only governors who were serving their first terms (or first consecutive series of terms) during the years 1950-1975 were included in the table. Governors who succeeded to the office, whether or not they were eventually elected in their own right, are counted in this table. Neither governors who died in office nor governors still serving in office as of 1976 are counted in N.

[c]This category includes judicial offices at all levels.

[d]At least one term intervened before the former governor was reelected to his previous post.

[e]Tabulation includes Nelson A. Rockefeller who, while not an official party nominee, filled the office of vice president by presidential designation, which is not unlike the selection process prevailing in party conventions.

[f]Joseph Schlesinger's tabulation of governors' careers for 1900-1909 combines these three categories; thus, only the single figure is available.

[g]If governors who merely succeeded to the office and never won election in their own right are eliminated from the tally, this figure decreases to 51.8 percent.

separate federal positions, of which 26 were major department or cabinet posts, 22 were more minor positions (subcabinet level), and 11 were ambassadorships.

In the last twenty-five years almost every cabinet post has been filled by at least one governor. Included in this number are Secretary of State Christian Herter (R-Massachusetts), Secretary of Health, Education, and Welfare Abraham

Ribicoff (D-Connecticut), Secretary of the Treasury John Connally (D-Texas),[61] Secretary of Housing and Urban Development George Romney (R-Michigan), Transportation Secretary John Volpe (R-Massachusetts), Navy Secretary John Chafee (R-Rhode Island), Secretary of Commerce Luther Hodges (D-North Carolina), Agriculture Secretary Orville Freeman (D-Minnesota), and Secretaries of the Interior Douglas McKay (R-Oregon), Walter J. Hickel (R-Alaska), and Stanley Hathaway (R-Wyoming). Although Cecil Andrus of Idaho is not included in the table's tabulation, in 1977 his name was added to the growing list of Western governors who have assumed the Interior Secretaryship.

Two of the U.S. ambassadors to the United Nations have been governors: Adlai Stevenson (D-Illinois) and William Scranton (R-Pennsylvania). Another governor, Averell Harriman (D-New York), has loomed large on the world scene as ambassador for and counsellor to numerous U.S. presidents. Regardless of position, few men have achieved the influence of Sherman Adams (R-New Hampshire) who was President Dwight Eisenhower's closest aide and was often called the "assistant president," with good reason.[62] In the wake of the Watergate scandals another former governor, Vernon Thomson (R-Wisconsin), assumed the politically critical chairmanship of the powerful, newly created Federal Elections Commission.

The proportion of governors who win seats in the U.S. Senate has remained fairly constant at about an eighth of the total. In all, there were 31 successful and 31 unsuccessful Senate candidacies by governors between 1950 and 1975—a remarkably good 50 percent success rate. Donald Matthews calculated that, on the average, 22 percent of all U.S. senators held the governorship as the last public office before their election.[63] Consequently he calls the governorship one of the two major channels to the Senate, with the House of Representatives being the other.[64] Lately, though, the number of ex-governor senators has dropped. In the U.S. Senate organizing in January, 1975, for instance, there were only 16 former governors, and this number was unchanged by the 1976 elections. This decline does not bode ill for the governorship, however.

An accepted axiom in American politics is that governors naturally aspire to the U.S. Senate. For a governor who aspires to the presidency, it is supposedly more advantageous to be located in Washington than in the hinterlands. Further, the suggestion is that the position of senator is more prestigious and the perquisites greater than the governorship. The first assumption will be examined in a later chapter, and the second one is effectively demolished in Matthews' investigation of the Senate:

A former governor who becomes a senator is often accustomed to a higher salary, more power and perquisites, a grander office, a larger staff, and more publicity than the freshman senator enjoys. He is likely to find the pace of legislative life slow and to be frustrated by the necessity of cooperating with ninety-nine equals. To move from the governorship of one of the larger states to the role of apprentice senator is, in the short run, a demotion. The result for the one-time governor is a frequent feeling of disillusionment, depression, and discouragement. . . . At the same time the other senators complain that the former governors "are the hardest group to handle; they come down here expecting to be big shots" and that they often are unwilling to realize that "they are just one of the boys."[65]

The unhappiness experienced by governors-turned-senators and the reluctance to be "one of the boys" have contributed to repeated refusals to run for the Senate by a number of recent governors. Governor Tom McCall of Oregon, who himself turned down three promising opportunities for a Senate candidacy, remarked that ". . . governors have got to quit collapsing when the Potomac waves its little finger at them! . . . States and cities are the trenches where the battle for a better society is being fought."[66] Governor Dan Evans of Washington, discussing his postgubernatorial future, flatly insisted: "My plans do not include running for Congress under any circumstances. I'd be totally frustrated. I wouldn't take the job if I were appointed to it."[67] Other governors voiced similar sentiments in separate interviews.

It may be that the original stereotype of the "Senate-hungry" governor derived in part from the overanxiousness of a few state executives to grab Senate seats. On a couple of well-publicized occasions in the last twenty-five years, a governor has used his power to fill Senate vacancies to appoint himself to the empty seat.[68] E.L. Mechem (R-New Mexico) did so in 1962, and J. Howard Edmondson (D-Oklahoma) followed suit in 1953. Both were chastised by the voters in the succeeding elections, and their Senate careers were quite short. The voters apparently do not take kindly to any manipulation of the power to appoint to vacancies that stacks the odds in the appointer's favor. For example, in 1954 Governor Robert Crosby (R-Nebraska) selected a "seat warmer" who would step down at the end of the uncompleted term so that Crosby would have a clear field for the seat. Nine years later Governor Frank Clement (D-Tennessee) did the same. Both Crosby and Clement were rebuked by their own state parties and were soundly defeated in party primaries for the Senate nominations. No governor repeated either maneuver (self-appointed or "seat warmer" selection) for more than a dozen years after Clement until 1976, when Governor Wendell Anderson (D-Minnesota) arranged for his own appointment to the seat vacated by Vice President Walter Mondale. The voters' verdict on the move will not be known until the 1978 elections.

More governors (7 percent from 1950-1975 compared to 2.6 percent from 1900-1909) have been going on to judicial offices after their statehouse terms. Normally the judicial posts are major ones (either the state supreme court or the federal district court). One recent governor used the judicial channel to leave an imprint on the country larger than that of all but a few presidents. Earl Warren (R-California), as chief justice of the U.S. Supreme Court from 1953 to 1969, led the Court to hand down precedent-shattering decisions in the fields of racial integration, rights of the criminally accused, and legislative apportionment. In the former and latter cases especially, Warren helped to reshape the political map of the United States. He set the stage for a new breed of governor in a South no longer held back by divisive segregation and a new breed of legislator across the country who, by being responsive to the severe urban problems faced by the states, would make the job of governor a bit less frustrating. Only three other governors in U.S. history had achieved Warren's post of chief justice: John Jay and Charles Evans Hughes of New York, and Salmon P. Chase of Ohio.

About 4 percent of all governors in the last twenty-five years have come back to serve again as governor after the elapse of at least one term after they initially left the post. Sometimes they had originally left of their own volition and other times involuntarily (because of a constitutional limit on the number of successive terms or a defeat at the polls). E.L. Mechem (R-New Mexico) was perhaps the most successful in this category: He was reelected after an interval, defeated for the next reelection, then reelected once more. Mills Godwin of Virginia, who served his first term as a Democrat, also managed a unique comeback after a four-year interval as the gubernatorial candidate of the Republicans. No one, though, has ever matched the feat of Sam Houston, the only person to serve as governor of two different states (Texas and Tennessee). Overall, from 1950 to 1975, more governors have won the governorship again and been major party presidential or vice presidential nominees (7 percent) than in the first part of the century (a maximum of 1.9 percent).[69]

Since a greater proportion of governors are attaining high elective and administrative posts after their governorships, it can be expected that minor and less prestigious offices are attracting fewer former state chief executives. Table 2-8 bears this out. Only four governors in the last two and a half decades have served in the House of Representatives, and just one governor has been initially elected to the lower house of Congress since 1960. While 8.9 percent of the former governors from 1900 to 1909 served in some state administrative post, just 1.2 percent were doing so in the last quarter-century. (No governor first elected since 1958 has accepted such a post.) No governors but two have recently run for city mayor after their governorships. (Republicans Theodore McKeldin of Baltimore and J. Bracken Lee of Salt Lake City were the only exceptions.) Only three governors, all of whom had first succeeded to the office, ever went back to serve in state legislatures again. Finally, two governors have served in lesser statewide elective offices after their terms, but both were exceptional cases. When Lester Maddox (D-Georgia) was constitutionally forbidden from seeking a consecutive reelection as governor in 1970, he sought the lieutenant governorship instead, as a preliminary to another term in four years. (He won the lieutenant governorship but lost his second race for governor.) The other governor in this category, Dwight W. Burney (R-Nebraska), succeeded to the governorship in an election year when he had already accepted a party nomination for a lesser office (the lieutenant governorship).

Major party offices, such as state chairman or national committeeman, have consumed the time of thirteen governors after they left office. One former governor, Kenneth Curtis of Maine, became chairman of the Democratic National Committee in 1977 at President Carter's invitation.[70] Many other governors accepted significant campaign posts from time to time. For example, Republicans Hugh Gregg of New Hampshire and Richard Ogilvie of Illinois headed up the 1976 primary election campaigns for President Ford in their crucial states. A number of other "public" activities have occurred but do not lend themselves to the categories listed in Table 2-8. For example, Terry Sanford (D-North Carolina) became the president of Duke University, while Albert "Happy" Chandler (D-Kentucky) became the commissioner of baseball, which was a job that paid a good deal more than any state political office at the time!

A small but noticeable minority of governors over the years have become residents, rather than the supervisors, of prisons. Otto Kerner (D-Illinois), W.W. Barron (D-West Virginia), and David Hall (D-Oklahoma) were all found guilty of crimes and sentenced to jail terms.[71] Tim Babcock (R-Montana) and Spiro Agnew (R-Maryland) got caught up in the Watergate scandals. Babcock received a fine and a suspended jail term for arranging an illegal contribution to the 1972 Nixon reelection committee, and Agnew pleaded guilty to a single count of tax evasion and lost the vice presidency in October 1973 in a plea-bargaining agreement that revealed Agnew's corrupt dealings with contractors while governor. Agnew's successor as governor, Democrat Marvin Mandel, was felled by federal mail fraud and racketeering charges in 1977 and thus became the first sitting governor convicted of a federal crime since 1924. Perhaps the saddest case over twenty-five years is that of William C. Marland (D-West Virginia), a promising young governor whose advocacy of a severance tax on coal led to personal collapse.[72] His hopes for a successful governorship destroyed by special interests opposed to the severance tax, Marland completed an unhappy term as governor and ran two losing campaigns for the U.S. Senate. Subsequently he became an alcoholic and disappeared from West Virginia. He was finally found in Chicago in 1965 driving a taxi cab and trying to rehabilitate himself. Marland was offered a good job and the chance to return to his native state, but tragically he died of cancer before he could begin a new life.

Defeated gubernatorial candidates also have impressive later careers despite their losses, although quite expectedly the average achievements are somewhat less spectacular than those of successful candidates. Federal administrative offices are often made available to the rejected gubernatorial nominees of the party in power nationally. Republican Richard Kleindienst, who lost a 1964 Arizona governor's race, stayed active in GOP politics. When the party returned to power in 1969, he came to Washington as well, first as assistant attorney general, then as John Mitchell's replacement as head of the Justice Department. (He, too, became entangled in the Watergate web.) Howard Calloway (R-Georgia) is yet another example. The defeated 1966 gubernatorial contender became secretary of the army under President Ford, then head of the Ford 1976 election committee for a brief time. At least thirteen other defeated candidates from 1950 to 1975 received federal posts of varying importance.

"If at first you don't succeed . . ." is the motto of most politicians. One defeat is hardly enough to stymie an inveterate office-seeker, and many defeated gubernatorial hopefuls try for other offices on the rebound. Senators Charles Percy (R-Illinois) and Pete Domenici (R-New Mexico) lost governorships only two years before winning their congressional seats. William Proxmire (D-Wisconsin) had lost three successive elections for governor before capturing a U.S. Senate seat in 1957, which he has held since with ease. Nevertheless, Senate posts are much less frequently won by gubernatorial losers than winners. By contrast, seats in the House of Representatives are more often sought and won by defeated candidates. Since 1950 seven defeated candidates have held House posts compared to only four governors. Of all the offices, though, defeated gubernatorial nominees clearly best like to try for governor again. In twenty-five years sixteen have won on the second or third try, but twenty-four have repeatedly lost in the general elections tallied here.

Judgeships are sometimes repositories for defeated gubernatorial contenders. Just as with federal administrative posts, judicial offices at the federal district level can be dispensed to reward those who fought the good fight for the party. At least six received judicial plums as consolation prizes since 1950.

Offices that are seen as below the dignity of a former governor to seek are sufficiently prestigious for defeated candidates. It is very common for a gubernatorial loser to return to the state legislature, for instance. Terms in the state senate often overlap that of the governor so that a senator does not have to relinquish his seat to run for governor. The same is true for mayoral terms of office. Defeated candidates will sometimes seek local elective positions, or statewide elective offices below the governorship. After unsuccessful gubernatorial bids Richardson Dilworth (D-Pennsylvania) became mayor of Philadelphia, and Jesse Unruh (D-California) and Palmer Burch (R-Colorado) became elected treasurers of their states. Occasionally, a former gubernatorial candidate will wind up in a state administrative post once his party regains power. One disappointed contender for governor received a vice presidential nomination, though not from a major party. William Dyke of Wisconsin, who ran as a Republican for the statehouse in 1974, received the American Party nod for the second spot on the national ticket in 1976.

Outstanding Governors

Duane Lockard, after studying the careers of sixty-six New Jersey governors, was moved to call his subjects:

an incredibly assorted lot.... Some were rogues and thieves; some were the mere agents of powerful outsiders (like business moguls or party bosses); some were amiable nonentities, adept at platitude and evasion, who served their term and passed into oblivion. But there were others. Some were men of firmness, ability, and principle....[73]

Lockard's description applies equally well to the broad sweep of governors nationally. It is a highly subjective yet a worthwhile and even imperative task to identify those governors of "firmness, ability, and principle."[74] In Table 2-9 is found a list of governors who served from 1950 to 1975 deemed outstanding by this author. Although most decisions for inclusion would not cause significant controversy, there will hardly be unanimity on all the choices, if only because the very definition of the "outstanding governor" is not agreed upon. Governor Tom McCall of Oregon defined his standard in this fashion: "A good governor's got to throw himself under the train every now and then."[75] Governor Terry Sanford of North Carolina used a different yardstick for the outstanding governor: "One who tried to make state government work for the benefit of the people."[76]

The judgments made here in determining outstanding governors were based on criteria not dissimilar from those implied by Sanford. In general, the outstanding chief executive was a governor of conspicuous ability and competence whose term was characterized by personal hard work and firm dedication and who diligently attempted (even if unsuccessful in part) to meet the needs of the people of his or her state. There are no stand-patters noted in Table 2-9; the problems that have faced states and governors are simply too numerous, intricate, and bedevilling for that, whatever one's philosophical approach to government. This is not to say that an ideological predisposition of "progressivism" has prejudiced the table's findings. Great care was taken to rate governors in terms of their political milieux as well as specific accomplishments. Each state was considered primarily as a self-contained unit. The governors of South Dakota were compared to one another far more than to the governors of New York, for example. Each governor is also examined in the context of his times. It would be absurd and unfair to judge governors of the early 1950s on their racial policies, while it is more reasonable that this factor should be weighed in the mid-sixties.

Underlying these subjective judgments was a compilation of material about each governor who served from 1950 to 1975, including personal characteristics, political background, career training, and accomplishments in public life and office before, during, and after the governorship. Evaluations of the political and administrative abilities of the state chief executives were sought from a wide assortment of sources. Many of the books and articles listed in the bibliography provided detailed appraisals of a single governor's record. The series of seven

Table 2-9
Outstanding Governors, 1950-1975

State	Governors (Party)	State	Governors (Party)
Alabama	James Folsom (D)	Massachusetts	Christian Herter (R)
Alaska	William Egan (D)		John A. Volpe (R)
	Walter J. Hickel (R)		Francis W. Sargent (R)
	Jay Hammond (R)		Michael Dukakis (D)
Arkansas	Sid McMath (D)	Michigan	G. Mennen Williams (D)
	Winthrop Rockefeller (R)		George Romney (R)
	Dale Bumpers (D)		William G. Milliken (R)
	David Pryor (D)	Minnesota	Orville Freeman (D)
California	Earl Warren (R)		Wendell R. Anderson (D)
	Edmund Brown, Sr. (D)	Missouri	Warren E. Hearnes (D)
	Edmund Brown, Jr. (D)		Christopher Bond (R)
Colorado	Steven McNichols (D)	Montana	Thomas L. Judge (D)
	John Love (R)	Nebraska	Norbert T. Tiemann (R)
	Richard Lamm (D)	Nevada	Grant Sawyer (D)
Connecticut	Chester Bowles (D)		Mike O'Callaghan (D)
	Abraham Ribicoff (D)	New Hampshire	Sherman Adams (R)
	Ella Grasso (D)	New Jersey	Alfred E. Driscoll (R)
Delaware	Russell W. Peterson (R)		Robert B. Meyner (D)
Florida	Le Roy Collins (D)		Richard J. Hughes (D)
	Reubin Askew (D)		William T. Cahill (R)
Georgia	Herman Talmadge (D)	New Mexico	Edwin Mechem (R)
	Carl E. Sanders (D)		David F. Cargo (R)
	Jimmy Carter (D)		Jerry Apodaca (D)
Hawaii	William F. Quinn (R)	New York	Thomas E. Dewey (R)
	John A. Burns (D)		Nelson A. Rockefeller (R)
Idaho	Robert E. Smylie (R)		Hugh Carey (D)
	Cecil D. Andrus (D)	North Carolina	W. Kerr Scott (D)
Illinois	Adlai E. Stevenson (D)		Luther Hodges, Sr. (D)
	Richard B. Ogilvie (R)		Terry Sanford (D)
Indiana	Matthew Welsh (D)		James E. Holshouser (R)
	Edgar Whitcomb (R)	North Dakota	William L. Guy (D)
Iowa	Harold Hughes (D)		Arthur A. Link (D)
	Robert D. Ray (R)	Ohio	Michael V. DiSalle (D)
Kansas	Frank Carlson (R)		John J. Gilligan (D)
	John Anderson (R)	Oklahoma	J. Howard Edmondson (D)
Kentucky	Earle C. Clements (D)		Henry Bellmon (R)
	Bert Combs (D)	Oregon	Mark O. Hatfield (R)
	Edward Breathitt (D)		Tom McCall (R)
Louisiana	Earl K. Long (D)	Pennsylvania	James H. Duff (R)
	Edwin W. Edwards (D)		George M. Leader (D)
Maine	Burton Cross (R)		William W. Scranton (R)
	Edmund Muskie (D)		Milton J. Shapp (D)
	Ken Curtis (D)	Rhode Island	John O. Pastore (D)
	James B. Longley (I)		Dennis J. Roberts (D)
Maryland	Theodore R. McKeldin		John H. Chafee (R)
	Marvin Mandel (D)		Philip Noel (D)

Table 2-9 (cont.)

State	Governors (Party)	State	Governors (Party)
South Carolina	J. Strom Thurmond (D)[a] Ernest Hollings (D) Robert McNair (D) John C. West (D)	Virginia	Deane C. Davis (R) Thomas P. Salmon (D) Mills E. Godwin, Jr. (D,R)[b] Linwood Holton (R)
South Dakota	Joe J. Foss (R) Richard F. Kneip (D)	Washington	Daniel J. Evans (R)
Tennessee	Gordon Browning (D) Frank C. Clement (D) Winfield Dunn (R)	West Virginia	William C. Marland (D) Cecil H. Underwood (R)
		Wisconsin	Gaylord A. Nelson (D) Warren P. Knowles (R) Patrick J. Lucey (D)
Texas	John B. Connally (D)[a]		
Utah	Calvin L. Rampton (D)	Wyoming	Milward L. Simpson (R) Clifford P. Hansen (R)
Vermont	Philip H. Hoff (D)		Stanley K. Hathaway (R)

D = Democrat; R = Republican; I = Independent

Source: The construction of this table was the cumulative product of all interviews and most of the bibliographic material. See the Preface.

Note: See the text for a full explanation of this table. No outstanding governors have been chosen for Arizona and Mississippi during the time period surveyed.

[a]Strom Thurmond and John Connally, though both are now Republicans, were elected to their gubernatorial terms as Democrats.

[b]Godwin's "outstanding" term was served as a Democrat from 1966 to 1970. His second term, as a Republican from 1974 to 1978, was lackluster.

volumes on all fifty states by Neal Peirce was especially helpful in that it briefly reviewed the impact of most governors on their state governments in the post-World War II era. Dozens of experts in the field of state government, academics, and officials of organizations such as the National Governors' Conference and the Council of State Governments were personally consulted. Every incumbent and former governor who was interviewed for this study was asked to identify fellow governors in and out of his state and party whom he considered to be the most exceptional (see the interview questions in Appendix A). The same request was made to many other persons—from journalists to long-time gubernatorial aides—in the course of travel.

In assessing each governor's record, the seven "job qualifications" for a chief executive suggested by Joseph Kallenbach were borne in mind.[77] In Kallenbach's view a governor should be evaluated on his ability as a judge of men, ability to make hard decisions and assume responsibility, political sensitivity and timing, political audacity and zest for combat, ability to inspire confidence and loyalty, sense of proportion and perspective, and ability to withstand unfair criticism. (To the latter, one might add the ability to recognize and accept well-directed criticism.) The governors listed in Table 2-9 appear to possess these talents and often excel at them.

Before proceeding to an analysis of the outstanding governors, several other provisos should be mentioned. First, the ratings of governors initially elected after 1973 are naturally tentative. Some promising new governors have not been included because their gubernatorial records are too sketchy at this point. A few, like Democrat Hugh Carey with New York's severe financial crisis of 1975-76, have already been sufficiently tested. Secondly, the evaluation of each person's record extended only over the gubernatorial term of office. Performance in prior or succeeding posts was not considered. Thus, Sherman Adams is appraised on his record as governor of New Hampshire, not on his accomplishments or duties as Eisenhower's "assistant president." Finally, a broad view of each governor is taken. If men were angels this would not be necessary, but some outstanding governors had ample character flaws to be considered. Their records outweighed their faults, however. As one source consulted for this study commented when asked his opinion of a prominent Border state governor: "He's outstanding, even if a crook."

Of the 312 governors who served between 1950 and 1975, 117 (or 37.5 percent) have been included in the list of outstanding state executives and 48 of the 50 states are represented. For such a large proportion to be termed exceptionally able—and there were no quotas—suggests that V.O. Key, Jr., was not so "perverse" to argue that "voters are not fools."[78] It may also suggest that voters, and their state governments, have been extraordinarily lucky in recent years. Competent persons have been attracted to run for governorships at least occasionally in almost all states. The quality of even outstanding governors varies quite a bit. Some governors are marginal inclusions when compared with the top dozen: Winthrop Rockefeller (R-Arkansas), Earl Warren (R-California), Reubin Askew (D-Florida), Harold Hughes (D-Iowa), Alfred E. Driscoll (R-New Jersey), Richard J. Hughes (D-New Jersey), Thomas E. Dewey (R-New York), Nelson Rockefeller (R-New York), Terry Sanford (D-North Carolina), Tom McCall (R-Oregon), Dan Evans (R-Washington), and Patrick J. Lucey (D-Wisconsin).

If governors have been fairly evaluated with each state and time period properly considered, then one might expect to see a distribution of outstanding governors by region, party, and decade that closely parallels the overall pattern. There are 46 Republican and 70 Democratic governors (and one Independent) listed in Table 2-9, and this nearly precisely equals the party split of all governors. Regionally, too, the percentages correspond, with only a slight proportional overrepresentation for the Northeast. Exactly half of the outstanding governors were first elected to office before 1963 (the midpoint year of this study) and half afterwards. This distribution should emphatically not be taken to imply that there has been no major improvement in the quality of governors over 1950 to 1975. For the purposes of Table 2-9 governors have been judged on the basis of unique political circumstances of time and place. However, if governors were measured against one another as individuals and on accomplishments, those elected to office after 1963 would have a decided edge. Not only would there be more recent outstanding governors, but there would be fewer black sheep. There were one or two embarrassments in the 1975 gubernatorial crop, but the number was considerably reduced from 1950. As author Neal Peirce asserted: "The general quality has risen, and there are fewer outrageous showmen, charlatans, and crooks in the barrel than there were a quarter-century ago."[79]

Earlier in this chapter data were presented that indicated that governors in the 1970s have been better educated, younger, and more religiously diverse than ever before, thereby accelerating a trend detectable for some time. These personal characteristics may or may not have any relationship to a governor's likely performance, but to judge by the group of outstanding governors, gubernatorial attributes are changing in the right directions. Outstanding governors are close to three years younger on the average (44.6 years) than governors as a whole (47.3 years) at the time of their first elections. There are slightly more Catholics (25.7 percent) and Jews (2.9 percent) among the outstanding governors, compared to 15.6 and 1.8 percent, respectively, in the total group.[80] The outstanding governors were also slightly better educated, with 17.8 years of school to 17.6 for all governors. (The education gap, and the age and religious differentials as well, are actually greater than these figures indicate since the data for outstanding governors are included in that for the total group of governors.) The fact that the percentage of businessmen and lawyers among the outstanding governors was a bit larger than for governors as a whole (83.8 percent to 82.5 percent) emphasizes that the lack of representativeness does not by itself mean poor government.

The importance of legislative skills to success as governor is underlined in Table 2-10. A greater proportion of outstanding governors had a state legislative office as their last public post before election to the governorship. More of them came directly from Congress as well. Table 2-10 also indicates law enforcement and local elective offices are relatively poor sources of outstanding governors.

Table 2-11 presents the comparative facts of postgubernatorial careers. As we discovered earlier, recent former governors in greater numbers are being selected for high federal posts and national party nominations for president and vice president, while many fewer are occupying their time in minor, less prestigious posts at all governmental levels. These statements are also true for outstanding governors. About 24 percent have served in federal administrative positions after their governorships while just 18.5 percent of all governors have done so. Moreover, 80 percent of the federal posts held by outstanding governors were major ones (cabinet level or the equivalent), compared to only 44 percent for the total group. The percentage of outstanding governors who received presidential or vice presidential nominations was double that of governors as a whole. In fact, eleven of the fourteen governors who were major party nominees or serious candidates for the two top posts since 1948 were in the outstanding category.

The U.S. Senate attracted many of the outstanding governors in the past, with about 22 percent proceeding there from the governorship (well above the

Table 2-10
The Penultimate Offices for Outstanding Governors

Penultimate Office	All Governors[a]	Outstanding Governors Only
Legislature	24.9	29.0
Law enforcement	18.9	12.3
Statewide	22.1	21.9
Congress	9.1	12.3
Administrative	9.1	9.6
Local elective	5.6	4.4
No prior office	10.2	10.5
	N=285	N=114

Source: Compiled from statistics in Figures 2-1 and 2-2, as well as ten additional frequency trees which were constructed by the author but which, because of space limitations, are not reproduced in this volume.
Note: The penultimate office is the last office held before election to the governorship. See Figure 2-1 for definitions of the offices listed in this table.
[a]The years surveyed are 1950 to 1975.

percentage for governors as a whole). Yet, as noted earlier, the number of former governors in the Senate has been declining lately and many of the ablest governors in the last decade have declined even to run for the Senate, which is no longer considered the most productive and appropriate place for former state chief executives. However, while they turn their backs on the upper house of Congress, these persons are participating in more significant public activities in their postgubernatorial years than ever before. This, too, is the direction taken by outstanding governors. About 62 percent have taken appointive or elective public jobs after their governorships, fully 16 percent above the total for all governors in the last quarter-century.

The Emerging New Breed

Gradually a picture emerges of a new type of person dominating gubernatorial elections of late. Governors are still an elite corps composed mainly of white, male lawyers and businessmen, but the group is becoming demonstrably more heterogeneous in several respects. Blacks and women are finally making inroads in the realm of gubernatorial politics. Their advances thus far, and the increase in the proportion of attorneys who are black or female, give reason to expect this trend to continue. Catholics and Jews are finding that their religious beliefs are no great bar to the governors' mansions any longer and are being elected in greater numbers. Divorced and single persons need not feel severe inhibitions about gubernatorial candidacies today.

57

Table 2-11
Outstanding Governors and Postgubernatorial Office

Office	Percent of Governors Holding Office, 1950-1975	
	Outstanding Governors	All Governors
U.S. senator	21.8	12.8
U.S. representative	1.2	1.6
Judicial office	5.7	7.0
Federal administrative	24.1	18.5
State administrative	1.2	1.2
Statewide elective (except governor)	0.0	1.2
State legislative	0.0	1.2
Local elective-mayor	1.2	0.8
Governor again	4.6	4.1
Major party presidential or vice presidential nominee	5.8	2.9
No postgubernatorial office	37.9	53.9
	N=87	N=243

Sources: Marquis Who's Who, Inc., *Who's Who in America, 1950 [-1975]* (Chicago: A.M. Marquis, 1950-1975); Paul A. Theis and Edmund L. Henshaw, Jr. (eds.), *Who's Who in American Politics, 1968 [-1975]* (New York: R.R. Bowker, 1967-1975); and Michael Barone, Grant Ujifusa, and Douglas Matthews, *The Almanac of American Politics, 1972 [1974, 1976]* (New York: E.P. Dutton, 1972, 1973, 1975).
Note: Governors who were currently serving as of 1976 were excluded, as were governors who served their first set of terms prior to 1950.

The governors themselves are much younger, better educated than ever, and more thoroughly trained for the specific responsibilities of the governorship. Greater numbers have concentrated beforehand on developing legislative expertise, while fewer come to the executive post directly from minor offices in law enforcement or local government that have less relationship to the responsibilities a governor faces. A more attractive and prestigious governorship has even induced more congressmen to trade their Washington offices for governors' chairs. The new type of person elected governor wants to continue significant undertakings after leaving the governorship and is willingly indulged by voters and presidents. More major federal administrative posts, judicial offices, and presidential and vice presidential nominations come to former governors. They are much less content with the less prestigious offices like U.S. representative. Comparisons with the outstanding governors of a quarter-century confirm many of these images of the new governors.

However, governors do not operate in a vacuum. They are the directors but also the products of state government. It is doubtful that all the significant changes in the governors themselves could have come about without equally wide-ranging alterations in the structure and functioning of state government, which now must be as thoroughly examined.

Notes

1. Interview with the author, September 23, 1976, Bloomfield Hills, Mich.
2. Interview with the author, August 10, 1976, Indianapolis, Ind.
3. Interview with the author, August 24, 1976, New York, N.Y.
4. Duane Lockard, *The New Jersey Governor: A Study in Political Power* (Princeton, N.J.: D. Van Nostrand, 1965), p. 1.
5. Godwin's metamorphosis is a story in and of itself. See the author's *Aftermath of Armageddon: An Analysis of the 1973 Virginia Gubernatorial Election* (Charlottesville: Institute of Government, University of Virginia, 1975). In the same election in which ex-Democrat Godwin was narrowly elected as a Republican, there was no Democratic nominee at all in the formerly secure Democratic stronghold of Virginia. Instead, an Independent candidate and former Democrat, Henry Howell, almost defeated Godwin.
6. Ralph G. Plumb, *Our American Governors* (Manitowoc, Wisc.: Manitowoc Printing and Lithographing Corp., 1956), pp. 47-48.
7. Bennett M. Rich, *State Constitutions: The Governor,* State Constitutional Studies Project, Series 11, No. 3 (New York: National Municipal League, 1960), pp. 9-10.
8. This computation does not include Alaska and Hawaii since they were not states over the entire period.
9. Joseph E. Kallenbach, *The American Chief Executive: The Presidency and the Governorship* (New York: Harper & Row, 1966), pp. 71-75.
10. Ibid., p. 72.
11. Congressional Quarterly, Inc., *Guide to U.S. Elections* (Washington, D.C.: Congressional Quarterly, Inc., 1975), pp. 363-64.
12. Kallenbach, *The American Chief Executive,* pp. 86-93.
13. Ibid., p. 88.
14. Neal Peirce, *The Border South States* (New York: W.W. Norton, 1975), p. 217.
15. Duane Lockard, *New England State Politics* (Princeton, N.J.: Princeton University Press, 1959), pp. 184-85.
16. Kallenbach, *The American Chief Executive,* p. 86.
17. Ibid., pp. 156-58.
18. 367 U.S. 486 (1961).
19. Michael Barone, Grant Ujifusa, and Douglas Matthews, *The Almanac of American Politics, 1976* (New York: E.P. Dutton, 1975), pp. 771-72.
20. William L. Riordan (ed.), *Plunkitt of Tammany Hall* (New York: E.P. Dutton, 1963), p. xxiv.
21. Plumb, *Our American Governors,* p. 49.
22. Interview with the author, August 10, 1976, Indianapolis, Ind.
23. Donald R. Matthews, *U.S. Senators and Their World* (New York: Vantage Books, 1960), p. 45.

24. In 1968 a black Republican candidate for lieutenant governor in the state of Washington lost only narrowly.

25. See the author's "Virginia Legislative Elections in 1975: Some Change, Much Continuity," *University of Virginia Newsletter* 53 (January 1977):3.

26. Neal R. Peirce, *The Mountain States of America* (New York: W.W. Norton, 1972), pp. 83-85.

27. These three were not the first of their sex to serve in the office of lieutenant governor, although they were the first to be elected to it. Maude Frazier of Nevada, a state legislator, was appointed in 1962 to serve the remaining year in the term of deceased Lieutenant Governor Rex Bell.

28. Council of State Governments, *The Book of the States, 1974-1975* (Lexington, Ky.: Council of State Governments, 1974), pp. 68, 407.

29. Interview with the author, August 5, 1976, Olympia, Wash.

30. Letter from Woodrow Wilson to Ellen Axson, October 30, 1883, as quoted by Ray Stannard Baker, *Woodrow Wilson, Life and Letters: Youth, 1856-1890* (London: William Heinemann, 1928), p. 109.

31. Matthews, *U.S. Senators,* p. 33.

32. Samuel R. Solomon, "Governors, 1960-1970," *National Civic Review* 60 (March 1971):128-29.

33. The lawyer-governor must have held an executive position or outright business ownership to be included in this category. Lawyers who were simply members of corporate boards are included in the "pure lawyer" category.

34. Any governor whose previous career included a position of executive responsibility in a business or who owned and operated an enterprise was included in this category.

35. The percentage of the total population is 7.4.

36. U.S. Bureau of the Census, *Statistical Abstract of the United States, 1974,* 95th ed. (Washington, D.C.: Government Printing Office, 1974), p. 31, Table 34.

37. Ibid., pp. 158-59, Tables 266-67.

38. Matthews, *U.S. Senators,* pp. 30-42.

39. Samuel R. Solomon, "United States Governors, 1940-1950," *National Municipal Review* 41 (April 1952):191.

40. U.S. Bureau of the Census, *Statistical Abstract,* p. 116, Table 186. The average number of years of education for the public was 9.3 in 1950, 10.5 in 1960, 12.2 in 1970, and a peak of 12.3 in 1975.

41. Ibid., pp. 46-48, Tables 64-66.

42. Ibid. Other religions accounted for 4.3 percent of the religious population as a whole and 1.8 percent of the governors.

43. Kallenbach, *The American Chief Executive,* p. 182.

44. *Newsweek* (International Edition), November 15, 1976, p. 13; and George Gallup, *Gallup Opinion Index: The Anatomy of Victory,* Report No. 42 (Princeton, N.J.: Gallup International, December 1968), p. 5.

45. Gallup, ibid.

46. *Time* (Europe Edition), November 15, 1976, p. 27.

47. Interview with the author, August 6, 1976, Detroit, Mich.

48. U.S. Bureau of the Census, *Statistical Abstract,* p. 66, Table 93.

49. Interview with the author, July 30, 1976, Trenton, N.J.

50. Correspondence with the author, July 22, 1976.

51. See Angus Campbell et al., *The American Voter* (New York: John Wiley and Sons, 1960), p. 25, Table 2.12. Remarks of voters indicated that Stevenson's family life was a campaign detriment in both his presidential bids.

52. Solomon, "United States Governors, 1940-1950," p. 192.

53. U.S. Bureau of the Census, *Statistical Abstract,* p. 31, Table 33. Voting population consists of all citizens twenty-one years of age or older from 1950-1970 and eighteen years or older from 1971-1975.

54. Correspondence with the author, July 22, 1976.

55. Interview with the author, September 8, 1976, Tallahassee, Fla.

56. See Chapter 6 for a fuller discussion of the relative merits of executive and legislative backgrounds for the presidency.

57. The career frequency tree concept is taken from Joseph Schlesinger, *Ambition and Politics: Political Careers in the United States* (Chicago: Rand-McNally, 1966), pp. 90-99.

58. The "leadership offices" are speaker, majority or minority leader, floor leader, and caucus chairman.

59. Paul L. Hain and Terry B. Smith, "Congress: New Training Ground for Governors," *State Government* 48 (Spring 1975):114-15.

60. Ibid.

61. Connally also served as Secretary of the Navy in the Kennedy administration.

62. See Patrick Anderson, *The President's Men* (New York: Doubleday, 1968), pp. 135-39, 152-57.

63. Matthews, *U.S. Senators,* p. 55, Table 27.

64. Ibid., p. 56.

65. Ibid., pp. 103-06.

66. Interview with the author, August 4, 1976, Portland, Ore.

67. Interview with the author, August 5, 1976, Olympia, Wash.

68. Actually a governor cannot directly appoint himself to the vacancy. Instead the governor resigns after having consummated an agreement with the lieutenant governor (or other "next-in-line" official) that he will be appointed by the new governor to the seat. Most lieutenant governors are more than happy to oblige so that they can drop the first part of their title.

69. The 1.9 percent figure includes former governors elected city mayors, as well as those elected governor again or nominated for president or vice president.

70. Curtis is not included in Table 2-8's tabulation since he was appointed after 1975.

71. Kerner was found guilty on federal charges of tax evasion, perjury, and mail fraud. Barron was sentenced to jail for bribery, as was Hall. Hall was also convicted on extortion charges.

72. Peirce, *The Border South States,* pp. 192-93.

73. Lockard, *The New Jersey Governor,* pp. 1-2.

74. See the Preface to this volume for a cautionary note.

75. Interview with the author, August 4, 1976, Portland, Ore.

76. Interview with the author, July 21, 1976, Durham, N.C.

77. Kallenbach, *The American Chief Executive,* pp. 257-67.

78. V.O. Key, Jr., *The Responsible Electorate: Rationality in Presidential Voting 1936-1960* (New York: Bantam Books, 1966), p. 7.

79. Interview with the author, September 13, 1976, Washington, D.C.

80. The religious affiliations, if any, of twelve outstanding governors could not be determined. Protestants accounted for 69.5 percent and other religions for 1.9 percent of the outstanding governors.

3 Changing Contours of State Government

A feeble Executive implies a feeble execution of the government. A feeble execution is but another phrase for a bad execution; and a government ill executed, whatever it may be in theory, must be, in practice, a bad government.[1]

—Alexander Hamilton, *The Federalist,* no. 70

Because of the colonial experience, Americans have historically been hesitant to place any significant concentration of power in the hands of one person. Hamilton and his associates had to struggle to insure that the presidency was not crippled from the start. Governors were far more limited in the early state constitutions than the president was by the federal constitution and thus forced to bear severe institutional handicaps on their powers. The weakness of the governors inhibited and sometimes wholly obstructed the proper exercise and influence of executive authority.

Gradually it became clear that the neglect of various problems caused by lethargic, fragmented, and diffused state governments was a greater evil than the potential for executive abuse. By degrees a frustrated citizenry learned:

Responsible government means more than elected government. It means a government which can be held responsible for its actions because it has the power to take action. A government of inaction is not a responsible government. A governor without power is not a responsible governor.[2]

Within the last fifteen years, there has been a virtual explosion of reform in state government. In most of the states, as a result, the governor is now truly the master of his own house, not just the father figure.

In 1958 William H. Young proposed four major remedies for the lack of capable leadership by governors.[3] First, he advocated thorough reorganization of the structure of state governments to make some administrative sense out of the incredible hodgepodge of boards, commissions, agencies, and special jurisdictions that had accumulated over the years. Secondly, an executive budget that was designed and submitted to the legislature by the governor and that included all the divisions in the executive branch was seen as imperative. The centralization of the management of and planning for state government as a whole was of equal necessity. Finally, the governor's term, of but two years duration in many states, would have to be lengthened to four years.

63

Bennett Rich added several more essentials in 1960.[4] Not only should the governor's term be lengthened, but the governor should also be able to run for at least two successive terms. (Some states refused their chief executives the privilege of serving more than a single consecutive term.) Statewide elected officers other than the governor should be made appointive, and the governor's power to select and remove the major department heads should be broadened. The malapportionment of the legislatures, which kept rural interests predominant in many states though a majority of residents were urban, urgently required correction, and a key executive check on the legislature, the veto, needed buttressing.

An October 1965 survey of thirty-nine governors demonstrated that the chief executives concurred in Young and Rich's prescriptions for reform.[5] Governors emphatically felt that they had inadequate control of their own branch of government, which they perceived as sadly in need of reorganization. Control was hardly the only complaint heard from governors throughout the years. Staffing of the governor's office was insufficient; the salary for the demanding position of chief executive was inadequate to attract top-notch candidates; and transition procedures during a change of administrations were often minimal or nonexistent and thus seen as wasting some of the new governor's valuable time and inadequately preparing him for his new responsibilities.

By 1975, however, governors could report differently on their perceptions of the office. Almost all the interviewed governors agreed that the powers, both formal and informal, of the office had increased over the last decade and in some cases very significantly. A bit surprisingly (since the political breed is presumed insatiably power hungry), the governors were also content with the powers and responsibilities currently ceded them. Few cited any specific or general grants of authority not now possessed that they believed still essential for a strong governorship. State governments, then, have changed drastically, and their treatment of the executive has been transformed too. The major reforms and their effects on the governor will be outlined in the following sections.[6]

Constitutional Revision

"The constitutions of the States are their greatest shame," moaned Robert S. Allen in 1949, and he was surely correct.[7] They were, for the most part, voluminous tomes, sometimes undemocratic in character, which prescribed toothless executives and nightmarish administrative structures for state governments. Many of these archaic and even outrageous features were truly "grotesque parodies on modern government."[8]

The era about which Allen wrote has fortunately passed into history. While only five states rewrote their constitutions from 1902 to 1963, ten states adopted completely new constitutions in just twelve years (1964 to 1976).[9] The newest state constitution, that of Louisiana (adopted in 1975), overhauled what was described as an "octopus-like" government by regrouping scores of agencies, boards, and commissions into nineteen compact departments.[10] Five states (Maryland, New York, North Dakota, Rhode Island, and Texas) were not so lucky; new constitutions were drafted, but rejected for varying reasons.

Less drastic but still substantial changes by amendments to state constitutions have become common recently too. In the last decade (1966 to 1976) twenty-seven states streamlined the process of amendment, thereby facilitating major and minor alterations of the constitutional framework as the needs of state government required.[11] The pace of this alteration is perhaps indicated by the total of almost 1,000 separate constitutional revision proposals of statewide applicability that were proposed in only six years between 1968 and 1973.[12] The governor, legislators, and state electorates have embraced the new order in state affairs to a degree that seems surprising for an instinctively conservative political society that is normally suspicious of wholesale change. About 67 percent of the proposed constitutional amendments were approved; almost three-quarters of the proposals dealt specifically with the executive branch.[13]

Governors were normally either the initiators or among the strongest and most vociferous supporters of the revisions and recastings. The constitutional overhauls engineered by some outstanding governors, like Republican Winthrop Rockefeller of Arkansas, were their greatest and most enduring accomplishments. The motive of self-interest can hardly be ignored, since governors were the direct and indirect beneficiaries of many of the constitutional reforms. While the direct gains, like reorganization powers, a strengthened lieutenant governorship, and legislative reapportionment, will be reviewed in detail in the following sections, brief mention should be made here of the less obvious but perhaps more crucial indirect advantages that were not even specifically included in the constitutional executive articles. For example, antiquated tax prohibitions that had effectively prevented a governor from presenting a sound budget derived from the legitimate needs of his state were abolished. One such prohibition in Arkansas, for instance, forbade the state from raising property, excise, privilege, or personal tax rates without a referendum of the people or, in an emergency, a three-fourths vote by both houses of the legislature. Other states had constitutionally declared that whole categories of taxes (income, estate, property, and so forth) could not be levied at all. These iron restrictions have fallen now, for the most part, as have outdated and wholly unrealistic limitations on borrowing by state governments, thereby giving the governor both wide latitude in devising state policies and greater opportunity for executive leadership. This is not to say that the governor or the state government in part or whole is no longer constitutionally constrained; there remains ample circumscription—too ample still—on the chief executive and all other officers and branches. Compared to only two decades ago, however, the restrictions are not overly suppressive.

Reorganization's Clean Sweep

The movement for governmental reorganization actually began long ago in the years immediately preceding World War I. The Progressive by-product had as its goal not simply the minimization of waste; rather effeciency was to be the derivative of a broader reform—that is, matching authority with responsibility.

Some of the early principles of reorganization were flawed.[14] For one, the reformers erred in attempting to apply immutable axioms of administration to all states in all situations. Nevertheless, some of the first reorganizations served as satisfactory illustrations of governmental restructuring's bounty.[15] Illinois was the first state to effect a thorough reorganization in 1917, when more than fifty independent agencies were consolidated into fourteen and made responsible to the governor. California, New York, Idaho, Maryland, Massachusetts, Minnesota, Pennsylvania, Virginia, and Washington soon followed. Strong governors often led the reorganization movements and engineered their successes. Governor Harry Byrd, Sr., of Virginia, for instance, threw his own and his organization's prestige and power behind major reorganization proposals and secured their passage in the legislature and popular referendum in 1926-1928. In the next two decades, Georgia, Kentucky, Missouri, New Jersey, and Rhode Island joined the cadre of reorganized states. Two-thirds of the states, however, never attempted a major reorganization at all, and deterioration rapidly began in those states that had, especially in the immediate post-World War II era, as legislatures (and governors, too) haphazardly established agencies and boards, usually with status independent of gubernatorial control.

Despite the efforts of the "little Hoover Commissions" that were modelled after the National Commission on Organization of the Executive Branch of the Government headed by former President Herbert Hoover and established in many states to suggest reorganizations in the late 1940s and early 1950s, not a single state undertook a comprehensive reorganization.[16] Yet the logic and argument of the Hoover Commission remained powerful. Its prescription for sound national government under the president applies equally to the states and their governors:

The President, and under him his chief lieutenants, the department heads, must be held responsible and accountable to the people and to the Congress for the conduct of the executive branch. Responsibility and accountability are impossible without authority—the power to direct. The exercise of authority is impossible without a clear line of responsibility and accountability from the bottom to the top.[17]

Gradually states saw the wisdom of reorganization, and a modern avalanche of reform began, with state government being much improved and the governor considerably strengthened in the process. In the late 1950s Tennessee undertook a major governmental restructuring, and the new states of Alaska and Hawaii, unfettered by tradition, produced model state organizations in their first constitutions. No such *tabula rasa* existed in other states, but reorganization, though more difficult because of entrenched interests and spheres of power, gained momentum.

In 1961 California devised umbrella departments headed by gubernatorially appointed and directed cabinet secretaries. This schema, further developed and advanced in 1968, consolidated a patchwork of boards, commissions, and agencies under a clearly defined chain of command. A key breakthrough came in Michigan in 1963 when a new Michigan constitution won approval in a referendum. Spearheaded by Republican Governor George Romney, the new constitution provided for a streamlined government and a full-scale reorganization, which was accomplished in 1965. Thereafter, an unprecedented number of states (twenty, including Michigan) underwent major reorganization in a single decade (1965-1975): Wisconsin (1967), California and Colorado (1968), Massachusetts and Florida (1969), Delaware and Maryland (1969-70), Arkansas, Georgia, Maine, Montana, and North Carolina (1971), Virginia (1972), Kentucky (1972-73), South Dakota (1973), Missouri and Idaho (1974), Arizona (1971-75), and Louisiana (1975-76).

Moreover, twenty other states took significant steps—such as wide-ranging consolidations of all agencies and groups in particular fields of policy (health, transportation, environment, and so forth)—towards reorganization that, while short of full-scale restructuring, have altered the pattern of government in major ways. In just the single year of 1975, sixteen states effected partial reorganizations of some consequence.[18] Maine, for instance, finally abolished its "executive council," a device dating from the colonial era designed primarily to hamstring the governor. Even more importantly, thirteen states now provide for the chief executive to reorganize his branch of government, subject only to legislative veto.[19] As outlined in the constitutions of ten states and the statutes of three more, this procedure simply entails presentation of the governor's proposals to the legislature. These proposals automatically go into effect after a specified time unless both legislative houses pass a resolution disapproving of them. This broad executive authority over the administrative branch has strengthened the governor's hand in Alaska, California, Georgia, Illinois, Kansas, Maryland, Massachusetts, Michigan, Minnesota, Missouri, New Jersey, North Carolina, and Vermont.

The basic purpose of all of this reorganization activity has not really changed since the movement first began. It is, simply, to increase the accountability and efficiency of government by giving the state governor the authority to match his responsibility in the executive branch. In order to achieve this goal, the number of agencies reporting to the governor is reduced and the power to appoint all the agency directors is granted to the governor. A clear chain of command is established, agencies are structured more logically by function, and antiquated organizations in state government are reformed or eliminated. Better government usually does result, but regardless, the governor is the clear winner in the power game. Most governors whose states have undertaken reorganization would agree with Governor Thomas Salmon of Vermont who believes: "The key to [the governor's strengthened] control is the reorganization of state government. . . ."[20]

As dull and dry as a "nuts-and-bolts" issue like governmental reorganization might seem on paper, it can sometimes arouse the reformist impulse in the populace. Governor George Romney of Michigan led such a "citizens movement" for a new constitution in 1963 and this feat has been duplicated in other states. The national electorate was treated to an extended discussion of reorganization's merits in 1976, when Democratic presidential candidate Jimmy Carter almost succeeded in making it a household word. Carter linked his successful reorganization of the Georgia state government to his planned moves to tame the semi-autonomous federal bureaucracy. In the post-Watergate "antigovernment" mood, the issue found considerable favor with the voting public.

There is one other major state-federal reorganization connection that is a bit ironic. While reorganizations have helped to rejuvenate and strengthen state government, sometimes at the expense of the federal government, many of the recent studies that led to the state reorganizations were funded through planning grants awarded by the federal Department of Housing and Urban Development.[21]

The Fractionalized Executive

Twenty years ago Coleman Ransone regretfully reported: "In most states the governor is not the only executive in the government and is the chief executive only in the sense that he is the first among many executives."[22] The situation has improved, but the governor is still hindered and frustrated by a multitude of competing, elective executives over which he has only indirect control. In fact, this area in state government organization is the one where progress toward an empowered governorship has been slowest.

The number of elected officials has been reduced since 1950. Excepting the governor and lieutenant governor, the states in 1950 had 242 constitutionally or statutorily elected statewide officials in 16 major offices and departments.[23] By 1975 the number of other elected officials had dwindled a bit to 187, or about a 25 percent reduction overall.[24] On the average, each state had 13 constitutionally elected officials in 1950 (when governor, lieutenant governor, and all other major and minor elected posts are included), and by 1975 about 10. The range was quite large, from just 1 (the governor) in Maine and New Jersey to 36 in Michigan (because the state board of education and university regents are elected.) For some offices there has been notable progress. The number of elected state superintendents of education has declined sharply, from 32 in 1946 to 18 in 1975. As recently as 1975 Oklahoma reduced its cluster of statewide officials from thirteen to eight and made the labor commissioner, secretary of state, and mine inspector gubernatorially appointive. (Another officer, the corrections examiner, was combined with the appointed corrections director.)

Although the shortening of the "long ballot" in state after state continues to occur, when the view of the National Municipal League (NML) is considered, the improvements do not appear so substantial. The NML's "Model State Constitution" declares that the governor should be the only popularly elected statewide officer.[25] The lieutenant governor, while elected, should be voted upon jointly with the governor, much as the vice president of the United States is an adjunct of the national party ticket. The NML insists that even the attorney general, now elected in forty-two states, "must be a part of the chief executive's administrative team."

Compounding the problem of the fractionalized elective executive is a discriminatory system of term limitation that exists in many states. While the governor is often limited to a maximum of one or two successive terms, the subsidiary elected officers are allowed perpetual reelection without interruption. Thus, they become exceedingly entrenched, and the governor finds it difficult to influence, much less control, them; they in turn, view the governor as a mere "interloper."[26] While it is true that the same statewide constituency that elects the governor votes for these subordinate officers, it is also true that public knowledge of the performance or even the identities of these officeholders is shockingly low. Some surveys have indicated that mere name recognition, even for some subgubernatorial statewide officials who have served for long durations, is below 10 percent. Thus, these persons can insulate themselves from public opinion as a whole and respond mainly to the wishes of special interests whose concerns center on their posts. Commenting on the effects of multiple elective officers and independent department heads, the American Assembly concluded: "The result is not one state government but twenty or thirty in the same state, each with a special function and with but a fragment of the public as its clientele and controller."[28]

The presence of independently elected officials in the executive branch does not usually cripple the governors by any means, but it can cause time-consuming difficulties and seemingly interminable headaches that deter the governor from more productive endeavors. Consider these frustrating examples:

The state auditor was extremely incompetent and mildly dishonest but I couldn't do anything about him.

I have had some problems with my Attorney General. . . . My perception is that the Attorney General essentially serves as counsel to the Governor, and his perception is that he is an autonomously elected public official and solely represents the interests of the public, and the office of Governor when he has adequate time and staff.

The State Superintendent of Education is elected and has shown no interest in educational reform because he is the prisoner of vested interests, i.e., the school superintendents and college education departments who want to avoid change or accountability.[29]

Matters can take a turn for the worse when governors are faced with a team of statewide officers not of their party. Democrat G. Mennen Williams of Michigan, among many others, experienced this unpleasantness for part of his tenure.[30] The public is not particularly discriminating when it comes time for the blame for inaction to be assigned. The failures may well have been caused by the footdragging of other elected officers, but the governor must bear the consequences as the "head" of state government. "The fact is that people look to the *governor* to get the job done," surmised Governor Reubin Askew of Florida. "In the field of education for instance, the responsibility as well as the authority . . . rest in the elected commissioner of education. But people look to the governor."[31] Askew does not reject the idea of subsidiary elected officers entirely: "I believe that having some collegial responsibility, particularly in the field of contracts and land transactions, is a healthy thing. You force visibility on the transactions."[32]

The fact should not be ignored that some of the elected officials are very minor in nature and present few problems to the governors as they go about fulfilling their primary responsibilities. (The state treasurer and secretary of state are two such positions.) In the great majority of states, important departmental and executive officials most closely associated with the administrative management of the state are appointed by the governor.[33] As early as 1963, a clear majority of all major administrative posts were filled by gubernatorial appointment,[34] and the recent spate of reorganizations has significantly increased that number.

In addition, as Duane Lockard pointed out, the existence of other elective officers does not necessarily mean that the governor is not the effective head of state government: "It does not follow that the lack of specific authority to control an agency implies actual inability to do so."[35] Indeed, most interviewed governors insisted that they had no serious difficulties with the vast majority of other elected officials. Not only were these officers generally cooperative but most seemed to defer to the governor as the rightful leader of state government— or so the governors perceived it. Since recalcitrant elected officials could also be brought into line by a proper manipulation of the budget allocations of staff and salary for their offices, as the governors have gained greater budget authority (to be discussed shortly), they have also found their positions greatly strengthened in dealings with fellow elected officials in the executive branch.

The persistence of the fractionalized executive in spite of the overwhelming opposition among administrative experts, scholars, governors, and others is easily explained. At base, the popular devotion to the long ballot is the culprit. Claimed Governor Tom McCall: "The people, if you gave them their choice, would like to elect everything clear down to dogcatcher."[36] There are supplemental reasons, too. Inertia is a potent force in politics as well as physics. Any successful elected official, especially one of long-standing, could have a devoted personal following and a political band whose influence often far exceeds its number. A clientele group that may have captured an elective official sometimes has the weight in finances, organization, and membership base to work its will and preserve its man. The official himself will certainly do all he can to resist the abolition of his job. The tremendous energy and expenditure of political capital that it takes to put an end to a given position is just not worth the price for most governors. The grudge that an official surviving an attempted purge would surely carry could prove damaging to more important parts of a governor's program. The trend now is, however gradually, to reduce the number of statewide officers, and this can only prove beneficial to the governor. In the meantime governors will have to rely on personal persuasion, gubernatorial influence, the benevolence of incumbents, and the power of the purse.

The Decline of Patronage

The question of gubernatorial control of the executive branch extends much further than the subsidiary statewide posts. Each state government, even the smallest, includes scores of boards, agencies, and commissions and requires the appointments of thousands of persons. Generally, as we have already seen, the governor's control of the key executive departments and their directors has grown more secure. In over two-thirds of the states, governors can appoint singly or subject to legislative confirmation well over half the most crucial administrative posts.[37] Normally governors can also remove the appointees at will, although judicial officers, subject to a formal impeachment process, are a notable exception.[38]

There is another category of appointments known collectively as "patronage." Under the patronage system, victorious governors reward their party members by distributing state jobs to them. The largest portion of the jobs are not important ones; rather, they can range from clerks and secretaries to agricultural field personnel. Patronage long sustained party organizations in many cities and states and was the essential stimulus to take part in politics for the average nonpolitical citizen, but in the late nineteenth century the institution of patronage became the focus of attack for the burgeoning Progressive Movement. An aversion to the widespread corruption and lack of skill that existed at all levels of government led to the gradual elimination of patronage and the substitution of standardized civil service examinations.[39] The theory of "neutral competence" replaced the earlier operating principle of "to the victors belong the spoils," as the Pendleton Act was passed for the federal government in 1883 and states began to adopt similar measures (commencing with the New York and Massachusetts Civil Service Acts).

These reforms struck at the very roots of political organizations, and the machine leaders fought civil service laws strenuously. As George Washington Plunkitt of New York's Tammany Hall saw it:

This civil service law is the biggest fraud of the age. It is the curse of the nation. There can't be no real patriotism while it lasts. How are you goin' to interest our young men in their country if you have no offices to give them when they work for their party? . . . I have good reason for sayin' that most of the Anarchists in this city today are men who ran up against civil service examinations. . . .

I see a vision. I see the civil service monster lyin' flat on the ground. I see the Democratic party standin' over it with foot on its neck and wearin' the crown of victory. I see Thomas Jefferson lookin' out from a cloud and sayin' "Give him another sockdologer; finish him." And I see millions of men wavin' their hats and singin' "Glory Hallelujah!"[40]

Plunkitt's vision never came to pass. The civil service reformers continued to prevail, and the impact of their campaign upon public opinion was durable. Even today, "Patronage is one of those words in the American political vocabulary which, like the word 'politician,' carries adverse connotations. Political leaders who use the system frequently find some other name for it. Those who claim not to use it often speak the word in the same way they use words such as 'murder' or 'corruption.' "[41]

The number of patronage positions has significantly decreased in virtually every state. While the progression of civil service has been steady, there has been a spurt of growth since the mid-sixties. In 1958, just slightly over half (50.7 percent) of all state employees were under merit systems of one type or another.[42] By 1963 the figure had increased slightly to 54 percent,[43] and by 1975 the proportion had jumped to almost two-thirds of all state employees (64.1 percent).[44] The Western states generally have many fewer patronage positions than those in the East. In Washington state, only about 300 of approximately 30,000 state employees are patronage appointments, and in Utah 95 percent are civil service employees.

In 1976 the U.S. Supreme Court delivered a major blow to patronage in a decision that banned many firings of patronage employees.[45] Holding that state and local government employees have a constitutional protection in the First Amendment against removal for partisan political reasons, the Court inflicted additional wounds on the few patronage machines that still exist (such as the Daley organization in Chicago, against whom the suit was filed). To those who claimed that the ruling damaged the political system, Justice William J. Brennan, Jr., responded that ". . . the political process functions as well without the practice, perhaps even better."[46]

Despite the fact that scholars have usually concluded that the decline of patronage lessened gubernatorial power, governors tend to agree, some of them vehemently, with Justice Brennan. Surprisingly, one finds that the more recent governors themselves have been responsible for much of the proportional increase in civil service employees. Governor William Scranton of Pennsylvania had the power to appoint persons to a massive 53,000 posts (of 85,000 total in the state's government) when he took office in 1963. He promptly secured passage of a civil service law eliminating 27,000 of his appointments. Scranton pointed out that for every post he filled, he would make one friend (the appointee) and several enemies (those who were considered but didn't get it). "It isn't the great blessing of political power that some people think it is!"[47]

Reubin Askew of Florida divested himself of much of his judicial appointment power by placing the decisions in the hands of a nonpartisan judicial commission, and by doing so Askew believes he has strengthened his hand politically. Daniel Evans of Washington abolished a category of patronage appointments (appraisers) in fulfilling a campaign pledge. Robert Ray of Iowa spearheaded a major civil service reform in his state. Calvin Rampton of Utah also requested and steered to passage Utah's first merit system. "I've asked for the bills," said Rampton. "I don't regard it as a weakening of the governor. Running government, in many respects, is running a business. And nobody would be naïve enough to say that the skills of running a business or a department of government are always going to coincide with the person who happens to be active in a political campaign."[48] While no hard data are available to sustain Rampton's conclusion, it is probably an accurate one. Persons selected by reason of mere party loyalty and activity will usually be less qualified and less capable of filling most governmental posts than persons who have been chosen for their skills.

This is not to say that the decline of patronage has not presented some thorny problems. Patronage has been replaced in some states not just with a civil service system, but a *unionized* civil service system, which has no doubt placed greater demands on the governor and the resources of the state. Moreover, the thrust of civil service reform, at least at the rhetorical level, has been to separate administration from politics, which is neither possible nor healthy. Tenured civil servants are less politically accountable, and while there are certainly schemes and devices designed to deal with this problem, governors are less able to apply pressure and put into effect their policies. Some of the chief executives, particularly in the Western United States, have been hindered by the excessive extension of civil service to some of the top policy-making positions.

Governors seem to believe, however, that on balance civil service is vastly more desirable and indeed a boon to the governor. "I think it's much better to have the employee morale that comes from tenure than to be able to put your own people in," asserted Governor Rampton.[49] The governors insist that patronage is more trouble than it is worth, especially given the lessening importance of party to an increasingly independent electorate. Politically it makes little sense to the governors to practice extensive patronage for the maintenance of party organizations that mean less and produce less on election day. The majority of voters not only have considerably loosened their party ties, but have come to resent the blatant partisanship that naturally characterizes patronage.

Most governors have initiated or welcomed civil service extension in their states, and some are actively encouraging the divestiture of more of their patronage. Governor Askew believes that despite the modern whittling of the Florida chief executive's patronage, he should be relieved of a cartload of minor appointments, including officers of library districts, drainage districts, and mosquito control districts.[50] These appointments absorb a governor's time far in excess of their importance. Far more important to the governors are the recent gains in appointment power where it really counts: at the top layer of the executive department. For the arm-twisting, "scratch my back" appointments that governors often find so useful in influencing the persons who are key to given programs, says Governor Terry Sanford, there are always noncompensatory but prestigious citizen advisory board positions or university trusteeships, scores of which are at the disposal of most governors.[51] Governor John Gilligan of Ohio concluded: "Patronage is important but it is also a pain in the neck, and I would happily give away a good deal of it."[52]

The Lieutenant Governor

A delegate to an early Virginia constitutional convention argued strenuously against the establishment of a lieutenant governorship. The office, he proclaimed, was "like the fifth wheel of a wagon . . . and much more useless."[53]

The Virginia delegate lost his battle, as did other like-minded constitutionalists in most of the states through the years. Eight of the thirteen original states had either a lieutenant governor or a deputy governor, and the practice was generally extended to the new states.[54] By 1900 only fourteen states had no lieutenant governor, and three-quarters of a century later, the total had shrunk to merely seven: Arizona, Maine, New Hampshire, New Jersey, Oregon, West Virginia, and Wyoming. Just within the past few years, Florida (1968), Maryland (1970), and Alaska (1970) added the post.

All of the lieutenant governors are constitutional officers and are popularly elected except two. In Tennessee a state statute provides that the lieutenant governor shall be elected by the state Senate from among its membership (with the joint titles of lieutenant governor and speaker of the Senate). Utah now designates the secretary of state as the official lieutenant governor. The age, citizenship, and residency requirements for the lieutenant governor parallel those for the governor. The length of the term is also identical to the governor's, and the two posts are filled in simultaneous elections.

The Virginia delegate who opposed the lieutenant governorship may have been on target in his criticism of the post's vapid responsibilities. Much like the vice presidency on the national level, the lieutenant governor long suffered from the perception of being mere stand-by equipment with no other purpose. Certainly that perception is not wholly inaccurate. The main significance of the lieutenant governorship is that the office is next in the line of succession to the governorship.[55] As we have already seen, the post is the main steppingstone to the chief executiveship among the statewide elective offices, and fifty-four lieutenant governors have become governor through succession and, primarily, election in their own right in the past twenty-five years (see Chapter 2).

Since so many lieutenant governors become governor, the governorship is itself strengthened if the second-in-commands are better trained. It is also reasonable to suggest that a more potent office of lieutenant governor with responsibilities of greater consequence will attract more qualified people to run for it. Many capable and outstanding potential governors will not agree to mark time for four years or more in a "do-nothing" office, even if it means an eventual crack at the governorship. Moreover, voters will also be likely to cast their ballots with greater care if they perceive that the post has some substance and significance of its own.

In the last ten or fifteen years, the lieutenant governor has been afforded a much improved program of training. Crucial to this development has been a relatively recent movement to remove the lieutenant governor as presiding officer of the state Senate in many states. In the past the lieutenant governor has been a hybrid "executive-legislator," but the abolition of his legislative duties has helped to make him a firm and integral part of the executive branch, with his allegiance clearly owed to the governor rather than a house of legislators. Nine states have now moved away from what one lieutenant governor called "the most frustrating and least desirable status."[56] Even in those states that still assign their second officer legislative duties, there has been a major shift of duties to the lieutenant governor's office. In a 1973 survey by the Council of State Governments, twenty-one of thirty-four lieutenant governors reported that their office had already become a full-time job.[57] This finding contrasts sharply with the part-time norm of lieutenant governors that existed as late as the mid-1960s.

The actual practice of assigning executive functions to the lieutenant governor was begun by Governor Paul McNutt of Indiana in 1933, when he appointed his lieutenant to the post of chief administrative officer of the Department of Commerce and Industries.[58] Now at least twenty states empower the governor constitutionally or statutorily to delegate executive duties to the lieutenant governor, and governors in other states have done it without explicit authority.[59] The lieutenant governor in Florida is now secretary of administration by gubernatorial appointment, a post described by Governor Reubin Askew as "the key appointed role in my whole administration."[60] The constitution of New Mexico assigns the ombudsman office to the lieutenant governor. In Hawaii, Alaska, and Utah, the lieutenant governors perform the duties of a secretary of state. Other lieutenant governors have also recently served as consumer affairs advisor, coordinator of industrial development, chief negotiator for state employee collective bargaining, an executive budget officer, and an advisor on intergovernmental relations. The lieutenant governor is formally a member of the governor's cabinet in at least twelve states.[61]

The salaries and other compensations provided lieutenant governors have increased greatly, thereby attesting to the growing importance of the position and helping to attract better-qualified persons to serve in it. As of 1972 the median salary range for the post was $15,000 to $19,999, plus *per diem* pay, travel expenses, and occasionally other perquisites.[62] This salary range contrasts with that of the destitute lieutenant governors of 1944, when only 9 states paid over $2,000 and 7 states did not even provide a nominal salary.[63] The budget and staffing of the lieutenant governor's office have been similarly expanded. There were 9 states in 1972 with lieutenant governor's office budgets exceeding $100,000, and California gave its second officer $393,000.[64] In 24 states there were separate budgets for the lieutenant governor and in 9 more the lieutenant governor's office is included as an item in the governor's budget. Finally, lieutenant governors averaged about 5 full-time clerical and professional staff members, and California's lieutenant governor again led the pack, with 30 clerical and 7 professional full-time employees.

In addition to training and attracting qualified potential governors, there is a second way in which the lieutenant governorship can strengthen the state's highest post. Lieutenant governors who have some popular following and appeal can often assist governors by allying themselves with the chief executives and their programs. While the ambition to drop the "lieutenant" from the title, shared by virtually all lieutenant governors, sometimes promotes such severe friction with the governors that close working relationships are impossible, an institutional mechanism that can minimize the chances of this occurrence is team election of the two top state posts, and this approach has been adopted by a growing number of states. Starting with New York in 1953, twenty states by 1975 provided for the joint election of the governor and lieutenant governor. Almost all (eighteen of twenty) have instituted the system just since 1962, and in each of these states but Connecticut, it is constitutionally mandated.

There is considerable support among both governors and lieutenant governors for team election in states that do not presently have it.[65] The reasons for team election's popularity are not difficult to determine. A greater party accountability for each administration would presumably result since the possibility of a party split in the two highest offices would be barred. Should lieutenant governors have to succeed to the governorship, the guarantee of policy continuity would be firmer, and the lieutenant governors would probably find themselves better utilized since they are more likely to be compatible with and have the confidence of the governors. Administration would be facilitated by the reduction in political tension that exists when two warring party camps inhabit the executive branch.[66]

With the party-switching, ticket-splitting proclivities of modern voters, a governor of one party with a lieutenant governor of another is hardly a rarity. In the 1960s alone, twenty-four instances of split party election were recorded.[67] Even in the best of these situations, the trust necessary between governor and lieutenant governor is absent. Governor Daniel Evans of Washington, a Republican who had a Democratic lieutenant during all of his gubernatorial terms, commented:

We've worked together reasonably well and he's never caused any undue problems, but by the same token, I've never felt comfortable in adding responsibility to the office and in making him a real member or part of the management responsibility in state government.[68]

At the worst, split party control of the governorship and lieutenant governorship can be chaotic, frustrating, and retarding to the governors' programs. Republican Governor George Romney of Michigan had this experience in his first term when his Democratic lieutenant governor was "... constantly trying to embarrass me. ... He enjoyed poking fun at me. ... He wasn't really an individual I could turn responsibilities over to. I couldn't even delegate ceremonial duties under the circumstances."[69] At a later reelection after the adoption of team election in Michigan, Romney's new Republican lieutenant governor, William Milliken, became a close adviser with major duties in the educational sphere. When Romney resigned the governorship to assume the post of secretary of Housing and Urban Development in Richard Nixon's cabinet in 1969, he clearly believed he had turned the reins of state government over to a thoroughly prepared and compatible person, and he even delegated the 1969 "State of the State" address to Milliken while he was still the lieutenant governor. (Milliken has since been elected twice in his own right.)

Team election doesn't always result in as consonant a pair as Romney and Milliken. Team *nomination* (i.e., nomination of the governor and lieutenant governor as a predetermined primary or convention slate or selection of the lieutenant governor nominee by the victorious gubernatorial standardbearer) exists in only a few states, and while it is certainly possible for intraparty political enemies to be nominated together, the likelihood of disruptive frictions is less than in the interparty case. In any event, at least a partially independent political base and following for the lieutenant governors should probably be retained in team situations so that they are not totally submerged by the governors.

The advent of team election, coupled with the assignment of weighty administrative tasks and larger salaries and budgets, has considerably strengthened the oft-maligned office of lieutenant governor. More important for our purposes here, the office of governor has been strengthened too as a result. One new symbolic aspect of the lieutenant governorship has lent credibility to the executive department as well. In the 1970s two blacks and three women were elected to the second highest posts in their states. Their proximity both to the governorship and the public press have helped to atone a bit for the unrepresentativeness of the group of governors.

Transition Procedures

The influence of lieutenant governors leads naturally to the question of gubernatorial transition. There is probably no more crucial time to incoming, just-elected governors than the two or three months between the election and inauguration. So much is done then that sets the course for the succeeding years of their terms: The state budget for the next two years is determined, initial preparations for legislative programs are made, key appointments in the executive branch are decided, and an image begins to form in the mind of the public. A tremendous amount of research, interviewing, and staff pairing with the incumbent administration is necessary if the transition is to be successful. With stakes as high as these, one may be amazed to discover that before about 1960, state funding and staffing for the governor-elect was virtually unheard of. In 1960, the governor-elect of Massachusetts was the first to request and be granted $25,000 for the transition, with the money being spent mainly for budget preparation and the inaugural. Shortly thereafter, Illinois, Minnesota, and Ohio also established transition funds.

By 1968 a survey by the Council of State Governments indicated how swiftly the merits of transition funding were recognized.[70] Budget, staffing, office space or equipment, or some combination of these had been made available in most of the states. Specific appropriations to the governor-elect were provided in 11 of the 35 states responding to the survey, and other states made funds available through contingency or special accounts. Office space in state buildings was made available to the incoming administration in 16 states, and in 18 states public personnel were assigned part-time or full-time to the governor-elect. A new survey published in 1972 showed that transition funding had gained even wider support, with half of the responding states (20 of 40) reporting that formal transition legislation was now on the statute books.[71] Three more states without statutory provisions made regular appropriations for transitions. In all, 26 states provided funds of some type through regular appropriations channels, and only 14 did not. Some in the latter category earmarked money for the governor-elect from the outgoing governor's contingency fund. Finally, 30 of the 40 states made provisions for the allocation of space to the nascent administration.

Involving the governor-elect in the preparation of the biennial budget still presents difficulties, since the responsibility for the budget squarely rests with the outgoing governor. Some governors-elect have used their transition monies to research and prepare budget alternatives or supplements of their own, while allowing the outgoing governors free rein with the formally presented budget. Several states, however, including Connecticut, Massachusetts, Oklahoma, and Wisconsin, have delegated to the governor-elect the forging of the formal budget, and the state budget directors and staffs are designated to work with the new governor directly. In more than a dozen states, the governor-elect is involved in the final adjustments of the budget—that is, "final" insofar as the document's contrivance is in the final stages even as the new governor is elected or is a formal participant in the budget hearings of the outgoing governor.

Major advances, then, have been recorded in the area of transition funding, an invaluable aid in strengthening the governorship as the foundation is laid for an entire term of office. An innovative example of recent transition funding that underlines its importance can be found in the heavily Democratic state of Missouri in 1972, when a Republican governor-elect, Christopher "Kit" Bond, recognized the pressing need for thorough transition planning in an alien political environment. Bond established a short-term, non-profit corporation called Missouri Transition Government, Inc., which collected funds from private sources and secured a federal grant for transition-planning.

The Strengthened State Legislature

If there is a new breed of governor, then there is a new breed of legislator as well. The state legislatures have yielded some of the finest recent state chief executives. There can be little doubt that court-ordered reapportionment—the redrawing of electoral districts to insure that every legislator represented approximately the same number of people and that each person's vote was thus about equal in weight—is responsible for the legislative transformation. The governor's job is more complicated, but also stronger for it.

Before proceeding to a discussion of reapportionment's effect, we should briefly review the legislative powers that the governor possesses. The most important of these has historically been, and continues to be, the veto. Prior to the turn of this century, the veto was virtually the only legislative function the governor had. Some, like Lord Bryce, suggested that it was the governor's predominant power: "The use of his veto is, in ordinary times, a governor's most serious duty and chiefly by his discharge of it he is judged."[72]

The veto is still a singularly valuable symbol of the governor's legislative authority. Governors in every state but North Carolina, which has no veto at all, have the right to reject any bill passed by the legislature within a prescribed period of time. The legislature still has the opportunity to override the governor's veto and pass the bill, but more than a majority of both houses is required in most states to do so. In 36 states a two-thirds majority is necessary; in one state, three-quarters; and in 6 states, three-fifths.[73] (Only 6 states require a mere simple majority to override.) Further, in 33 states the legislature may recall a bill before the governor acts to veto. Alterations to suit the governor's specifications or fulfill a compromise agreement can then be made, thereby salvaging the bill and valuable time and effort on everyone's part.

The veto power, already substantial, has been strengthened over the last quarter-century.[74] Five more states (bringing the total to 43) have added the "item veto" on appropriations bills to the governor's arsenal. With this authority the governor can veto single items in a money bill without rejecting the bill *in toto*. Without the item veto, the governor is usually forced to accept objectionable parts of appropriations measures because the bill as a whole is simply too important and too urgent to be vetoed. Eight states have gone a step further and now permit the governor to reduce the appropriated amounts for specific items rather than apply the veto, thereby allowing for even more executive discretion.

While in 1950 only four states—Alabama, Virginia, Massachusetts, and New Jersey—permitted the process of "executive amendment," whereby the governors can return a vetoed bill to the legislature with suggested amendments for a "veto-proof" measure, fifteen now do. Lastly, six states—California, Florida, Illinois, Massachusetts, Michigan, and Virginia—have given the governors a longer time to decide whether they will sign or veto bills while the legislature is in session.[75] All of these measures have buttressed the gubernatorial veto, which is almost absolute and very rarely overridden in any state.[76] The threat of a veto is often enough to kill a bill or alter it to the governor's liking.

Other powers add to the legislative lustre of the modern governor. All governors have the authority to call special sessions of the legislature, and in nineteen states the legislators must limit their actions to the subjects for which the governor assembled them.[77] Most governors have the right to address their state legislatures at least once a year (for the "state of the state" message), and the chief executives have become adroit at using the occasion for their own purposes (for example, to focus on their top priority programs).

It is hardly improper that governors should play a major legislative role even if they are the head of the executive branch. Governors are the representatives of entire statewide constituencies, while legislators represent only tiny parts. Since the whole is greater than the aggregated interests of the parts, governors are able to contribute broader perspectives to the legislatures' pursuits. As President Harry S Truman was fond of interjecting in his dealings with Congress: "The president is the only lobbyist all of the people in this country have!" This statement applies as well to the governor on the state level. As full-time chief administrators who travel constantly around their states and receive reports from the administrators in state agencies, governors are probably in a better position than most part-time legislators to perceive the urgent and underlying needs of the states. Moreover, governors are elected on platforms that are theoretically ratified by the people when they are elected. Almost every political platform depends heavily on legislation for its implementation, and governors must rightly involve themselves in order to fulfill their pledges.

The veto, identified here as the governor's most potent legislative tool, is a negative power, useful to governors in that it can prevent legislative actions that they oppose. Since problems usually require positive approaches to effect solutions, the veto is inadequate; the governor must rely on the competence, foresight, and representativeness of the legislature. Until little more than a decade ago, governors were apt to be very disappointed with the legislatures for two basic reasons. First, the legislatures were so malapportioned that rural districts could elect a majority of the legislature even when a large majority of the state's population was urban. The governors and legislatures of many states, then, were elected by different constituencies. Urban areas provided the margin for many governors who depended on a statewide majority for victory. Rural areas had a considerable edge in the legislatures, which thereby represented interests differing more than a bit from those of the governors. Stalemate often resulted, and urban sores inevitably festered.

The second reason for the governors' legislative frustrations involved the structure and functioning of most state legislatures. The legislative committees were a jumble of overlapping principalities. Annual sessions were infrequently held. The compensation, staffing, budget, and facilities provided legislators were extremely poor. Researching and bill drafting were primitive processes. Court-ordered reapportionment decisions, which came in a floodtide after the Supreme court's landmark decision *Baker* v. *Carr* (March 1962), revolutionized the executive-legislative relationship by reforming the legislatures at their roots. The principle of "one-man, one-vote" became virtually absolute. No person's vote could count for more in a district than a fellow citizen's vote in another. Every legislator would have to represent close to the same number of people.

By the 1970s, clarifying court decisions made the mathematical calculations for determining legislative districts just about as precise as possible. Every state reapportioned its legislature after the 1970 decennial census, and in only sixteen of fifty lower houses and thirteen of forty-nine state senates was there a deviation of more than 10 percent between the largest and smallest per-seat population.[78] The urban-suburban majority became predominant in the legislatures just as it was in the population as a whole. For the first time, governors and the legislature were elected by and represented the same weighted constituency— a development that could only help them to find a community of programmatic interests.

Infused with an imposing group of new legislators representing long-frustrated constituencies, legislatures went about the task of reinvigorating their structures and operations with some fervor, aided by organizations like the Council of State Governments and the Citizens' Conference on State Legislatures (CCSL, now called Legis 50).[79] The CCSL's "elements of independence" became the universal guideposts for the state legislatures as they struggled to awaken themselves from a long slumber:

1. [It] must control its own life. It must decide how long and how often it meets, and establish its own procedures, programs, expenditures, and apportionment.
2. It must be, in practice as in principle, able to operate as a separate and coequal branch of government relative to the executive branch.
3. It must be able to oversee and evaluate the programs and expenditures which it has authorized.
4. It must be free from undue influence on the part of special interest groups and representatives.
5. It must be free from conflicts or dilution of interests on the part of individual legislators.[80]

In 1940 only four states held annual legislative sessions; the number had grown to nineteen by 1960, and by 1976 forty-two legislatures met on an annual basis. The unwieldy committee systems, the heart of the legislative process, have been thoroughly overhauled. The number of committees in each house has been reduced, while the breadth and depth of their subject matter has increased. Legislators serve on fewer committees, which thus permits them greater concentration on a few subjects so that they may develop expertness. Facilities and staffing for committees have been improved, and the committee meetings have been opened to press and public with advance notice of times and places. More than two-thirds of the state legislatures have now adopted formal rules of procedures for their committees.

The compensation and perquisites offered legislators have swelled in kind and number, thereby assisting in at least the partial liberation of many legislators from the control of well-financed lobby groups. In 1973 alone, for example, six states increased legislative salaries and eight more raised expense allowances.[81] The average state legislator now has his own staff, however small, of clerical and professional assistants. Computerization of bill information at a legislator's fingertips and professionalized bill drafting are commonplace. Much better office facilities are also provided. In just two years, between 1970 and 1972, forty-three states improved staff and forty-one enhanced legislative facilities.[82]

This tremendous internal strengthening of the legislature, combined with its more prestigious and representative character since the termination of malapportionment, has not been wholly advantageous to governors; some of the changes have come at the expense of their prerogatives. As the legislators became more professional and their duties more time consuming, they requested a correspondingly greater voice in state government. For instance, the governor has had to work more closely on financial matters with the legislature of late, since forty-five legislatures now have full-time, year-round staffing of their appropriations committees.[83]

Yet the gains for the governor far outweigh the losses. Governors have gladly traded a share of their decision-making authority for the informed, independent, representative, and accountable legislatures that by and large work far more closely and are vastly more in tune with the chief executives than those of only a decade ago. Governor Reubin Askew of Florida, who listed the rise of state legislatures as one of the three primary causes of a strengthened governorship, expressed the view of many governors when he claimed that the legislative reform "has not adversely affected the governor; it's resulted in the strengthening of the whole system. . . ."[84]

A revitalized legislature has been as important as an empowered governorship in the recent reclaiming by state government of authority and responsibility from Washington. Herbert Wiltsee reports that one of the major themes of the new legislatures is "a concern . . . for the development of a better means by which the states can have greater impact on the policies and programs developed by Congress and the President, and the manner of their implementation by the federal executive establishment."[85]

It is doubtful whether the legislature can ever really gain the upper hand over the executive if the present basic structure of politics and government remains intact.[86] Any legislature of several hundred persons is normally at a severe disadvantage when pitted against a single executive. The governor, far more capable of decisive action, is the focus of the people's expectations and is viewed by them as the commander-in-chief of state government. No single legislator or the legislature as a whole can command the personal allegiance that accrues to the governor. Furthermore, a fractionalized legislature cannot manipulate the news media as any governor worth his salt is adept at doing. The media are usually at the governor's beck and call; even legislative leaders do not have the resources or the prestige to compete. In experience, too, the governor is in a better position to dominate. While the legislative committee system encourages, if not requires, specialization, the governor has a statewide perspective on issues and their priorities and is thus more familiar with a broad sweep of policies than most legislators and probably situated in a better post to judge the impact of any single policy on the government as a whole. Despite the decline in patronage, the governor's appointive powers are still substantial levers that more than once have brought a recalcitrant legislator into line.

All of these factors combine to insure executive supremacy in normal conditions. Alan J. Wyner, examining executive-legislative relations in fourteen states in the mid-1960s, testified that ". . . when the stakes are high, when he wants to win, and if his party is not a hopeless minority, the probability is large that the governor will be extremely influential in legislative actions."[87] A governor's legislative "batting average" (or percentage of his program acceded to by the legislature) was on the average a quite high 71 percent.[88]

Perhaps too much emphasis has been placed in this analysis on competition for power between the executive and legislative branches. A Louisiana committee studying the question properly concluded: "We feel that it is not necessary to weaken one branch, in its proper sphere, in order to strengthen another. . . . We believe the goal of equal and coordinate branches can be achieved and developed by making each branch strong in the exercise of functions inherent in each."[89] At least in the American experience the best government seems to be a properly balanced one, where neither the executive nor the legislative branch is weak and debilitated and where each has the authority and the resources to fulfill its responsibilities. The emergence of both governor and legislature in this mold is a new and propitious phenomenon in state government.

A note about the third branch of government should be added here before continuing. The state judiciary has not been immune to reform in the last two decades.[90] The advance of greatest consequence has been the conversion to a unified, integrated judicial system under the general supervision of the state supreme court, which three-quarters of the states have now accomplished. Just as with legislatures, there have been great strides in staffing and technology. A coordinating officer of state court administration now exists in forty-three states, and computers have been introduced to speed the flow of judicial information and decision. Selection of judicial personnel has also absorbed the energy of reformers. Since the first state did so in 1940, forty states have now adopted some type of "merit system" for choosing judges, thereby removing the selection from a strictly political realm and introducing a degree of screening. Like its coordinate executive and legislative branches, a more logically organized and better executed judicial branch has contributed to the rejuvenation and renewal of modern state governments.

Powers and "Perks"

Not all a governor's powers are the stuff that television news spots are made of, but they are hardly insubstantial items. Indeed, some of the budgeting, planning, and managerial powers are among the governor's mightiest as they have developed over the last couple of decades. The executive budget may well be the single most important tool possessed by the chief executive. The executive budget gives the governor hegemony in the financial realm, especially when it is combined with an item veto for legislative appropriations. It is also a device for exerting gubernatorial control of (or at least influence over) other statewide elective officers. One governor has suggested that the development of the executive budget is the weightiest factor in the advent of the invigorated modern governor.[91]

The formalized budget process was first developed by New York City and the state of Ohio in the early part of the twentieth century, and this step was copied by the federal government in 1921 with the passage of the national Budgeting and Accounting Act.[92] Progressives encouraged the budgetary movement out of concern for efficiency and control, but the purposes expanded through the decades to include a stress on financial planning to achieve goals deemed desirable by elected representatives. Several programmatic methods of budgeting were developed and refined by both federal and state governments. The Planning-Programming-Budgeting (PPB) System of the Rand Corporation is the most widely known, if only because of former Secretary of Defense Robert S. McNamara's ill-fated use of it in his department during the Kennedy and Johnson administrations. The Management by Objective (MBO) method, adopted by the Nixon administration and Governor Christopher Bond of Missouri among others and Zero-Based Budgeting popularized by Governor Jimmy Carter of Georgia are two additional illustrations of programmatic systems.

In their adaptations on the state level, the governor is the key figure in budgetary decisions. The ideal set forth by the National Association of State Budget Officers has been realized in most states: "The Governor should be the supreme budget authority. The budget director should be responsible to him directly or through an intervening agency head appointed by the Governor and serving at the Governor's pleasure."[93] As of 1975 31 states assigned the primary budgetary authority as well as the actual preparation of the budget to the governor.[94] In 14 more states, an agency under the command of the governor was given the responsibility for the budget. In 21 states the budget director was appointed by the governor directly; in 11 additional states the budget department chief appointed the budget director with the approval of the governor; and in 2 states the governor appointed the director subject only to the confirmation of the state senate.[95]

Just 2 states out of 50 have not now adopted the major aspects of the executive budget system. South Carolina has an executive-legislative budget board to make its financial decisions, and Mississippi is the only state that gives the executive no budgetary role (members of the state's legislature comprise the budget authority). In 1950, 10 states did not give the governor alone the budget-making power, and there were 6 such states as late as 1967.[96] Further, the officials and agency heads preparing the budget were commonly not appointed by the governor. It is evident, then, that a great deal of progress has been made.

In fact, the governor's budgetary influence is still waxing. S. Kenneth Howard concluded in his study of state budgeting practices:

Gubernatorial powers appear to be growing. Governors are being consulted and given more information about federal grants, their approval may be necessary before an agency may apply for a grant, and their approval is increasingly being required for some other program matters; consolidation among federal categorical grants is taking place so that supported agencies can less readily obtain money independently of the governor; additional responsibilities and authority for meeting pressing domestic problems are devolving upon the states; budgetary innovations are being initiated that can strengthen a governor's participation in these matters; and efforts at state constitutional revision emphasize administrative integration under the governor.[97]

The governor's budgetary authority is increasing because of other factors as well. Ira Sharkansky found in 1969 that governors' chances of success in securing legislative approval of the budgets and of raising expenditures are maximized in states where governors can succeed themselves, where there are relatively few other statewide elected officials, and when total spending is relatively high.[98] At least two of these factors (succession and spending) are present in a larger number of states than ever before.

Lest the budgetary picture be perceived as an unspoiled rose-colored one, it should be noted that governors constantly are forced to snuff out brush fires that threaten their prerogatives. Legislatures always are searching for new footholds, and agencies sometimes attempt to contravene gubernatorial authority or to obscure their financial balance sheets.[99] Such is the nature of the political power game. Howard also cautioned: "The power of the governor should not be overestimated. He cannot fight every battle that he might wish. He must spend his limited political capital selectively—he must cash his Green Stamps where he feels they will do the most good according to his scale of values."[100] Nevertheless, the executive budget has become fundamentally one of the governor's most formidable and widely acknowledged powers.

The governor has made striking advances in the planning and managerial fields too. In twenty-eight states the chief executives are now formally assigned the planning function for state government,[101] but their powers are extensive in virtually all the states. A detailed Council of State Governments' survey in 1970 found that "The various governors either through their own office or through a department directly responsible to them are responsible for most of the central management functions administered by the states."[102] Only a few central functions, most of a minor nature (like the preparation of checks, custody of state funds, and postaudit) are administered more than half the time by someone other than the governor.[103]

Among the central functions controlled almost entirely by the governor are the budget preparation and execution; capital improvement planning and budgeting; management studies; data processing policies, services, and systems: central purchasing; mail, telephone, and other communications; duplicating and printing; the motor pool; building planning and construction; comprehensive state planning; labor-management relations; and, crucially, federal aid coordination, including grant review and approval authority. Singly these items are important, and together they extend the governor's influence by quite a measure. Even a novice governor quickly becomes skilled in their manipulation and can sometimes trade perquisites for vital support of his programs.

A governor's own "perks" include staff and salary, and these two will be used here to illustrate the enrichment of the chief executive's working environment over the last quarter-century. Coleman Ransone decided that most governors were understaffed in the early 1950s.[104] More clerical and professional assistance was deemed necessary both to increase the workload handled by the governors' offices and to reduce the governors' personal workload and some of the detail with which they often had to involve themselves. In these ways additional staff could help to broaden the governor's influence and power, thereby permitting the governor to concentrate on basic policies and their executions. A governor less distracted by minutiae can be more effective. New developments, however, suggest a revision of Ransone's conclusion.[105] In 1956 the average staff size in a governor's office was 4.3 persons. By 1966 the number had grown to 6.6 (a 54 percent increase), and just two years later another increment of 11 percent (to 7.3 persons) was recorded. The growth of state government since then has been more than matched in gubernatorial offices. The staff members themselves were exceptional in both education and dedication.[106] Almost three-quarters of them had at least one college degree.

A governor's salary might not strike one as particulary crucial, but it is precisely that. If the salary is set too low, directly or indirectly corrupt relationships between a governor and private persons or groups are encouraged. In and out of politics, you normally get what you pay for. There can be no better example of this than Spiro Agnew. When Agnew became governor of Maryland, the office's salary ($15,000) was one of the lowest in the country. The infamous associations Agnew made with state contractors for the purpose of supplementing his pay are well known. Arkansas, the only state with a lower gubernatorial emolument ($10,000) than Maryland provides another illustration of the effects of low pay. One of the state's governors, Orval Faubus, became wealthy off subsidies from special interests like the Arkansas-Louisiana Gas Company, which coincidentally got most of the rate increases it desired.[107] Even if a low salary does not result in corrupt practices, it has an undesirable inhibiting effect in a democracy, since it permits only a very few in any society the luxury of running for and serving in the governorship. Moreover, a minimal salary can discourage even members of the upper strata from gubernatorial candidacies; government must at least approach the rewards of industry if able persons are to be enticed away from the private sector.

Government does differ from industry in that money is not the primary remuneration for service. The keen desires for power and prestige, which are fairly universal among politicians and find satisfaction in public service, mitigate the need for exactly competitive compensations. Also, if the salary was set too high, people with the sole motive of financial advancement might be attracted to run. As always, the search for the golden mean is an arduous one. It is clear, however, that salaries for governors in the 1950s were distinctly on the low side of the ideal. The average gubernatorial salary in 1950 was a mere $11,512.[108] By 1975 gubernatorial pay had climbed to an average of $40,963, an increase of 256 percent. The salary swell is substantial even after accounting for inflation, and when standardizing in terms of 1958 dollars, a 68 percent rise is still observed. Not computed here but also noteworthy is the accretion over the years of perquisites like large expense accounts and travel allowances and executive housing of some type, which is normally provided as well.

Twelve states now have salaries for governors of $50,000 and above, with

New York ($85,000), Texas ($65,000), and New Jersey and Pennsylvania ($60,000) at the top. For their sizes the states of Georgia, Tennessee, and Virginia (at $50,000), and Colorado and Iowa (at $40,000) pay quite well. States like California, Massachusetts, Michigan, New Jersey, and New York have had top salaries throughout the last quarter-century. Other states, including Florida, Illinois, Minnesota, Ohio, Wisconsin, Nevada, Kansas, and Texas, have shown vast improvements. The present salary levels do not appear unreasonable at all. There is a major financial sacrifice involved in running for and holding the governorship. Campaigning alone requires a full-time commitment of a year or more, and personal election costs may amount to several times the annual gubernatorial salary. The demands of the office are great too. Some authorities have suggested that the present salaries may be minimal in light of the burdens carried by candidate and governor,[109] for despite the advances that have been made, there are still a few underpaid governors, including Arkansas (with a low of $10,000), North Dakota ($18,000), and Maryland ($25,000).[110]

Watergate and the State Executive

The Watergate scandals on the national level certainly resulted in a rollback of presidential power and influence. Americans lost some of their naïveté about the Oval Office, and the presidency's aura was noticeably dimmed. As Congress reasserted itself and partially retook powers like the war-making authority long ago ceded to the president, many suggested, as their colonial brethren once had, that a mighty executive was inherently untrustworthy. A series of new curbs and checks on executive power was prescribed at the national level.

Did the Watergate-fed suspicion of executives carry over to the states? Did state legislatures or the people through referenda attempt to place controls on governors similar to those enacted by Congress to restrain the president? It might appear to follow logically, but the answer to these questions is "No." In a 1974 study of New York state, Eugene Gleason and Joseph Zimmerman found:

The recent challenges of the strong executive concept at the Presidential level have not produced a similar challenge in New York State. While predicting the future is a hazardous business, the lack of public debate challenging the strong executive concept in New York State and the noticeable absence of a movement based on this theme in the legislature suggest that the strong executive concept is secure in the State in the forseeable future.[111]

Of more than two dozen governors queried in this study, only one saw a connection between Watergate and a specific action on the state level. Governor Thomas Salmon of Vermont reported that Watergate was "the only significant reason" that a 1974 statewide referendum on lengthening the governor's term from two to four years was narrowly defeated.[112] The other governors perceived no direct effects on the executive that were not felt by politicians generally. Certainly, coverage of the new financial disclosure and ethics laws includes the governor, and the negative connotations conferred by Watergate on all politicians make life more difficult for any public officials, but, again, none of this is particular to the governor. In fact, it was the governor in many states who, responding to the Watergate scandals, initiated the proposals for public campaign finance laws and conflict-of-interest prohibitions. Most of the governors elected for the first time in 1974 were themselves part of the reform tide generated by Watergate.

All in all, the governors and the states appear to have gained from Watergate's national devastation by what David Broder has called the "teeter-totter effect."[113] As the national government in Washington fell from popular favor and the extent of the corruption became apparent, the status of the states was enhanced. The 1976 Harris Survey quoted earlier seems to support this theory (see Chapter 1).

A Concluding Note on Gubernatorial Power

An index of the governor's formal powers is useful and vital in any assessment of changing gubernatorial strength.[114] The examination of the rapid and basic transformation of state governments in this chapter indicates that the governor now works in a political and structural environment less inhibiting than ever before. The recent pace of constitutional revisions and reorganizations has been nothing short of astounding in states that were static for decades. The major hurdle remaining is the reduction in the number of other statewide elective offices. There has been some progress in fusing the fractionalized executive, but it has been gradual for reasons already reviewed.

The decline of patronage has been judged, somewhat surprisingly, as a boon for governors, since it has liberated them from a tedious, time-consuming, and frustrating chore that is outmoded in the modern political system. At the same time the governor has gained appointive powers where it really matters, at the top-level in policy-making positions. Of particular and ever-increasing assistance to the chief executive is the lieutenant governor, whose office has been buttressed with better pay and staffing and whose job has been expanded to incorporate significant executive duties. A more consonant relationship between the two top officers is the promise of team election of governors and lieutenant governors—a widespread practice in the states of late. Governors feel more comfortable in delegating chunks of executive responsibility to lieutenant governors in these circumstances, and the lieutenant governors are thereby trained for the day when they might well acquire the governorship. If they win it, they can also be assured of a better-funded transition between their teams and the preceding administrations.

In the executive sphere, governors have done quite well, not only in successfully orchestrating constitutional revisions and reorganizations but also in consolidating and fortifying their control of administration. The executive budget is a formidable and almost universal gubernatorial lever. Lesser planning and management tools have also been strengthened and are at the governor's disposal. The governorship as an office draws a better salary and is more adequately staffed now than in the past.

Legislatively, the governor has advanced in the last quarter-century, with gubernatorial veto power, always near-invincible, being further enlarged. Far more important, though, is the fact that the governor's programs fall on more sympathetic legislative ears since reapportionment. The governor and legislature now represent the same constituency, and while they will never agree on everything, they presently have at least similar general outlooks and orientations. More responsive state government has also resulted from the internal strengthening of the legislatures that are now better equipped to grapple with the perplexing issues facing the states and localities.

Again, one should be cautioned against overgeneralization of fifty very diverse political entities. As Samuel K. Gove has warned, it is foolhardy and even dangerous to equate each state's governor with all others and to insist that all governors should be "identical in power and scope."[115] Nevertheless, there are some common administrative elements that every chief executive should possess to have the potential for effectiveness, and the concentration in this chapter has been on these components.

Only the formal powers have been (and can be) comparatively surveyed, but the significance of informal factors cannot be ignored. A governor's personality is chief among them. Leslie Lipson concluded his discussion of gubernatorial weakness in 1949 by suggesting: "The ultimate solution lies beyond the scope of mere institutional reform. Provisions of law can ordain hierarchies and confer authority. But true leadership, which inspires the willing confidence of men, cannot be crystallized into constitutional grants of power. Each governor must win it anew."[116] Ultimately, then, an individual governor's degree of power, success, or failure, will depend on his or her competence, ability, and personality. Perhaps at its base, gubernatorial power, like the presidential variety, is the power to persuade.[117] Governors must command respect in their governments and among their people to have the chance to accomplish their goals. A brief incident from the career of Governor Tom McCall of Oregon can illustrate this point. During the 1973-74 energy crisis, McCall issued an executive order that all display lighting in Oregon was to be extinguished. His action was without legal foundation, and McCall expected to be taken to court and to lose. Surprisingly, though, he was never challenged and his order was respected. His recognized authority was such that he was able to use powers he didn't have.[118] Governor G. Mennen Williams of Michigan put it this way:

The Governor's power, I found, results only in part from the constitution and statutes. As in all else in a democracy the ultimate source of power is the people. If the people are not with you, you cannot, or can only with the greatest difficulty, exercise many of the powers that are yours under law.[119]

In sum, in Chapter 2, we discovered that governors of greater capacity and better training were being elected in the last decade, and the evidence from the states and nation suggests that they are well-respected. Thus, they have the foundations of persuasive power, but that is not enough for success. The brightest, ablest governors could be stopped dead in their tracks by the multitude of institutional obstacles placed in their way. The point of this chapter is that most of those institutional barriers have been dislodged and swept away. The new governors are in a position to use their appreciable talents and to work relatively unhindered, and that is no small gain for the governors and the states.

Notes

1. As quoted in Louis Lambert, "The Executive Article," in W. Brooke Graves (ed.), *Major Problems in Constitutional Revision* (Chicago: Public Administration Service, 1960), p. 185.
2. Coleman B. Ransone, Jr., *The Office of Governor in the United States* (University: The University of Alabama Press, 1956), p. 402.
3. William H. Young, "The Development of the Governorship," *State Government* 31 (Summer 1958):181.
4. Bennett M. Rich, *State Constitutions: The Governor*, State Constitutional Studies Project, Series 11, No. 3 (New York: National Municipal League, 1960), pp. 30-33.
5. Thad L. Beyle, The Governor's Formal Powers: A View from the Governor's Chair," in Donald R. Sprengel (ed.), *Comparative State Politics: A Reader* (New York: Charles E. Merrill, 1971), pp. 293-99.
6. One major reform, that of the governor's term, will not be discussed here, but in Chapter 4.
7. Robert S. Allen, *Our Sovereign State* (New York: Vanguard Press, 1949), p. xv. See pp. xv-xx for a description of the inadequacies of state constitutions existing at the time.
8. Ibid.
9. Neal R. Peirce, "Structural Reform of Bureaucracy Grows Rapidly," *National Journal Reports* 7 (April 5, 1975):504. The states are Connecticut, Florida, Hawaii, Illinois, Louisiana, Michigan, Montana, North Carolina, Pennsylvania, and Virginia.

10. Neal R. Peirce, "The States: Innovative Solutions to the Recession," *The Washington Post*, February 27, 1976.

11. Peirce, "Structural Reform of Bureaucracy Grows Rapidly."

12. Council of State Governments, *The Book of the States, 1974-1975* (Lexington, Ky: Council of State Governments, 1974), pp. 3-23.

13. Ibid.

14. See Charles S. Hyneman, "Administrative Reorganization: An Adventure into Science and Theology," *Journal of Politics* 1 (February 1939):66.

15. Peirce, "Structural Reform of Bureaucracy Grows Rapidly," pp. 502-08.

16. Ibid., p. 502.

17. Commission on the Organization of the Executive Branch of Government, *General Management of the Executive Branch* (Washington, D.C.: Government Printing Office, 1949), p. 1, as quoted by Lambert, "The Executive Article."

18. Peirce, "The States: Innovative Solutions to the Recession."

19. Advisory Commission on Intergovernmental Relations, *State Legislative Program* (Washington, D.C.: ACIR, November 1975), pp. 28-29.

20. Correspondence with the author, July 22, 1976.

21. Peirce, "Structural Reform of Bureaucracy Grows Rapidly," p. 506.

22. Ransone, *The Office of Governor,* p. 223.

23. Compiled from Council of State Governments, *The Book of the States, 1952-53* (Chicago: Council of State Governments, 1952), p. 156.

24. Compiled from Council of State Governments, *The Book of the States, 1976-77* (Lexington, Ky.: The Council of State Governments, 1976), pp. 155-57.

25. National Municipal League, Committee on State Government, *Model State Constitution with Explanatory Articles* (New York: National Municipal League, 1948).

26. Rich, *State Constitutions,* p. 14.

27. Duane Lockard, *The Politics of State and Local Government* (New York: Macmillan, 1963), p. 323.

28. The American Assembly, *The Forty-Eight States: Their Tasks as Policy Makers and Administrators* (New York: The American Assembly, Graduate School of Business, Columbia University, 1955), p. 140.

29. Interviews and correspondence with the author. Due to the sensitive nature of the quotations, governors are not quoted by name.

30. A. James Reichley, *States in Crisis: Politics in Ten American States, 1950-1962* (Chapel Hill: University of North Carolina Press, 1964), pp. 198-99.

31. Interview with the author, September 8, 1976, Tallahassee, Fla.

32. Ibid.

33. Lockard, *The Politics of State and Local Government,* p. 349.

34. Ibid., p. 348.

93

35. Ibid., p. 355.

36. Interview with the author, August 4, 1976, Portland, Ore.

37. Council of State Governments, *The Governor: The Office and Its Powers* (Lexington, Ky.: Council of State Governments, 1972), pp. 14, 16-18.

38. Ibid., p. 19.

39. Thad L. Beyle, "State Executives," in Richard H. Leach (ed.), *Compacts of Antiquity: State Constitutions* (Atlanta: Southern Newspaper Publisher's Association's Foundation, 1969), p. 28.

40. William L. Riordon (ed.), *Plunkitt of Tammany Hall* (New York: E.P. Dutton, 1963), pp. 11, 89.

41. National Governors' Conference, *The Critical Hundred Days: A Handbook for the New Governor* (Washington, D.C.: National Governors' Conference, 1975), p. 45.

42. Council of State Governments, *The Book of States, 1958-59* (Chicago: Council of State Governments, 1958), pp. 140-42. The total of 1,321,759 state employees includes full and part-time employees. See also Frank Sorauf, "The Silent Revolution in Patronage," *Public Administration Review* 20 (1960): 28-39.

43. Lockard, *The Politics of State and Local Government*, p. 351.

44. Council of State Governments, *The Book of the States, 1976-77,* pp. 155, 522-25. The total number of full-time and part-time state employees was 2,020,783.

45. *Elrod* v. *Burns*, 96 S.Ct. 2673 (1976). See also *The Washington Post*, June 29, 1976, p. A-1.

46. Ibid.

47. Interview with the author, August 24, 1976, New York, N.Y.

48. Interview with the author, August 3, 1976, Salt Lake City, Utah.

49. Ibid.

50. Interview with the author, September 8, 1976, Tallahassee, Fla.

51. Interview with the author, July 21, 1976, Durham, N.C.

52. Correspondence with the author, November 4, 1976.

53. Thomas R. Morris, *Virginia's Lieutenant Governors: The Office and the Person* (Charlottesville: Institute of Government, University of Virginia, 1970), pp. 9-10.

54. Council of State Governments, *The Lieutenant Governor: Office and Powers* (Lexington, Ky.: Council of State Governments, 1973), p. 1.

55. In the states without lieutenant governors, either the popularly elected secretary of state, or the president of the state senate or speaker of the house (both of whom are elected by their colleagues representing all areas of the state), are designated next in the line of succession. In a few states special elections are called when the vacancy occurs before the mid-point of the term.

56. Council of State Governments, *The Lieutenant Governor: Office and Powers,* p. 29.

57. Ibid., p. 8.

58. R.F. Patterson, *The Office of Lieutenant Governor in the United States* (Vermillion: Governmental Research Bureau, University of South Dakota, 1944), pp. 10-11.

59. Council of State Governments, *The Lieutenant Governor: Office and Powers* p. 20. Specific assignments to lieutenant governors noted here were culled from the author's interviews.

60. Interview with the author, September 8, 1976, Tallahassee, Fla.

61. Council of State Governments, *The Lieutenant Governor: Office and Powers,* p. 21.

62. Ibid., pp. 8-12.

63. Patterson, *The Office of Lieutenant Governor,* pp. 10a, 10b, 17.

64. Council of State Governments, *The Lieutenant Governor: Office and Powers,* pp. 12-14.

65. Ibid., p. 7; see the poll of lieutenant governors. The opinions of governors were secured in the author's interviews.

66. These arguments and others are thoroughly discussed in the following report that recommended the adoption of team election in Massachusetts: Massachusetts Legislative Research Council, "Report Relative to Joint Election of Governor (Proposed Constitutional Amendment)," Commonwealth of Massachusetts, Senate Document No. 949, March 3, 1965.

67. Samuel R. Solomon, "Governors: 1960-1970," *National Civic Review* 60 (March 1971):133.

68. Interview with the author, August 5, 1976, Olympia, Wash.

69. Interview with the author, September 23, 1976, Bloomfield Hills, Mich.

70. Council of State Governments, *The Governor: The Office and Its Powers,* pp. 26-27.

71. Council of State Governments, *Gubernatorial Transition in the States:* (Lexington, Ky.: Council of State Governments, 1972).

72. James Bryce, *The American Commonwealth* (New York: Macmillan, 1928), i, p. 500.

73. Council of State Governments, *Book of the States 1974-1975,* pp. 80-81.

74. Ibid., and Council of State Governments, *The Book of the States 1952-1953,* p. 103.

75. Council of State Governments, *The Governor: The Office and Its Powers,* p. 20.

76. Rich, *State Constitutions,* pp. 20-22, and Frank W. Prescott, "The Executive Veto in American States," *The Western Political Quarterly* 3 (March 1950):99.

77. Council of State Governments, *The Governor: The Office and Its Powers,* p. 21.

78. Herbert L. Wiltsee, "The State Legislatures," in the Council of State Governments, *The Book of the States, 1976-1977,* p. 32.

79. Ibid., pp. 33-39. Information is also taken from National Governors' Conference, *The State of the States* (Washington, D.C.: National Governors' Conference, 1974), pp. 21-22.

80. Citizens' Conference on State Legislatures, *The Sometime Governments: A Critical Study of the 50 American Legislatures* (New York: Bantam Books, 1971), pp. 121-22.

81. National Governors' Conference, *The State of the States,* p. 21.

82. A CCSL study quoted in ibid.

83. Ibid., p. 22.

84. Interview with the author, September 8, 1976, Tallahassee, Fla.

85. Wiltsee, "The State Legislatures," p. 31.

86. See The American Assembly, *The Forty-eight States,* pp. 59-60.

87. Alan J. Wyner, "Gubernatorial Relations with Legislators and Administrators," *State Government* 51 (Summer 1968):200.

88. Ibid., p. 202.

89. State of Louisiana, "Report of the Louisiana Governor's Committee to Consider Changes in the Powers, Duties, and Responsibilities of the Governor," Office of the Governor, Baton Rouge, May 11, 1966, pp. B-1 to B-2.

90. National Governors' Conference, *The State of the States,* p. 22.

91. Reubin Askew in an interview with the author, September 8, 1976, Tallahassee, Fla.

92. Peirce, "Structural Reform of Bureaucracy Grows Rapidly," pp. 507-08.

93. National Association of State Budget Officers, *Principles for State Executive Budget Officers* (Lexington, Ky.: Council of State Governments, 1975), p. 3.

94. Council of State Governments, *Budgetary Processes in the States (A Tabular Display)* (Lexington, Ky.: Council of State Governments, 1975).

95. Ibid.

96. Council of State Governments, *Budgeting by the States* (Chicago: Council of State Governments, 1967), pp. 9-11.

97. S. Kenneth Howard, *State Budgeting Practices* (Lexington, Ky.: Council of State Governments, 1973), p. 269.

98. Ira Sharkansky, *The Politics of Taxing and Spending* (Indianapolis: Bobbs-Merrill, 1969), p. 111.

99. Advisory Commission on Intergovernmental Relations, *State Legislative Program,* pp. 30-31.

100. Howard, *State Budgeting Practices,* p. 269.

101. Council of State Governments, *Book of the States, 1976-1977,* p. 110.

102. Council of State Governments, *Central Management in the States* (Lexington, Ky.: Council of State Governments, 1970), p. 8.

103. Ibid., pp. 14-15. For a state-by-state accounting of the governor's role in planning and management, see pp. 17-83.

104. Ransone, *The Office of Governor,* pp. 302, 362.

105. Donald R. Sprengel, "Patterns of Organization in Gubernatorial Staffs" in Sprengel (ed.), *Gubernatorial Staffs: Function and Political Profiles* (Iowa City: Institute of Public Affairs, University of Iowa, 1969), pp. 308-30.

106. Ibid., p. 308.

107. Neal Peirce, *The Deep South States of America* (New York: W.W. Norton, 1972), pp. 130-32.

108. Average salaries quoted in the text were compiled from state-by-state figures contained in the biennial Council of State Governments' publication, *The Book of the States.*

109. David R. Berman, *State and Local Politics* (Boston: Holbrook Press, 1975), p. 105.

110. A proposal to raise the salary of Maryland's governor to $60,000 after 1978 was approved by the state salary commission in 1977. The proposal was made in the wake of Governor Marvin Mandel's conviction on charges that he traded official favors for valuable gifts used to supplement his salary.

111. Eugene J. Gleason, Jr., and Joseph F. Zimmerman, "Executive Dominance in New York State," a paper presented to the Northeastern Political Science Association, Saratoga Springs, N.Y., November 9, 1974.

112. Correspondence with the author, July 22, 1976.

113. David S. Broder, "The Rise of the Governors," *The Washington Post,* June 12, 1976.

114. The indexing method used in this chapter was extended description; but others have attempted a strict quantitative analysis of gubernatorial power. See Joseph Schlesinger, "The Governorship," in Herbert Jacobs and Kenneth Vines (eds.), *Politics in the American States: A Comparative Analysis* (Boston: Little, Brown, 1971), pp. 220-34; and also Thad L. Beyle, "The Governor's Formal Powers: A View from the Governor's Chair," in Donald P. Sprengel (ed.), *Comparative State Politics: A Reader* (New York: Charles E. Merrill, 1971), pp. 292-99.

115. Samuel K. Gove, "Why Strong Governors?" *National Civic Review* 53 (March 1964):131-36.

116. Leslie Lipson, *The American Governor: From Figurehead to Leader* (Chicago: University of Chicago Press, 1949), p. 268.

117. See Richard Neustadt, *Presidential Power* (New York: John Wiley and Sons, 1960), passim.

118. Interview of Ron Schmidt, former administrative assistant to Governor McCall, Portland, Ore., August 4, 1976.

119. G. Mennen Williams, *A Governor's Notes* (Ann Arbor: Institute of Public Administration, University of Michigan, 1961), p. 1.

4 Winning in the Election Game

While the foregoing emphasis on administration has been rightly placed, governors do not operate solely within the confines of the governmental apparatus. They are political creatures who shape and conform to the electoral environment in their states. Before they can accomplish anything at all, they must convince first their parties (unless they are Independent) and then enough of the general electorate that they are worthy of the governorship. Yet, the nomination and election hurdles, once cleared, do not signify by any stretch of the imagination the conclusion of political influences on the chief executives. The degree of success governors achieve during their terms is often determined as much by the climate of party competition, their ability to succeed themselves, and the voting habits of their constituents as by anything else. These topics and others in the political realm will be surveyed in this chapter. The electoral realignments over the past quarter-century, as we shall see, have had a major impact on the identity and the effectiveness of America's state governors.

Governor's Tenure

From the beginning of the republic, citizens have argued fiercely about the proper length and maximum number of terms any governor should serve. The designers of early state constitutions believed firmly in the advisability of the two-year term. It was considered more democratic, since the governor was subjected to the judgment of the people at more frequent intervals. With a two-year term there was less likelihood of a governor's building a political machine to perpetuate himself in power—or so it was supposed. The governor and his policies were also considered better off, since a fresh mandate could justify the continuance and expansion of a chief executive's program. These arguments, coupled with the colonial experience, were convincing enough so that ten of the thirteen original states instituted a gubernatorial term of a single year. Two others had a two-year term, and only one allowed the governor so much as three years.

Gradually the states came to see the folly of these extreme limitations on gubernatorial terms. Reformers urged a four-year term of office, and they found support in the decision of the federal constitutionalists to give the president such a tenure.[1] A two-year term, it became clear, resulted in eternal, almost full-scale electioneering for governor. "I am running for office 365 days a year," declared

Governor E.L. Mechem of New Mexico.[2] An Ohio state commission in 1951, recommending the lengthening of that state's gubernatorial term from two to four years, concluded: "A two-year term in office for the governor leaves him in the situation where, in the first term, he must spend the first year getting acquainted with his position and the second year in campaigning for re-election. These necessities pose a severe limiting factor to his administrative contribution."[3]

A four-year term gives a governor the opportunity to develop a thorough program and a real record that can be presented to the voters for a reelection judgment if successive terms are permitted. With only two years, there is but a single biennial budget to be devised and administered (and the preceding governor has usually done the lion's share of the decision making on this first budget). Long-range program and policy planning is exceedingly difficult under these conditions, and a governor is less likely to develop the administrative expertise needed to do a good job. The chief executive's control of state government is considerably lessened under a two-year term limitation. Many state administrators who are under the merit system or otherwise insulated from the gubernatorial appointment power may rightly take the attitude that they can survive any governor, however obnoxious to them or their interests, if the governor's term is but two years. The prospect of a gubernatorial stretch of four years, uninterrupted by the rigors and stresses of politicking, might tend to make them a bit more flexible. A governor, too, often has to possess extraordinary persuasive powers to procure outstanding department heads if a tenure of only two years is assured. Highly trained persons in most fields expect, and get, a much greater degree of job security in private industry. Finally, in addition to the tremendous energy that an election consumes among those in state government, there is a significant personnel turnover whenever the governorship changes hands. Administrative efficiency and continuity would thus seem to require a duration greater than two years.

The people, it is true, are deprived of half their opportunities to pass on the performance of their governors when terms are lengthened from two to four years. Yet this not trivial price appears more than balanced by the better government that probably results from extended tenure. Moreover, an indirect method of gauging voter sentiment on a governor's program does exist at midterm when at least one house of the state legislature is elected, for the contests can and often do reflect public attitudes on gubernatorial policies and directives.

Nevertheless, the states, ever reluctant to change, clung to limited terms until very recent times. While the one-year term was finally abolished in Rhode Island in 1911 and Massachusetts in 1918 (the last states to retain it), the two-year term was far more persistent. As Table 4-1 shows, the two-year term was still found in twenty-one states in 1950. By 1975 only four (Arkansas, New Hampshire, Rhode Island, and Vermont) were still included in this outmoded category; seven states switched to the four-year term just since 1970. (Table 4-2 records the shift to longer terms throughout U.S. history.)

As important as the length of gubernatorial terms is the question of consecutive succession. Should the governor be permitted to succeed himself, and if so, how many times? The rooted distrust of executive power in many of the early states meant only one answer: more severe strictures on the governorship. Refusing the governor succession supposedly prevented him from abusing his powers and perpetuating himself in office. A governor who could not run for a consecutive term was freed from political partisanship and given the luxury of rising above the fray, proponents argued. They further contended that new leadership was encouraged and political dynasties were barred. These arguments have not been and cannot be wholly discounted, and they have tended in part to be more persuasive than the propositions set forth in defense of the two-year term. Of course, while chief executives cannot perpetuate themselves in the governor's office, they can easily use the position to propel themselves toward the U.S. Senate or the presidency. And it is to be doubted whether governors are ever liberated from political considerations—nor should they be. Rare is the governor forbidden another term who does not meddle in the selection of a successor; some actively attempt to anoint one.

A severe term limitation can also serve the interests of political machines as often as it inhibits them.[4] One has only to look at the experiences of Virginia and Georgia in this century for proof. The one anti-Byrd machine governor elected in Virginia before 1969, James H. Price, was prevented in a single four-year term from significantly disrupting the structure and flow of the machine. The same was true in the case of Governor Ellis Arnall of Georgia, who proved ineffective in the long-term against the entrenched Talmadge organization. If Price and Arnall had been allowed to serve a consecutive term, their efforts might have met with greater success.

While executive abuse of power is always a possibility and a term limitation of some sort can help to check the dictatorial tendencies of any particular governor, it is well to remember that term limitation is only one way of many to balance the executive. A fixed term in and of itself is a check; governors are aware that, at a given time, their powers dissipate unless their electoral mandate is renewed by their constituencies. As politicians, their eyes are always focused on a real or potential electoral majority. Hardly to be ignored either are the several constitutional limitations in all the basic documents of state: separation of powers, bill of rights, specific limitations on and parameters of gubernatorial authority. Joseph Kallenbach wrote, prophetically in light of Watergate, in 1952:

The fundamental problem toward which constitutional limitations on executive tenure are advanced as solutions is the dangerous accretion of power in the hands of the chief executive. . . . It may be seriously doubted, however, whether

Table 4-1
Term Limitations, by States, 1950-1975

	Length of Term		Maximum No. of Consecutive Terms[f]	
State	1950	1975	1950	1975
Alabama	4	4	1	2
Alaska[d]	–	4	–	2
Arizona	2	4	NL	NL
Arkansas	2	2	NL	NL
California	4	4	NL	NL
Colorado	2	4	NL	NL
Connecticut	2	4	NL	NL
Delaware[c]	4	4	2	2
Florida	4	4	1	2
Georgia	4	4	NL	1
Hawaii[d]	–	4	–	NL
Idaho[e]	4	4	NL	NL
Illinois	4	4	NL	NL
Indiana	4	4	1	2
Iowa	2	4	NL	NL
Kansas	2	4	NL	2
Kentucky	4	4	1	1
Louisiana	4	4	1	2
Maine	2	4	NL	2
Maryland	4	4	NL	2
Massachusetts	2	4	NL	NL
Michigan	2	4	NL	NL
Minnesota	2	4	NL	NL
Mississippi	4	4	1	1
Missouri[c]	4	4	1	2
Montana	4	4	NL	NL
Nebraska	2	4	NL	2
Nevada	4	4	NL	2
New Hampshire	2	2	NL	NL
New Jersey	4	4	2	2
New Mexico[a]	2	4	2	1
New York	4	4	NL	NL
North Carolina[g]	4	4	1	1
North Dakota	2	4	NL	NL
Ohio	2	4	NL	2
Oklahoma	4	4	1	2
Oregon	4	4	2	2
Pennsylvania	4	4	1	2

Table 4-1 (cont.)

State	Length of Term		Maximum No. of Consecutive Terms[f]	
	1950	1975	1950	1975
Rhode Island	2	2	NL	NL
South Carolina	4	4	1	1
South Dakota	2	4	NL	2
Tennessee[b]	2	4	3	1
Texas	2	4	NL	NL
Utah	4	4	NL	NL
Vermont	2	2	NL	NL
Virginia	4	4	1	1
Washington	4	4	NL	NL
West Virginia	4	4	1	2
Wisconsin	2	4	NL	NL
Wyoming	4	4	NL	NL

NL = No Limitation

Source: Compiled from Council of State Governments, *The Book of the States, 1950 [-1975]* (Chicago and Lexington, Ky.: Council of State Governments, 1952-1976).

[a]After 2 consecutive terms (4 years) have intervened, reelection is permitted.

[b]No person can serve as governor more than 6 terms (12 years), and no person can serve as governor for more than 6 of any consecutive 8 years.

[c]Delaware and Missouri have an absolute two-term limitation.

[d]Alaska and Hawaii were not admitted as states until 1959. Governors were not popularly elected until that time.

[e]Idaho imposed a one-term limitation (with reelection permitted after an intervening term) from 1953 to 1959. In the latter year, the state abolished the one-term limit.

[f]Almost all states permit the relection of a governor who has served the maximum number of consecutive terms after he has been out of office for at least one term.

[g]The voters of North Carolina, in a November 1977 referendum, approved a state constitutional amendment that permits the governor to succeed himself once. The amendment applies to the incumbent, Jim Hunt, who will be able to seek re-election in 1980.

a constitutional limitation on executive tenure offers any substantial measure of relief. The causes for the recent growth of executive power and influence are to be found in the expansion of the functions of government generally, in the increasing complexity of the matters with which government must grapple in a period of worldwide economic and political dislocation induced by two world wars in one generation, and in the increasing reliance which must be placed upon a bureaucracy functioning under the immediate direction of the chief executive to effectuate the purposes of government. . . . Constitutional limitations on executive tenure fail to come to grips with the basic issue. By promoting a false sense of security, they may actually hinder the development of those types of safeguards in which salvation against the evils of an overweening executive power

Table 4-2
Length of Term of Governors, 1780-1975

Year	No. of States	1-Year Term	2-Year Term	3-Year Term	4-Year Term
1780	13	10	1	2	0
1820	24	10	6	4	4
1860	34	5	16	2	11
1900	45	2	21	1	21
1940	48	0	24	1	23
1964	50	0	15	0	35
1975	50	0	4	0	46

Sources: For the years 1780-1964, data are taken from Joseph E. Kallenbach, *The American Chief Executive: The Presidency and the Governorship* (New York: Harper & Row, 1966), p. 187, Table 2. For the year 1975, data are taken from Council of State Governments, *The Book of States, 1975* (Lexington, Ky.: Council of State Governments, 1976).

really lies. A reshaping of our political institutions to make the opposition party a more effective instrument for holding the administration to account, reexamination by the legislative branch of the question of its proper role and function in the government process and the devising of means and methods to give it a more powerful voice in various areas of high-level policy-making, and insistence upon a rigid regard for the right of the people generally to criticize and oppose within the broad limits assumed by the democratic dogma—these are lines of action which offer far greater promise as safeguards against the threat of "dictatorship."[5]

A limitation on successive terms can serve a state as well as a governor badly. An outstanding governor may be forced to retire at his peak or when his talents are most needed. At base, term limitation could be considered undemocratic, since it deprives the citizenry of leaders they may well want to continue in office. As Governor Dan Evans of Washington insisted, "The people themselves are the best limiters. They can judge whom they want for governor or any other office."[6]

Executives under term limitation are also critically hindered in their dealings with legislatures. Any term limitation implies that the governor will be a "lame duck" for his last term. It is known by all the political actors that the governor will without question vacate his office and cease to exercise his influence on a certain date, and the legislature, and the bureaucracy as well, can "mark time" until he is gone. The early maneuvering of his potential successors is distracting for the governor since it absorbs so much time and energy in the political system. Although appointment authority and other powers can sometimes compensate for these problems, the lame duck status is truly crippling when the governor is allowed only a single term. Governor Bob Scott of North Carolina, barely halfway into his sole four-year term, was informed that some state department leaders were obstructing his projects. Replied Scott: "I can understand this because I sense it as a governor going out of office. Allegiances are already being switched, although it shouldn't be that way."[7] Often, the one-term governors must choose one or two major programs at most and cash their political chips to insure passage at the first legislative sessions of their terms. In this fashion a governor as resourceful and ambitious as Jimmy Carter had to pick between reorganization of state government and revising Georgia's antiquated constitution when he took office in 1971.[8] (Carter of course, selected reorganization, successfully accomplished it, and made it a hallmark of his 1976 presidential campaign.)

Still, not all academicians or even governors are convinced that the executive should be allowed an unlimited number of successive terms. While virtually all agree that the possibility of one successive election should be provided for, many stop there and agree in principle with the Twenty-Second Amendment to the U.S. Constitution that prohibits presidents from seeking a third full term.[9] Despite all the safeguards, it is hardly beyond reason that an executive would use the authority that accumulates over successive terms far beyond what was intended. Some have argued that over the last twenty-five years there have been several cases of such abuse in one state or another, often where the governor has served more than ten consecutive years.

Favors, of both a substantial and minor nature, dispensed over a number of years, combined with name recognition and financial contacts that are usually fringe benefits of major office, can result in the continued reelection of a governor who, while once outstanding, has aged in outlook and vigor. "After eight years," commented New Jersey's Richard J. Hughes, "a governor can become stale."[10] Term limitation forces a turnover, thereby elminating the direct bias of incumbency. As one governor suggested, "There is always a need for fresh leadership, new thrusts, a sweeping out of cobwebs."[11] This executive thus supported a two-term limit and noted that one term was "too short to accomplish in-depth administrative oversight and impact." Most of the states have come to agree with this governor since 1960 and have found the four-year term with one possible reelection a good compromise (see Table 4-1). While thirteen states restricted their governors to a single term in 1950, only eight did so in 1975.[12] (All eight had a term duration of four years.) Most of these one-term states were and are in the Southern and Border regions. The two-term allowance has gained greatly, from five to nineteen states over twenty-five years. All of the two-term states also have four-year term lengths.

Even where there is no constitutional two-term limit, an informal prohibition sometimes exists that is similar to the presidential tradition at the national level first established by George Washington. Just as Franklin Roosevelt felt free to break the White House tradition in 1940, so governors contravene state custom when circumstances permit. Orval Faubus of Arkansas, for example, used the cry of segregation to override the informal two-term bonds in the 1950s and 1960s, and won six successive terms.[13] The only way actually to insure adherence, then, is to set the limit in constitutional stone.

It should be noted that a fair number of governors have managed to surmount the term obstacles placed in their paths. Over twenty-five years fourteen governors from one-term states (eleven of them from the South) served nonsuccessive terms. Accomplishing this none-too-easy feat were James Folsom (D-Alabama), George Wallace (D-Alabama), Henry Schricker (D-Indiana), Albert "Happy" Chandler (D-Kentucky), Earl Long (D-Louisiana), Jimmie Davis (D-Louisiana), Hugh White (D-Mississippi), Phil Donnelly (D-Missouri), Edwin Mechem (R-New Mexico), James Rhodes (R-Ohio), Gordon Browning (D-Tennessee), Frank Clement (D-Tennessee), Buford Ellington (D-Tennessee), and Mills Godwin (D-R-Virginia). The most famous of these are probably Clement and Ellington, who "leap frogged" each other several times by arrangement. No governor, though, has ever duplicated Sam Houston's trick of serving as governor of two separate states, Tennessee (in the 1820s) and Texas (in the 1850s)—an airtight loophole in the term limitation scheme.[14]

Tenure in Practice

From the data presented in Tables 4-1 and 4-2, it is clear that the opportunities for governors to serve longer terms of office have been provided. Whether or not that potential has been fulfilled is another matter. As a spate of states expanded their terms in the 1960s, Joseph Schlesinger perceived: "If tenure potential is turned into the reality of governors with long terms, the gubernatorial office could become a true position of political leadership in the states."[15]

If tenure is any measure of gubernatorial strength, then governors for most of America's history needed weight-lifting courses. Coleman Ransone estimated that, at best, the average tenure for a governor up to the 1950s was three years.[16] His sad conclusion was inevitable: "The average governor is, therefore, a bird of passage who comes from other walks of life and after a short stay in the governor's office moves on to other places."[17] The governorship, as a direct result of stringent term limitations, could only be seen as a steppingstone to higher office or a way station to bide one's time. No governor, no matter how able, could develop a well-coordinated program and leave an integrated legacy in such a short space of time. Politicians holding the office were sometimes encouraged to make easy choices to secure a transient popularity that would propel them to a more substantial public position. Accountability for irresponsible actions would be difficult, and the damage might not appear until several terms had elapsed. In any event a future governor would have to pay the piper.

Table 4-3 indicates how much this pattern has been altered. Tenure

Table 4-3
Tenure of Governors, Selected Decades, 1800-1969

No. of Years Spent as Governor	1800-1809 (%)	1820-1829 (%)	1850-1859 (%)	1870-1879 (%)	1900-1909 (%)	1920-1929 (%)	1950-1959 (%)	1960-1969[a] (%)
10 plus	14.3	3.5	0.8	0.0	1.3	1.0	4.6	10.0
5-9	16.1	14.0	5.6	11.8	8.5	15.1	24.1	26.0
3-4	30.3	40.2	40.4	49.1	54.4	53.5	50.0	46.0
1-2	39.3	42.3	53.2	39.1	35.7	30.4	21.3	19.0
N	56	92	124	154	154	185	108	100

Sources: For all years between 1800 and 1929, the figures are taken from Joseph A. Schlesinger, "The Governor's Place in American Politics," *Public Administration Review* 30 (January/February 1970):4. For the years 1950-1969, figures were computed from Appendix B.

Note: The figures in the table include only those governors who were elected to their first terms during each time span listed. The tenures of those who succeeded to the office of governor are included in the tabulations.

[a]Governors elected in the 1960s who are still serving are counted for tenure to the end of their present elected term.

potential has come closer to fulfillment. Through the decades tenure has naturally fluctuated, but a considerable extension is apparent since 1950 and especially in the decade of the 1960s. In earlier periods, a third to over a half of all governors were serving two years or less but only a fifth of the total group were so categorized after 1950. More than 28 percent of all governors in the 1950s served five years or more, and fully 36 percent did so in the 1960s, the highest proportion ever. Tenure potential has not been fully realized by any means. In the 1960s 65 percent of the governors still held the office for four years or less, but this was reduced from 71 percent in the 1950s and percentages that ranged up to 94 percent earlier.

Regionally, the Midwest has shown the largest increase in tenure, followed by the West (see Table 4-4). The Western governors, holding office on an average of about six years, have the longest tenures of any region in the later time periods. The substantial change in the Midwest is not unexpected since much of the constitutional lengthening of terms took place there. Not all of the expansion in tenure, however, is due to constitutional alterations of the term. More governors are completing the terms to which they have been elected. From 1900 to 1949, 80 of the 634 persons elected to governorships (12.5 percent) did not complete their terms: 31 died in office, 38 resigned, 4 were ejected by the impeachment process, 2 were removed by the courts as constitutionally unqualified, 1 was voted out in a popular recall, 2 were ousted following election recounts, and 2 died between their elections and their scheduled inauguration.[18]

From 1950 to 1975, only 8 percent (25 of 312) did not complete their

Table 4-4
Tenure of Governors, by Region, 1950-1969

No. of Years Spent as Governor	Region									
	Northeast		South		Border		Midwest		West	
	1950s (%)	1960s[a] (%)	1950s (%)	1960s[a] (%)	1950s (%)	1960s[a] (%)	1950s (%)	1960s[a] (%)	1950s (%)	1960s[a] (%)
10 plus	4.3	5.0	5.3	4.2	7.1	9.1	0.0	12.0	6.9	20.0
5-9	21.8	35.0	15.8	16.7	21.4	18.2	13.0	28.0	37.9	25.0
3-4	52.2	50.0	57.9	62.5	71.4	63.6	60.9	32.0	24.1	30.0
1-2	21.8	10.0	21.0	16.7	0.0	18.2	26.1	28.0	31.0	25.0
Average tenure	4.7	5.0	4.2	4.3	5.3	5.1	3.8	5.0	5.7	5.9
N	23	20	19	24	14	11	23	25	29	20

Source: Figures were computed from Appendix B.
Note: The figures in the table include only those governors who were elected to their first terms during each decade. The tenures of those who succeeded to the office of governor are included in the tabulations.
[a]Governors elected in the 1960s who are still serving are counted for tenure to the end of their present elected term.

terms, with 8 vacating through death and 17 by resignation. The difference lies primarily in the death rate, which attests both to the greater health of the population as a whole and to the election of younger governors in recent years. It may also be a tribute to the governors since 1950 that none have been impeached or recalled (though the smattering of criminally charged governors cannot be ignored).

Overall it is not likely a mere coincidence that 66.7 percent of the oustanding governors served more than one term.[19] That there is a link between longer tenure and the opportunity to develop an exemplary program is reasonable conjecture. The important point here, however, is that the governorship, while still a transitory office, is becoming a more extended stage in a political career and presumably the focus of more of the politician's energies and talents.

Election Issues

Tenure for governors is determined not only by the length of their constitutional term but by their political skills. Unless they succeed to office, governors initially have to win a popular mandate and then seek to preserve the majority for subsequent reelection battles. On what kinds of issues do gubernatorial elections, especially those involving incumbents, turn?

On the state level no issue has been more prominent (and more widely discussed nationally) than tax policy. With the advent of the 1960s, governors have been faced with revenue dilemmas more complicated than the Gordian knot. A cacophony of demands from urban residents, minorities, educators, mental health professionals, and scores of others has been heard, and they have usually reflected real and pressing human needs. While other state leaders had sometimes swept the problems under the rug in past years, the newer governors felt an obligation to act. Even if they had wanted to hold back, they would not have been able to do so. The urban morass, for one, had become too critical and conspicuous to be ignored.

Satisfying so many wants and desires could mean only one thing: raising taxes. Governor Arthur B. Langlie of Washington, in his capacity as chairman of the National Governors' Conference, summed the situation up for fellow and future chief executives:

I dare say that there is not a legislator or a Governor in this nation who will not have to face the question, in the months immediately ahead—where is the money coming from? ... There is no question that these demands must be met, and that these services must be paid for. ... No single man in a state is in a better position to sell the story of financial responsibility than the Chief Executive of the State. It is not a popular story to sell. It does not assure votes. You win no popularity contests by telling your people they must pay more taxes ... [but it is] the greatest responsibility of Governors.[20]

The difficulty with taxes did not simply lie with the raising of them. It was as much the kind and quality of taxes that had to be levied due to the restrictive and outdated state constitutions in existence at the time.[21] Regressive assessments like the property tax were constitutionally encouraged, while tax rates were many times defined too precisely. The inadequacy of state revenue powers was heightened by narrow restrictions on the amount and kind of borrowing in which states could indulge, as well as provisos on the uses to which the borrowed funds could be put. The resourcefulness of strong governors, aided by constitutional revisions, overcame these obstacles in some states, but even where the taxing limits were closely circumscribed, governors raised taxes. Researchers Deil Wright and David Stephenson concluded that the states had been "hyperactive" in the taxing field from 1959 to 1971, with an average of one tax increase in each state every time a state legislature met.[22]

The state legislators passed the taxes, but the governors proposed and cajoled, and accepted public responsibility for the actions because they rightly saw no alternative. Governor Richard Hughes of New Jersey, in the wake of his state's severe urban riots in 1968, offered a major program to attack the problems at the root of the disorders. He proposed a graduated personal income tax to fund it and soberly told the legislature:

Like you, I dislike taxes of any kind and, if such a thing were possible, might prefer to go on from year to year, stringing the beads and balancing the mirrors, a little excise boost here and a little gimmick there. But we have seen with our own eyes, in our political lifetimes, the result of such equivocation. It has brought us to a very sorry pass, and unless we wish to hurt our State and its communities and its people severely, we must come to our senses and, like other states, begin to pay our own way, provide for the needs of our own citizens, fulfill our own destiny. . . .

I think we have come to the end of that happy road when the citizens of the most tightly run state government in the nation can be looked in the eye by a politician and blandly told that imaginary economies in government or tightening the belt against make-believe extravagancies, or buying time with another study or tax convention, or getting past another election year, or finding some mysterious kind of non-tax revenue, can solve our problems.

We have reached the day of reckoning. And I tell you very seriously and respectfully that we must act in these two months before us or this State over the next six years will sink into stagnation and despair that will take a quarter of a century to overcome.[23]

Hughes was nearing the end of his second term and, ineligible to run again, could not be rebuked by the voters. Others were not so fortunate. The number of what Terry Sanford called "tax-loss" governors (i.e., incumbent governors who lost reelection after proposing or securing tax increases) mounted through the years. The toll included Governors Pat Brown (D-California), Stephen McNichols (D-Colorado), Russell Peterson (R-Delaware), Robert Smylie (R-Idaho), Richard Ogilvie (R-Illinois), Norbert Tiemann (R-Nebraska), John Gilligan (D-Ohio),

Michael DiSalle (D-Ohio), and John Chafee (R-Rhode Island), among many others. More than a little talent was lost to the states on this issue. All of the governors named above, for example, were on the list of "outstanding governors" presented in Chapter 2.

State chief executives who dared to raise taxes were seen to be putting their political lives in extreme jeopardy. Louis Harris, after examining poll data on 1960 gubernatorial elections in fourteen states, surmised that governors were "getting the daylights knocked out of them for simply trying to make ends meet."[24] In the phrase coined by New Jersey political boss Frank Hague, "Taxes is losers." Or are they? Gerald Pomper surveyed thirty-seven states and found no statistical connection between tax or spending increases and electoral success for governors. "Although the relationship between taxes and electoral results is commonly assumed, it is not clearly proven," Pomper concludes. "Voters do not evidence a consistent concern for fiscal issues. Moreover, their party preferences complicate their policy choices."[25]

It is certainly true that dozens of governors have survived tax increases made at their behest. (The percentage of incumbent governors defeated for any reason, in fact, is quite low, and the average governor seeking reelection has a better than eight in ten chance of winning (see Table 4-12). John Volpe of Massachusetts not only won reelection despite his 3 percent sales tax, but he got the voters to approve it in a referendum by a 5-to-1 margin. Tom McCall of Oregon was as lucky as Volpe in a 1970 reelection race, even though his state's electorate was put off by McCall's proposed sales tax. The Oregon progressive easily got another term in the statehouse despite the results of an earlier referendum on the sales tax, where in McCall's words, "Under my charismatic leadership, campaigning day and night, we got beaten 8-to-1."[26]

Many other governors provide illustrations as well. George Romney of Michigan won reelection despite his proposed and enacted income tax. Richard Hughes of New Jersey vehemently advocated a 3 percent sales tax for New Jersey, but kept his job anyway. The champion foe of "big government," Ronald Reagan, requested and secured the largest tax increase in California's history. At the other end of the Republican spectrum, Nelson Rockefeller of New York survived several tough election battles although he had multiplied the Empire State's taxes. Daniel Evans of Washington was handsomely reelected in spite of his advocacy of a very progressive graduated net income tax for his state. Calvin Rampton, a Democrat in the heavily conservative and Republican state of Utah, served three terms even though advocacy of tax increases of one sort or another was a staple of his tenure. Brendan Byrne of New Jersey managed to convince voters of the necessity of his state income tax in 1977 and reversed his opponent's seemingly insurmountable lead to score a landslide victory. Thus many governors have survived tax increases they initiated or supported in reelection races. Other issues and party identification certainly played crucial roles in many of these gubernatorial elections, but to deny that tax policy was a leading, if not predominant, issue in state politics is folly. An examination of the key issues in the reelection defeats of governors will provide evidence to support this contention.

In Table 4-5 one hundred cases occurring between 1951 and 1975 when an incumbent or former governor was defeated for reelection in either the primary or general election are reviewed. In each case an attempt was made to determine the single issue most responsible for the governor's loss. Usually this issue was the one that dominated the headlines and the contenders themselves treated as fundamental. Sometimes, however, especially when the issue fell in the categories of scandal, race, intraparty and two-party politics, the electorally decisive undercurrent was not really expressed. Also, in a few cases (sixteen of one hundred total), there appeared to be two equally weighted issues, and the electoral defeat of the governor has been attributed to both of them. The results of this issue analysis are summarized by decade, party, and region in Tables 4-6 and 4-7.

The pivotal finding is that tax policy after 1960 is the most prominent issue in gubernatorial politics that results in incumbent defeats. When the fifty-four incumbent governors defeated after 1960 are taken as a group, more than a third (35.2 percent) are found to have lost on the single issue of taxes. If we consider only substantive issues (eliminating intraparty and two-party politics), then taxes account for an even greater proportion of incumbent losses. This total actually understates the number of "tax-loss" governors since some governors, after a successful battle to raise levies, saw the electoral handwriting on the wall and retired voluntarily. Frank Licht (D-Rhode Island), for example, threw in the towel in 1972 (at the behest of party leaders) after he broke a campaign promise and pushed an income tax to passage. Knotty tax problems, in fact, felled three Rhode Island governors in a row. John Notte (D) was beaten for proposing an income tax in 1962 by John Chafee (R), who got the boot in 1968 for suggesting the same thing. Chafee then lost to Frank Licht. Massachusetts voters were very sensitive very early to tax increases. In 1952 a small income tax increase resulted in Paul Dever's defeat for reelection. At the end of the decade, advocacy of a sales tax caused a shattering Democratic primary defeat for Governor Foster Furcolo against a virtually unknown candidate.[27]

Taxes have not just deprived governors of their statehouse chairs but also stymied them when they ran for other offices. Former Governor Louie Nunn (R-Kentucky) managed to lose a Senate seat in the midst of an overwhelming 1972 Nixon landslide in his state because of a sales tax on food and some medicines that he had instituted during his term. Other governors, not noted in the accompanying tables, have barely scraped by in reelection struggles due to tax issues. Mills Godwin of Virginia won but a narrow reelection in 1973 due, in part, to his opponent's constant hammering at the regressivity of Godwin's sales tax on food and nonprescription drugs.

Even in elections where no incumbent is running, taxes loom large. The

Table 4-5
Key Issues in the Defeats of Governors, by State, 1951-1975

State[a]	Defeated Governors	Year of Defeat	Primary or General Election	Key Issue of Election[b]								
				Taxes	Intraparty Politics	Two-Party Politics	Scandal	Race	Political/ Administrative Incompetence	Environment	Farm Policy	Others
Alabama	James E. Folsom (D)	1962	P				X	X				
	Albert P. Brewer (D)*	1970	P					X				
Alaska	William A. Egan (D)*	1966	G									X
	Keith Miller (R)*c	1970	G									X
	Walter J. Hickel (R)	1974	P							X		
	Keith Miller (R)c	1974	P		X							
	William A. Egan (D)*	1974	G							X		
Arizona	Howard Pyle (R)*	1954	G	X								
	Sam Goddard (D)*	1966	G						X			
Arkansas	Sid McMath (D)*	1952	P				X					
	Francis Cherry (D)*	1954	P									X
	Sid McMath (D)	1962	P					X				
	Orval Faubus (D)	1970	P					X				
	Winthrop Rockefeller (R)*	1970	G				X					
California	Edmund G. Brown, Sr. (D)*	1966	G	X								
Colorado	Stephen McNichols (D)*	1962	G	X								
	John Vanderhoof (R)*c	1974	G							X		
Connecticut	John Lodge (R)*	1954	G			X						
Delaware	Elbert Carvel (D)*	1952	G			X						
	Charles Terry (D)*	1968	G									X
	Russell Peterson (R)*	1972	G	X								
Florida	Charley Johns (D)*c	1954	P		X							

Table 4-5 (cont.)

State[a]	Defeated Governors	Year of Defeat	Primary or General Election	Taxes	Intraparty Politics	Two-Party Politics	Scandal	Race	Political/ Administrative Incompetence	Environment	Farm Policy	Others
	Fuller Warren (D)	1956	P		X							
	Haydon Burns (D)*	1966	P				X					
	Claude Kirk (R)*	1970	G		X		X					
Georgia	M.E. Thompson (D)[c]	1954	P		X							
	Marvin Griffin (D)	1962	P				X	X				
	Ellis Arnall (D)	1966	P					X				
	Carl Sanders (D)	1970	P					X				X
	Lester Maddox (D)	1974	P					X				
Hawaii	William Quinn (R)*	1962	G		X	X						
Idaho	Robert E. Smylie (R)*	1966	P	X	X							
	Don Samuelson (R)*	1970	G							X		
Illinois	William G. Stratton (R)*	1960	G				X					
	Samuel H. Shapiro (D)*[c]	1968	G			X						
	Richard B. Ogilvie (R)*	1973	G	X								
Indiana	Matthew Welsh (D)	1972	G			X						
Iowa	Leo Hoegh (R)*	1956	G								X	
	Norman Erbe (R)*	1962	G	X								
Kansas	George Docking (D)*	1960	G		X	X						
	William Avery (R)*	1966	G	X								
Kentucky	Albert B. Chandler (D)	1963	P		X							

State	Governor	Year	Type	1	2	3	4	5	6
	Albert B. Chandler (D)	1967	P						X
	Albert B. Chandler (D)	1971	P		X				
	Bert Combs (D)	1971	P	X	X				
Louisiana	Robert F. Kennon (D)	1964	P	X	X				
	Jimmie H. Davis (D)	1970	P	X	X				
Maine	Burton Cross (R)*	1954	G				X		
	John Reed (R)*	1966	G				X		
Massachusetts	Paul Dever (D)*	1952	G	X	X				
	Foster Furcolo (D)*	1960	P	X	X				
	John Volpe (R)*	1962	G		X		X		
	Endicott Peabody (D)*	1964	P				X		
	Francis Sargent (R)*	1974	G		X	X			
Michigan	John Swainson (D)*	1962	G				X		
Minnesota	C. Elmer Anderson (R)*	1954	G			X			
	Orville Freeman (D)*	1960	G	X					
	Elmer L. Andersen (R)*	1962	G			X			
	Karl F. Rolvaag (D)*	1966	G		X		X		
	Fielding Wright (D)	1955	P		X				
Mississippi	Ross Barnett (D)	1967	P		X				
Montana	John Bonner (D)*	1952	G		X				
	Tim Babcock (R)*	1968	G	X	X				
Nebraska	Victor Anderson (R)*	1958	G					X	
	Val Peterson (R)	1966	P		X				
	Norbert Tiemann (R)*	1970	G		X				
Nevada	Charles Russell (R)*	1958	G						X
	Grant Sawyer (D)*	1966	G						X
New Hampshire	Walter Peterson (R)*	1972	P	X					
New Jersey	Robert B. Meyner (D)	1969	G		X		X		

State[a]	Defeated Governors	Year of Defeat	Primary or General Election	Taxes	Intraparty Politics	Two-Party Politics	Scandal	Race	Political/ Administrative Incompetence	Environment	Farm Policy	Others
	William T. Cahill (R)*	1973	P		X		X					
New Mexico	John Simms (D)*	1956	G		X				X			
	Edwin Mechem (R)*	1958	G			X						
	John Burroughs (D)*	1960	G		X		X					
	Edwin Mechem (R)*	1962	G	X								
New York	Averell Harriman (D)*	1958	G						X			
	Malcolm Wilson (R)*c	1974	G			X	X					
Ohio	C. William O'Neill (R)*	1958	G									X
	Michael DiSalle (D)*	1962	G	X								
	John J. Gilligan (D)*	1974	G	X								
Oklahoma	Dewey Bartlett (R)*	1970	G	X								
	David Hall (D)*	1974	P				X					
Oregon	Elmo Smith (R)*c	1956	G			X						
	Robert Holmes (D)*	1958	G		X							
Rhode Island	Dennis J. Roberts (D)*	1958	G				X					
	Christopher DelSesto (R)*	1960	G			X						
	John Notte (D)*	1962	G	X								
	John H. Chafee (R)*	1968	G	X								
South Dakota	Ralph Herseth (D)*	1960	G			X						
	Frank Farrar (R)*	1970	G				X					
Tennessee	Gordon Browning (D)*	1952	P		X							

Key Issue of Election[b]

State		Year						
	Gordon Browning (D)	1954	P				X	X
Texas	Price Daniel (D)*	1962	P			X		
	Preston Smith (D)*	1972	P		X			
Utah	J. Bracken Lee (R)*	1956	P		X			
Vermont	F. Ray Keyser (R)*	1962	G					X
Washington	Albert Rosellini (D)*	1964	G			X		
Wisconsin	Vernon Thomson (R)*	1958	G	X				
	John Reynolds (D)*	1964	G	X				
Wyoming	Milward Simpson (R)*	1958	G			X		
	Jack R. Gage (D)*c	1962	G			X		

D = Democrat, R = Republican, P = Primary, G = General Election

Sources: A determination of the key issue or issues for each election was made after reference to numerous books, magazines, newspapers, and government publications. Among the most important sources were the following: *Congressional Quarterly Weekly* and *Congressional Quarterly Almanac, The New York Times, The Washington Post, Newsweek, Time,* and *U.S. News and World Report.* Six books were particularly helpful in constructing this table: John H. Fenton, *Politics in the Border States* (New York: Russell and Russell, 1974); Frank Jonas, *Western Politics* (New York: Holt, 1966); William C. Havard (ed.), *The Changing Politics of the South* (Baton Rouge: Louisiana State University Press, 1969); Duane Lockard, *New England State Politics* (Princeton, N.J.: Princeton University Press, 1959); and James Reichley, *States in Crisis: Politics in Ten American States, 1950-1962* (Chapel Hill: University of North Carolina Press, 1964). The six-volume series on state politics by Neal R. Peirce, *People, Politics and Power in the American States* (New York: W.W. Norton, 1970-1976), was especially useful. Many other more specialized works contained in the bibliography were also consulted.

Note: All elections—primaries as well as general elections—in which an incumbent governor or a former governor was defeated for the governorship between 1950-1975 are listed in this table. See the text for a further explanation of methodology and a description of the issue categories. Succeeding tables provide additional breakdowns of this data.

*Denotes that governor was the incumbent at time of defeat. Unstarred governors, then, were attempting comebacks after a term or more had intervened since they had left office.

aThe eight states that are not listed in this table had no incumbent or former governors defeated during the years surveyed. Those eight are Maryland, Missouri, North Carolina, North Dakota, Pennsylvania, South Carolina, Virginia, and West Virginia.

bIn 16 of the 100 elections two issues are indicated as the key, or electorally decisive, issues. In all other elections only one such issue is indicated.

cSucceeded to the governorship and had not been elected in his own right.

Table 4-6

Key Issues in the Defeats of Governors, by Decade, 1951-1975

Issue Category	Years Surveyed (% of N)[a]			Totals N=100
	1951-1959 (N=28)	1960-1969 (N=44)	1970-1975 (N=28)	
Taxes	7.1	29.5	25.0	22.0
Intraparty politics	32.1	27.3	21.4	27.0
Two-party politics	28.6	18.2	10.7	19.0
Scandal	7.1	15.9	25.0	16.0
Race	0.0	9.1	14.3	8.0
Political and/or administrative incompetence	10.7	11.4	0.0	8.0
Environmental	0.0	0.0	14.3	4.0
Farm policy	7.1	0.0	0.0	2.0
Other issues	10.7	9.1	10.7	10.0

Source: Compiled from statistics in Table 4-5.

Note: All elections–primaries as well as general elections–in which an incumbent governor or a former governor was defeated for the governorship were surveyed. See the text for a further explanation of methodology and a description of the issue categories. See Table 4-5 for a state-by-state breakdown of the elections summarized in this table.

[a]Totals add to more than 100 percent since, in some elections, there were two key issues that played decisive roles in the defeat of governors.

1962 Wisconsin gubernatorial race turned on the varying tax proposals of the major party contenders. Democrat John Reynolds (who won) advocated an income tax to raise new revenues while Republican Philip Kuehn proposed a sales tax.[28] Normally, tax debates in gubernatorial politics center on the merits of proposed or enacted sales and income taxes, but there are variations. In the 1962 Iowa race incumbent Republican Norman Erbe and successful challenger Harold Hughes, a Democrat, squared off on how best to redistribute the tax burden. Another incumbent Republican, Dewey Bartlett of Oklahoma, lost in part because of tax breaks he had sponsored for industry.

In emphasizing taxes, other issues that have spearheaded triumphant challenges to incumbents should not be ignored. During the decade of the 1950s, taxes caused only 7.1 percent of gubernatorial defeats. Two-party politics and competition (which includes the presidential "coattail" factor as well as party organizational strength) alone comprised almost a third of the total. When taken altogether with intraparty politics (i.e., party factional in-fighting), more than 60 percent of incumbent losses are explained. Political machinations can exert their greatest influences over election outcomes when there are no overriding substantive issues.

Scandals caused about as few defeats as taxes in the 1950s. It is to be

Table 4-7

Key Issues in the Defeat of Governors, by Region and Party, 1951-1975

Issue Category	Region (% of N)[a]					Party (% of N)[a]	
	Northeast (N=20)	South (N=22)	Border (N=8)	Midwest (N=23)	West (N=27)	Democratic (N=57)	Republican (N=43)
Taxes	30.0	0.0	25.0	34.8	22.2	17.5	27.9
Intraparty politics	15.0	40.9	62.5	13.0	33.3	33.3	18.6
Two-party politics	30.0	0.0	0.0	30.4	8.5	12.3	27.9
Scandal	20.0	31.8	12.5	8.7	7.4	17.5	14.0
Race	0.0	36.4	0.0	0.0	0.0	14.0	0.0
Political and/or administrative incompetence	20.0	0.0	0.0	8.7	0.0	10.5	4.6
Environmental	0.0	0.0	0.0	0.0	8.5	1.8	7.0
Farm policy	0.0	0.0	0.0	8.7	0.0	0.0	4.6
Other issues	10.0	9.1	12.5	4.4	8.5	8.8	9.3

Source: Compiled from statistics in Table 4-5.

Note: All elections—primaries as well as general elections—in which an incumbent governor or a former governor was defeated for the governorship were surveyed. See the text for a further explanation of methodology and a description of the issue categories. See Table 4-5 for a state-by-state breakdown of the elections summarized in this table.

[a]Totals add to more than 100 percent since, in some elections, there were two key issues that played decisive roles in the defeat of governors.

doubted that there were no scandals lurking about in those days; rather, it was a matter of their not being exposed by a press that was not quite so investigative as today. One "scandal" was well-publicized. Democratic Governor Dennis Roberts of Rhode Island was accused of "stealing" the 1956 election when he got a court to invalidate enough absentee ballots to tip a close election to him. The state's people remembered and ousted Roberts in 1958 by seating the Republican to whom he had denied the governorship earlier.

The race issue, overtly or symbolically, was ever present—certainly after 1954—but its concentration was almost wholly in the South. Interestingly, not a single Southern governor lost his office on the issue, mainly because most of them were on the popular, prosegregationist side. Incompetent gubernatorial leadership in either political affairs or state administration was responsible for about one of ten defeats nationwide, and disputes over state farm policies accounted for 7.1 percent of the incumbent losses. Environmental concerns, from land development and land-use planning to air and water pollution, were not in evidence at all. A few issues were unique to a particular state or election. Ohio's 1958 gubernatorial loss centered on a right-to-work law referendum, and violating the informal two-term tradition proved fatal to several Nevada governors through the years. McCarthyism on the state level did not match its ugly national dimensions in the 1950s. It appears that only one gubernatorial race was determined by it, and in that one case the "red scare" backfired. Governor Francis Cherry accused his 1954 Democratic primary opponent, Orval Faubus, of having maintained Communist affiliations, but the sympathy generated by Faubus' rebuttal carried the challenger to victory.[29]

The 1960s present quite a contrast with the preceding decade. Tax policy as the crucial issue in a governor's defeat had soared to 29.5 percent of the cases, thereby supplanting two-party politics as the overlord of the gubernatorial graveyard. The scandal issue was emerging into the sunlight, and the divisive racial turmoil was bubbling up and spilling over into the electoral realm. Several former Southern governors from an earlier era when race did not predominate politically were defeated in comeback attempts by strong segregationists in Democratic primaries. The number of governors brought down by incompetence increased slightly, but environmental matters were still absent from the campaign turf. While anticommunism was the national election standard of the 1950s, Washington's battle cry in the late 1960s was "law and order." Just as McCarthyism proved electorally impotent earlier, the new shibboleth was equally ineffectual. Only one governor, Charles Terry of Delaware, went down to defeat thanks to the "law-and-order" theme.

In the first half of the 1970s, taxes still accounted for a quarter of all governors' defeats, but the issue began to wane a bit, for reasons to be examined shortly. Internecine party rivalry continued its gradual subsidence; party realignments in many states as the result of civil rights and other domestic upheavals and the wrenching Vietnam war had probably neared completion. Interparty politics, while more competitive in more states than ever (see the following section on the spread of two-party competition), became less prominent as the singular cause of a governor's defeat, both because of the increase in independent voting and ticket splitting and the rise of substantive issues subordinating mere party affiliations. Politics became a good deal more issue oriented after the mid-1960s, and party was the sole determinant of an election much less frequently.

One of these new issues was the environment. From Earth Day in 1970 onwards, environmental concerns helped to defeat some pro-growth, pro-industry governors. About one-seventh of all gubernatorial defeats after 1969 could be traced to a concentration on environmental preservation. Another issue that gathered considerable momentum in the 1970s was scandal, a byproduct of the Watergate affair. An energized press and a more exacting public demanded, and got, more personal information about governors' family finances and campaign funding than ever before. A few governors apparently had a lot to hide, too, since fully a fourth of all incumbent defeats in the 1970s were a result of scandal.

The ascension of race to a slightly more prominent position in the 1970s (14.3 percent as opposed to 9.1 percent in the previous decade) is superficially surprising. The difference is, however, that the tables were being turned. The old segregationist order was being routed by a Southern division of the new gubernatorial breed. Hard-line racists like Orval Faubus of Arkansas and Lester Maddox of Georgia were crushed by men who were representative of a nascent nonsegregationist majority. As judged by Earl Black, after a study of all Southern governors from 1950 to 1969: "By the end of the 1960s, then, many Southern governors could be differentiated from their predecessors by a comparatively reduced preoccupation with the principle of racial segregation and by a heightened interest in adaptive economic development policies."[30]

Since Black wrote those words, Southern politics has changed even further. One or more moderate, progressive "New South" governors has been elected in Virginia, North Carolina, South Carolina, Georgia, Florida, Mississippi, Louisiana, Arkansas, and Tennessee. Both parties have supplied these men, and the fact that one of their number, Jimmy Carter of Georgia, was elevated to the presidency is more than a symbol that the South has joined the national political mainstream once again.

The basic causes of the regional transformation are varied, but the major alterations both in cultural patterns wrought by the Civil Rights Act of 1964 and in the Southern electorate brought about by the Voting Rights Act of 1965 rank high on any list. The political translation was clear: Blacks would be integrated into society and their votes would count the same as white ballots. Old politicians who valued survival more than tradition changed their ways. And a South freed of the bondage of race could encourage young men with new issues and fresh ideas to take up the reins of leadership. As Earl Black persuasively argues, "National stateways can indeed modify regional folkways."[31] It may be a measure of the new breed of governor in the South and throughout the country that not a single chief executive from 1970 to 1975 was defeated by charges of administrative or political incompetence. At least one of every ten gubernatorial losses in the twenty years previous had been tied to this issue.

Issues, as so many other factors in gubernatorial politics, follow regional patterns (see Table 4-7). In the Northeast, where the economic base has been crumbling, taxes have been a greater concern than in most areas. Making ends meet, as well as coping with rising demands for a shrinking financial pie, has become a full-time occupation in itself for many Northeastern governors. In these conditions, it is relatively easy to mishandle politics or administration, which perhaps explains the high proportion of gubernatorial defeats for incompetence. Scandal has also played an above-average role in gubernatorial politics in the Northeast. The public airing of scandal and incompetence is probably also related to the vigorous two-party competition that exists there.

In the South, by contrast, the competition has been primarily intra-party in the Democratic primaries until recently, and factional politics have accounted for 40.9 percent of Southern gubernatorial defeats. Still, two issues—scandal and race—together are the root at least in part of almost 70 percent of governors' unsuccessful reelection campaigns. Incompetence did not defeat a single Southern governor from 1951 to 1975, although many were qualified for the description. Usually it was segregationist rhetoric that saved them. Southerners permitted their governors to be maladroit at administration so long as they would preserve the "Southern way of life." Tax issues were electorally negligible since, first of all, taxes were rarely raised (with state services maintained at abysmally low levels), and secondly, even if a governor did raise additional revenues, there was a one-term limit that denied the electorate a chance to pass on his stewardship. If he ran again, a Southern governor would have to wait a term or two out of office, and tax passions would have cooled or been forgotten entirely by many voters. (Astute opponents seldom forget, though.)

Intraparty politics also predominated in the Border states. Taxes and scandals were the supplementary issues there. In the Midwest taxes were more than a subsidiary topic and accounted for the highest proportion of gubernatorial defeats (34.8 percent) in that category of any region. Like the Northeast, the Midwestern states have a more muted form of intraparty politics due to the high degree of two-party competitiveness. Naturally enough, the only two cases of decisive farm policy disputes occurred in this "breadbasket" region. It seems remarkable at first that so few governors have been beaten in farm states on farm policies, but when one considers that most major decisions affecting farmers are made at the national and international levels, it is understandable. The farm belt tends to vent its frustrations against party presidential candidates (which, however, can still affect gubernatorial nominees at least as far as "coattails" extend).

The West, location of some of America's most magnificent unspoiled landscape, has been the sole preserve of the environmental issue, at least as it has been effectively employed against incumbent governors. Factionalism has been quite prevalent in this region, too, a product perhaps of the personality-oriented, individualistic nature of Western politics. Governors have been a bit luckier than in some regions with tax increases here.

Republicans have felt the tax axe more frequently than Democrats. The GOP governors have also been regarded as more unsympathetic to environmental concerns, while Democrats have borne the incompetence and scandal labels a greater number of times. Primarily because of the Southern political structure that existed for most of the period studied, the Democrats tended to suffer intraparty knifings, while Republicans were ravaged to a greater degree by two-party competition.

In the broad sweep, though, nothing has had the national significance of the tax issue. The circumstances and personalities of two-party or factional politics may be momentarily fascinating, a scandal may be tantalizing, but none of these can compare with taxes as a national common denominator of state politics. The vulnerability of governors is emphasized by the tax issue defeats, and since a "tax-loss" governor is a common denominator, his plight is publicized country-wide. The vise that has squeezed so many outstanding governors requires more of a chief executive's time and energy and produces harried governors with less opportunity to develop a strong political base. Governors are less available, and less pursued, for party presidential nominations as a consequence.

However, the once-bleak tax picture has brightened considerably for governors in the last few years, even as economic conditions worsened nationally. (There have been only two "tax-loss" governors since 1972.) Paradoxical as it may appear, governors have fewer electoral tax worries today because they have been so successful in securing new taxes. By far the most vicious and vengeful public outcry comes with the imposition of heretofore unknown major taxes like income or sales taxes. In 1950 only 17 states had both an income and a sales tax, while 7 had neither.[32] In ten years' time the number of states with both taxes had hardly increased at all to only 19.[33] It was in the decade of the 1960s that the tax piper was paid, the political blood was shed, and the gubernatorial scapegoats were sacrificed. By 1971 only one state, New Hampshire, had neither major tax. Personal income taxes had been established in 40 states; 45 had a broad-based sales tax; and 36 had both.[34] Primary tax initiation, then, has neared completion. Only one state (New Jersey) has adopted either sales or income taxes since 1971.

Instead, today, the National Governors' Conference reports: "The thrust of the tax policies advocated by the Governors is to remove the regressive taxes, avoid tax increases where possible by increasing the effectiveness of already existing taxes, and where increases are necessary, levy them on those most able to absorb the additional burden (businesses and higher income classes)."[35] These measures may be good government but they are certainly good politics. Governors, now that most are equipped with the basic taxing tools, can afford the relative luxury of mere tax adjustment. Small revenue holes can be plugged by specialized levies, like severance taxes on minerals and national resources (proposed by several governors in 1975).

Governors have also begun to concentrate on the politically popular item of tax reform. By 1974, twenty-four states had adopted exemptions for food or medicine or had instituted tax rebates or credits to reduce the regressivity of the sales tax.[36] Some form of property tax relief, including the establishment of a maximum percentage of income that can be paid in property taxes, has now been instituted by every state, with thirty states so acting in 1973 alone.[37] Not all tax reforms sponsored by governors recently have deprived state treasuries of funds. Abolition of oil depletion allowances, the closing of other loopholes, and the increase of the income tax's progressivity have all infused additional funds while helping to make the tax system more equitable.[38]

Tax increases (both sales and income varieties) will continue to be necessary from time to time, of course, but the risk for the governor will not be the same as before. The basic taxing modes already exist statutorily or constitutionally in most states. Equally significant is the fact, as Neal Peirce points out: "People are getting so hardened to more taxes and inflation . . . that I don't think a governor who puts in a one percent sales tax increase is about to get dismembered quite as rapidly as in the old days."[39]

Revenue-sharing monies from the federal government are an assist (see Chapter 5), and an ex-governor in the White House may prove more sympathetic to states' fiscal plights than the Washington-trained presidents of the last several decades. A new approach to their constituencies by several new governors (most notably Jerry Brown of California) might also reduce the demand for more services that spawns many tax increases. Preaching an "era of limits," Brown and others encourage citizens to expect less from government, though human nature would suggest that they will always want more. Still, for a governor at least, it is an attractive philosophy and a seductive sermon for the public pulpit!

The Spread of Two-Party Competition

Espousing popular causes hardly insures any candidate's election. An aspiring and capable politician can be on the "right" side of every issue and lose miserably. The element most lacked in such an event is probably political organization—that is, the electoral machinery that readies the precincts, distributes the literature, mans the polling booths, and gets out the vote. For a vigorous party organization to exist in the United States, a party must have a reasonable chance to win elections and offices. Few indeed are the people who will dedicate vast amounts of their time and energies to lost causes and foregone defeats and least of all ambitious office-hopefuls. People who desire public office will go where pragmatism leads them, and a very weak party suffers a shortage not only of workers but also of talent and leadership.

A one-party system is undesirable for a state because it can easily result in second-rate government. If a party is assured of victory regardless of whom it chooses to nominate for governor, then it is likely to treat the governorship more as a "reward" for dedicated service to the party than as a public trust where the best qualified men and women should be placed. On the other hand, if a strong, competitive party system exists, a party will logically seek out the strongest and ablest candidate available, whether he or she be in or out of the party. Better governors and superior state governments result. (A bit of evidence will be offered shortly to support this conclusion.) A one-party state can make no such claim even though factions that resemble competitive parties normally develop. As V.O. Key convincingly contended, the resemblance between party and faction is superficial; in fact, their characteristics are contradictory.[40]

In 1950 the competitive condition of two-party politics in the states was unhealthy. The "Solid South" was overwhelmingly Democratic, as were the

Border states, and the Northeastern and Midwestern states were heavily Republican (though not as predictable as their Southern brethren). Coleman Ransone found at the time that only 14 of the 48 states had a party balance sufficient enough so that each party could capture the governorship and at least one state legislative house from time to time.[41] From merely a cursory glance at Table 4-8, one might assume that party competitiveness has deteriorated even further. In 1951 the GOP actually held one more than a majority of the governorships, while in 1975 only 13 of 50 were in Republican hands. The vagaries of party governorship totals, however, are deceptive. Just a few years earlier, after Republicans won off-year elections in Virginia and New Jersey, the GOP controlled 32 statehouses. Over the entire 1950-1975 period Democrats held 58 percent of the governorships—exactly their proportion during the 1940s and slightly under their margin in the 1930s.[42]

The governorship has changed hands several times in most states over a quarter-century, although one of the parties has predominated in at least half the states. Figure 4-1 ranks the states by the number of years they have had Democratic governors since 1950. The first 15 states are heavily Democratic, and 13 of them are, as expected, Southern and Border states. The last 15 lean Republican, having had Democratic governors for ten years or less over the past twenty-five. These states are all located in New England, the Midwest, or the West. Figure 4-2 graphically represents party control of governorships in the states over the last quarter-century.

Table 4-8
Party Balance in Governorships, 1951-1975

| | | No. of Governors[a] | |
Year	Democratic	Republican	Independent
1951	23	25	0
1953	18	30	0
1955	27	21	0
1957	29	19	0
1959	34	16	0
1961	34	16	0
1963	34	16	0
1965	33	17	0
1967	24	26	0
1969	20	30	0
1971	30	20	0
1973	31	19	0
1975	36	13	1

Source: Compiled from Appendix B.

[a]Governors in office as of December 31 of the years shown.

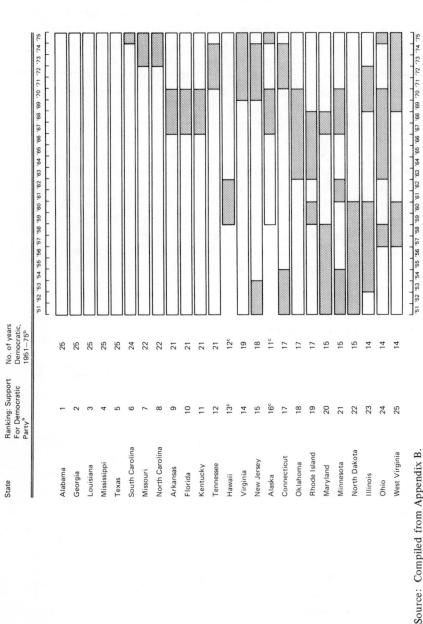

Source: Compiled from Appendix B.

[a]On a scale of 1 (most Democratic) to 50 (least Democratic). This ranking is based solely on the number of years each party has controlled the governorship from 1951-1975.

[b]The number listed is the total number of years in which the Democratic party held the governorship in each state from 1951 to 1975. The highest possible "score" would, of course, be 25.

Figure 4-1. Party Control of Governorships, by State, 1951-1975

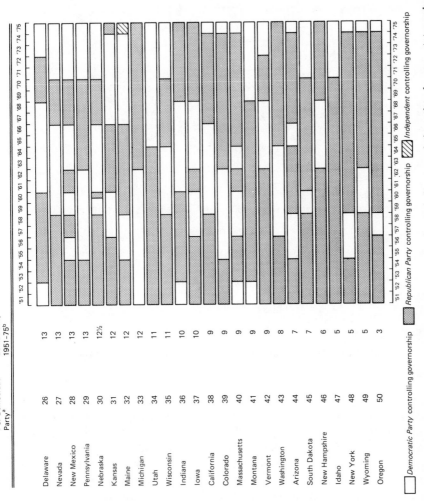

State	Ranking: Support For Democratic Party[a]	No. of years Democratic, 1951–75[b]
Delaware	26	13
Nevada	27	13
New Mexico	28	13
Pennsylvania	29	13
Nebraska	30	12½
Kansas	31	12
Maine	32	12
Michigan	33	12
Utah	34	11
Wisconsin	35	11
Indiana	36	10
Iowa	37	10
California	38	9
Colorado	39	9
Massachusetts	40	9
Montana	41	9
Vermont	42	9
Washington	43	8
Arizona	44	7
South Dakota	45	7
New Hampshire	46	6
Idaho	47	5
New York	48	5
Wyoming	49	5
Oregon	50	3

☐ *Democratic Party* controlling governorship   ▦ *Republican Party* controlling governorship   ▨ *Independent* controlling governorship

Figure 4-1 (cont.)

[c] Alaska and Hawaii have had elected governors for only 16 of the 25 years in the period surveyed since they became states only in 1959. Thus, their rankings are weighted accordingly. Alaska has had a Democratic governor for 11 of 16 years, and this is the equivalent of about 17 years of Democratic control over a quarter-century. Similarly, Democrats have held the Hawaiian governorship for 12 of 16 years, which is equated with 19 years in a 25-year period.

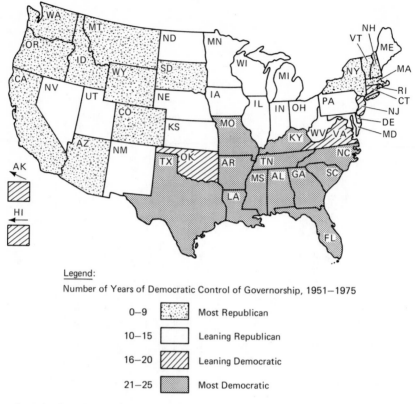

Legend:

Number of Years of Democratic Control of Governorship, 1951–1975

0–9		Most Republican
10–15		Leaning Republican
16–20		Leaning Democratic
21–25		Most Democratic

Source: Compiled from Appendix B.

Figure 4-2. Map of Party Control of Governorships, 1951-1975

If the later years depicted in Figure 4-1 are examined, though, the first hint of changing party relationships in some states becomes apparent. As Figure 4-3 shows, the North Central and some Western states had been transferring their allegiances to the Democrats, while Southern and Border states are far more likely to be found in the Republican column in 1975 than 1950. Nine of the 15 heavily Democratic states have elected at least one Republican governor since 1965, and 14 of 15 strong Republican states have been under Democratic rule at least a few years during the same period.[43] The transformations become more obvious when the number of elections won by each party in the states is compared for recent years with the rest of this century. The basic party characters and attachments can still be discerned from 1950 to 1975, but in general heavily Democratic states are electing more Republicans and GOP-leaning states are electing more Democrats since 1950 than has been the case in the previous half-century.

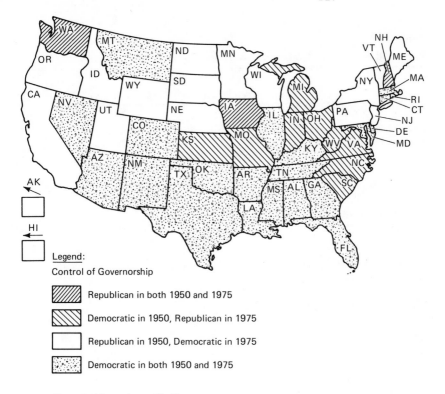

Source: Compiled from Appendix B.
Note: Alaska and Hawaii did not become states and popularly elect their governors until 1959. Thus they cannot be included in this figure's depiction. Maine had a Republican governor in 1950 and an Independent governor in 1975.

Figure 4-3. Party Control of Governorships, 1950 and 1975

Further, the proportion of party change-overs has been increasing steadily by decade after 1950, as Table 4-9 shows. Only 23.6 percent of all gubernatorial elections resulted in a party change in the 1950s, but that percentage grew to 35.3 in the 1960s and an even larger 37.5 in the first half of the 1970s. Only the Northeast and West (the latter especially) had large numbers of party turnovers, as well as incumbent defeats, in the 1950s. Twenty years later, however, the Border states had surpassed all regions in party changes, and the Midwest had drawn even with the Northeast. The South, still lagging considerably behind other areas, nonetheless saw a 20 percent party turnover in the 1970s, compared to none at all in the 1950s.

Clearly, a substantial shift in the level of state party competition has taken place in the last quarter-century. Since this alteration of political patterns has major implications for the governorship and the type of person nominated and elected to fill it, an attempt should be made to measure the extent of the shift.

Table 4-9

Party and Personnel Changes in Governorships, 1950-1975

	U.S. Overall	Northeast	South	Border	Midwest	West
1950-1959						
No. of gubernatorial elections	174	38	31	17	49	39
Percent of elections with party change[a]	23.6	28.9	0.0	17.6	18.4	46.2
Percent of elections with defeat of incumbent[b]	12.2	15.8	0.0	5.9	10.2	25.7
Percent of elections with a personnel change in the office of governor[c]	61.5	57.9	74.2	82.4	42.9	69.2
1960-1969						
No. of gubernatorial elections	156	34	30	14	43	35
Percent of elections with party change[a]	35.3	44.1	10.0	28.6	44.2	40.0
Percent of elections with defeat of incumbent[b]	19.2	20.6	0.0	0.0	27.8	31.4
Percent of elections with a personnel change in the office of governor[c]	61.5	61.8	73.3	85.7	51.2	54.3
1970-1975						
No. of gubernatorial elections	96	22	20	10	22	22
Percent of elections with party change[a]	37.5	36.4	20.0[d]	60.0	36.4	45.4
Percent of elections with defeat of incumbent[b]	14.6	13.6	10.0	10.0	18.2	18.2
Percent of elections with a personnel change in the office of governor[c]	64.6	59.1	70.0	80.0	63.6	59.1

Source: Data was compiled from official election results of gubernatorial contests from 1950-1975.

[a]An election with a "party change" is any election where the control of the governorship passes from one *party* to the other. The 1974 election in Maine is counted as a "party change" election, though the victorious candidate was not the nominee of any party.

[b]Incumbents include those persons who succeeded to the governorship upon the death, disability or resignation of the elected governor. It should be noted, however, that some "incumbents" had never been elected to the office of governor in their own right. Only defeats of incumbents in *general* elections are counted.

[c]An election with a "personnel change" is any election where the control of the governorship passes from one *person* to another, regardless of party affiliations.

[d]The Georgia election of 1966, is *not* counted as a "party change" election. Although the Republican candidate secured a plurality of the vote, the Democrats held onto the governorship.

This gauging is neither a simple nor a precise task. Many political scientists have tried to classify state party balance by utilizing a multitude of statistical techniques at electoral levels ranging from the presidency and congressional seats to state legislative and minor statewide posts.[44] The classification that will be described in the following pages is based primarily on gubernatorial elections and the metamorphosis in party control of the statehouses that can be traced from 1930 to 1975.

First, the decline of party regularity in the Democratic South and two one-party Republican Northeastern states is capsuled in Table 4-10. Between 1930 and 1950 the Democrats controlled every single governorship continuously in the twelve states listed, and the GOP was just as successful in its strongholds of Vermont and New Hampshire. But how things changed over the next twenty-five years! The Democrats still dominated the executive branch in the South, but Republican victories were hardly unheard of, having occurred at least once in seven of the twelve states. Significantly, the Democratic percentage of the major party vote for governor declined in every state, most drastically in Virginia, North Carolina, and Oklahoma. The monolithic "Solid South" (despite Jimmy Carter's 1976 "favorite son" showing) exists no longer on the state or national level.

Democrats have made even deeper inroads in New England. It is not uncommon at all for a Democrat to sit in the governor's chair, and amazingly the Democrats have almost exactly split the overall gubernatorial vote with the once-supreme GOP. "When I came to Vermont eighteen years ago, the Democratic Party in my community met in a phone booth," reported Democratic Governor Thomas Salmon of Vermont. "Today we send two Democratic legislators to Montpelier [the state capital] and have twice elected Democrats as governor."[45]

The increase in two-party competition in the South has had its effects on that venerable old institution of Confederate Democracy, the primary. The Democratic primary, for certain, is still almost universal as the gubernatorial nomination method. Between 1946 and 1975, of 98 elections for governor in 10 Southern states and 1 Border state, the Democrats held contested party primaries to make all but 5 nominations. Interestingly, these 5 exceptions occurred only because just one or no candidate filed for the party nomination. Thus, contested primaries were the staple political fare in the South, whether incumbent governor was seeking renomination or not. In close to half (44 of 98) of the elections, Southern voters were treated to not just one, but two primaries for governor, due to party or statutory provisions requiring run-offs when no candidate gained a majority in the first round. (Only Tennessee has never adopted the run-off rule.)

For all of this frantic electoral activity that has continued uninterrupted through the years, the primary has sharply declined in importance in most Southern states. Just as the South is no longer solid, the primary is no longer

Table 4-10
Metamorphosis in Party Control in the One-Party States, 1930-1975

	Years 1930-1950		Years 1951-1975	
Democratic States	% of Gubernatorial Elections Won by Democrats	Average % Democratic of Major Party Vote for Governor	% of Gubernatorial Elections Won by Democrats	Average % Democratic of Major Party Vote for Governor
Georgia	100.0	100.0	100.0	95.8
Mississippi	100.0	100.0	100.0	83.2
South Carolina	100.0	99.9	85.7	79.6
Louisiana	100.0	99.2	100.0	85.4
Alabama	100.0	90.6	100.0	81.5
Texas	100.0	89.0	100.0	72.1
Arkansas	100.0	88.6	84.6	68.6
Florida	100.0	78.5	87.5	63.5
Virginia	100.0	74.0	66.7	54.1[a]
Tennessee	100.0	73.8	87.5	66.9
North Carolina	100.0	68.5	83.3	57.8
Oklahoma	100.0	57.7	71.4	54.9
Republican States	% of Gubernatorial Elections Won by Republicans	Average % Republican of Major Party Vote for Governor	% of Gubernatorial Elections Won by Republicans	Average % Republican of Major Party Vote for Governor
Vermont	100.0	68.5	61.5	51.1
New Hampshire	100.0	58.6	76.9	49.9

Sources: For the years 1930-1950, the statistics are taken from Coleman B. Ransone, Jr., *The Office of Governor in the United States* (University, Alabama: University of Alabama Press, 1956), p. 13. For the years 1951-1975, the information was compiled from official election results for all gubernatorial elections.

[a]Figure includes the percentage won by Henry Howell in 1973. Howell, though officially an Independent, received the "commendation" of the Democratic party. If Howell's percentage is excluded, the column figure becomes 45.8 percent.

tantamount to election.[46] As the Republican party has become more competitive statewide and has either threatened Democratic hegemony or won the governorship outright, voter interest in the primary has waned. The primary was, rightly, no longer perceived as the point of final electoral decision; the general election now deserved that status, and citizens delayed their balloting participation until November when it "really" mattered. Coupled with this change was the loosening of party ties and the growing independence of the electorate that made voters less inclined to take part in a strictly party affair.

Thus, as Table 4-11 indicates, the vote in gubernatorial primaries as a proportion of the general election vote shrunk considerably, as party activists assumed a greater role in determining their organization's nominees. Between 1930 and 1950, for instance, the Democratic primary vote was ten times the general election total. Only in North Carolina (the only state on the list to hold all its gubernatorial elections in high-turnout presidential years) was the turnout in the primary below that of the November election. Participation in the two elections was nearly equivalent in Virginia and Tennessee, which, together with North Carolina, were the states of the old Confederacy with the most potent Republican parties. Since 1950 the electoral pattern has been quite different. Primary interest has dwindled in every state surveyed, drastically in some. Just

Table 4-11
The Fading Gubernatorial Primary in One-Party Democratic States, 1930-1975

	1930-1950 Primary Interest	1951-1975 Primary Interest
South Carolina	1009.1	121.0
Mississippi	550.1	160.4
Louisiana	511.1	153.0
Georgia	315.8	137.7
Alabama	211.1	132.8
Texas	194.8	79.9
Arkansas	139.4	83.7
Florida	111.4	65.9
Tennessee	108.2	92.2
Virginia	101.5	50.8
North Carolina	54.4	48.3

Sources: For the years 1930-1950, the statistics are taken from Coleman B. Ransone, Jr., *The Office of Governor in the United States* (University: University of Alabama Press, 1956), p. 17. For the years 1951-1975, the information was compiled from official election results for all Southern gubernatorial primaries.

Note: Figures show the total vote in the gubernatorial primary as a percentage of the total vote for governor in the subsequent general election, on the average. If no primary was held in a given year, the general election vote in the same year was not used.

five of the eleven states had average gubernatorial primary turnouts exceeding general election totals, and in elections since 1971 only Alabama and Mississippi have persisted in this.

As they have grown in strength and stature, some state Republican parties have instituted their own primaries, thereby ironically shoring up the primary method of nomination at the same time as they were weakening it. In the period 1950 to 1963, only eight contested GOP gubernatorial primaries were held in the South, and six of these were in Florida. After 1963 there were seventeen contested Republican primaries in Southern states, four of which included run-offs, and only Alabama, Mississippi, and Virginia have not experienced at least one of these "Grand Old Primaries."

The one-party states are extreme cases where, until recently, Democrats or Republicans have been able virtually to monopolize the governorship. There are other states where one party dominates the political system, but not excessively. These are the "normally Democratic or Republican" states in which, as Coleman Ransone characterizes them, ". . . one of the two major parties has seemed unusually strong and has captured what might be considered more than its fair share of the gubernatorial elections."[47] In this category, too, while the trend is not as uniform as in the one-party states, movement toward more competitive party politics can be observed (see Table 4-12). Arizona's Democratic edge has dissipated to a greater degree than any other normally Democratic state, with the party's vote percentage declining from a heavy majority to under half. The Democratic share of the vote in New Mexico, Rhode Island, and West Virginia has fallen off a few percentage points, which has been enough to deny the party several gubernatorial terms in all three states. Fewer Democrats serve as chief executive in yet another Western state, Utah. (The Democratic vote percentage has risen a bit in recent years, but this is wholly due to the repeated good showings of long-time Democratic Governor Calvin Rampton.) On the other hand, Democrats have entrenched themselves further, votewise, in Nevada, Missouri, and Maryland, although only in Missouri was this reflected in the percentage of elections actually won by Democrats.

All eleven of the normally Republican states have become more competitive. California, having eliminated a heavy Republican bias in gubernatorial elections, is now closely divided between the two parties. Pennsylvania, Maine, South Dakota, Kansas, Iowa, North Dakota, and Minnesota all show a lower percentage of elections won and votes garnered by Republicans. In Nebraska the GOP vote has held fairly constant but more Democrats have served as governor. In Oregon, the reverse is true, but the average Republican vote has fallen several percentage points. Finally, Republicans have been much less successful in winning election as governor in Wisconsin, where the nominal increase in the GOP vote is illusory, since before 1950 many normally Republican votes had been siphoned off by a then-active Progressive Party.

The third category of states are the most competitive of all politically. In the two-party states no party is ever assured of control of the governor's office for a long period of time, and full-scale efforts to win it must be waged at almost every election.[48] The two-party states that existed from 1930 to 1950 have been further categorized in Table 4-13 into Democratic-leaning, Republican-leaning, and evenly divided states.

One would expect that politics would be volatile in the two-party states, and the data confirms this view. After 1950, only Connecticut has seen a marked improvement in Democratic fortunes, while seven of the eight Democratic-leaning two-party states at least nominally slipped into the Republican-leaning group. Democrats have experienced a decline in both the number of governorships they have held and the average percentage of the vote they have received in Indiana, Montana, Massachusetts, Ohio, Colorado, and New York. In Idaho Democrats won fewer elections proportionally while increasing their overall vote percentage. This paradox, however, illustrates the skewing effect on the data of a landslide such as that won by Democratic Governor Cecil Andrus of Idaho in 1974. Andrus' case also points up the folly of total reliance on statistics, and the necessity for subjective judgment in constructing a general classification of contemporary party competition in the states.

Subtle but significant shifts in the vote can be detected as well in the Republican-leaning two-party states. Delaware has moved from a marginally GOP state to the site of the most closely contested gubernatorial races in the country. With only a couple of exceptions (1976 being one), statehouse control in Delaware has been decided by an electoral whisper, and the figures in Table 4-13 reflect this. New Jersey has gone a step further and completely switched allegiances, but still within a strong two-party framework. Democrats have shaved five percentage points from the New Jersey Republican vote and reaped the gubernatorial spoils as a consequence. Only Michigan could still be classed as Republican-leaning, but just barely. There has been an almost even division of the vote in the last two elections for governor in the state.

There has been as much movement out of the ranks of evenly split states as there has been movement in. Only Illinois has retained its earlier designation as an evenly divided state in later years. Wyoming has gradually inched its way to the Republican-leaning two-party states, as has Washington. The latter case indicates the influence that a single, very popular incumbent may have upon gubernatorial political patterns in a state. Three-term Republican Daniel Evans won repeated, solid victories in Washington and singlehandedly reversed the state's Democratic leanings. The same thing has occurred in New York (Nelson Rockefeller), Utah (Calvin Rampton), and other states. Especially in this age of personality-oriented independent politics, a "party trend" may in fact be only an attachment to a single person. Once that person has passed from the scene, old ties may bind once more. New York and Washington elected Democratic governors when Rockefeller and Evans, respectively, left office. Utah, though, elected another Democrat, Scott Matheson, but it was again a personal victory in

Table 4-12

Metamorphosis in Party Control in the Normally Democratic or Republican States, 1930-1975

Democratic States

	Years 1930-1950		Years 1951-1975	
	% of Gubernatorial Elections Won by Democrats	Average % Democratic of Major Party Vote for Governor	% of Gubernatorial Elections Won by Democrats	Average % Democratic of Major Party Vote for Governor
Arizona	90.9	64.1	36.4	47.6
New Mexico	90.9	53.3	54.5	51.4
West Virginia	83.3	54.6	50.0	50.2
Kentucky	83.3	54.5	85.7	55.5
Utah	83.3	53.6	50.0	55.6
Rhode Island	81.8	55.4	66.6	52.0
Nevada	66.6	55.5	66.6	58.9
Missouri	66.6	54.0	83.3	55.1
Maryland	66.6	52.0	66.6	56.7

Republican States

	Years 1930-1950		Years 1951-1975	
	% of Gubernatorial Elections Won by Republicans	Average % Republican of Major Party Vote for Governor	% of Gubernatorial Elections Won by Republicans	Average % Republican of Major Party Vote for Governor
California	83.3	66.7	50.0	50.8
Pennsylvania	83.3	53.1	33.3	48.8
Maine	81.8	59.0	33.3	48.2
South Dakota	81.8	55.9	66.6	53.0

State				
Kansas	81.8	54.5	50.0	48.7
Iowa	72.7	55.2	58.3	49.8
Wisconsin	72.7	47.2[a]	54.5	50.6
Oregon	66.6	59.4	71.4	53.1
North Dakota	63.6	56.3	44.4	54.4
Minnesota	63.6	49.8[a]	33.3	47.2
Nebraska	54.5	50.1	40.0	50.8

Sources: For the years 1930-1950, the statistics are taken from Coleman B. Ransone, Jr., *The Office of Governor in the United States* (University: University of Alabama Press, 1956), p. 41. For the years 1951-1975, the information was compiled from official election results for all gubernatorial elections.

[a]The Republican percentages are low due to the presence of active third parties in both Wisconsin (the Progressives) and Minnesota (the Farmer-Laborites) during much of the period surveyed.

Table 4-13
Metamorphosis in Party Control in the Two-Party States, 1930-1975

Democratic-Leaning

	Years 1930-1950		Years 1951-1975	
	% of Gubernatorial Elections Won by Democrats	*Average % Democratic of Major Party Vote for Governor*	*% of Gubernatorial Elections Won by Democrats*	*Average % Democratic of Major Party Vote for Governor*
Indiana	66.6	52.2	33.3	47.5
Montana	66.6	51.6	33.3	50.3
Massachusetts	63.6	51.4	40.0	49.0
Ohio	54.5	50.1	50.0	49.4
Colorado	54.5	52.8	50.0	47.9
New York	54.5	52.8	33.3	47.9
Idaho	54.5	51.8	33.3	52.1
Connecticut	54.5	49.8	83.3	54.6

Republican-Leaning

	% of Gubernatorial Elections Won by Republicans	*Average % Republican of Major Party Vote for Governor*	*% of Gubernatorial Elections Won by Republicans*	*Average % Republican of Major Party Vote for Governor*
Delaware	66.6	51.8	50.0	50.0
New Jersey	62.5	51.1	16.7	45.7
Michigan	54.5	51.6	50.0	50.7

Evenly Divided

	% of Gubernatorial Elections Won by Democrats	*Average % Democratic of Major Party Vote for Governor*	*% of Gubernatorial Elections Won by Democrats*	*Average % Democratic of Major Party Vote for Governor*
Washington	50.0	54.5	33.3	48.1
Illinois	50.0	51.7	50.0	50.7
Wyoming	50.0	49.7	33.3	47.5

Sources: For the years 1930-1950, the statistics are taken from Coleman B. Ransone, Jr., *The Office of Governor in the United States* (University: University of Alabama Press, 1956), p. 75. For the years 1951-1975, information was compiled from official election results for all gubernatorial contests.

the mold of Rampton. Even as Matheson won in 1976, Utah was unseating an incumbent Democratic senator and giving the Republican presidential candidate his highest vote percentage in the nation.

Overall, what classification of state party competition can be made that will account for the convulsions catalogued in the previous tables? If we retain the labels of "one-party," "normally Democratic or Republican," and "two-party," then a reasonable grouping of states appears in Table 4-14. Some qualifications concerning the table should be made explicit. First, the table's classifications are based in large measure, but not wholly, on the data presented in Tables 4-10 through 4-13. Some subjective judgments could not have been avoided, nor should they have been since the quantitative material gives an incomplete and occasionally misleading picture of state political complexities. Secondly, the classification in Table 4-14 is a gubernatorial model, derived first and foremost from statehouse elections and meant to apply primarily to them. In determining each state's classification, reference was made to party balance in the state legislatures as well as to congressional and presidential voting trends, although much less weight was given to these elections than to gubernatorial results. This is not to say that, for most states, there is no applicability beyond the vote for governor. There usually is, but not always, since a few state parties, for reasons unique to their environments, are competitive for state offices but ineffectual in national or purely local contests. Finally, there is a "time bias" in the table, for it is only, as Austin Ranney described his model, "a snapshot of an object moving in time."[49] Politics is more fluid today than ever before, and drastic revisions will undoubtedly be required in just a few years (if they are not already necessary). While the party balance for the entire 1950-1975 period was reviewed, the final classification naturally followed the more current trends.

Now that the provisos have all been made, the classification itself can be examined. More than a slight shift has occurred, with 31 of 48 states either changing categories or subcategories since the earlier 1950 grouping. (Alaska and Hawaii have, of course, been added to the new classification as well.) Clearly, the states are much more competitive than in the past. Whereas just 14 states were included in the two-party competitive category before 1950, 31 states are now. In 1975, 6 states (double the previous number) were so closely divided in their party vote patterns that they could not be safely assigned as leaning to either party. The one-party group has shrunk by half, from 14 to 7, and no one-party Republican states remain at all. There are 8 fewer normally Democratic or Republican states. The ranks of the one-party states will probably be further reduced in future years. The 1975 gubernatorial election in Mississippi saw 49 percent of the vote go to the Republican nominee, and Texas has a GOP senator and the Republican candidate for governor came close to victory in 1972.

These one-party states still have a long way to go, however, before they can be characterized as even minimally competitive, as are Louisiana, Georgia, and Alabama. Arkansas remains solidly Democratic despite the fact that it twice

Table 4-14
Party Competition in the American States, 1950-1975

Classifications for 1950-1975	No. of States	
	1930-1950	1951-1975
Group I: One-Party States	14	7
A. Democratic one-party states	12	7
Alabama		
Arkansas		
Georgia		
Louisiana		
Mississippi		
South Carolina		
Texas		
B. Republican one-party states	2	0
None		
Group II: Normally Democratic or Republican States	20	12
A. Normally Democratic states	9	6
Florida (one-party Democratic)		
Hawaii (none)		
Kentucky		
Maryland		
North Carolina (one-party Democratic)		
Tennessee (one-party Democratic)		
B. Normally Republican states	11	6
Arizona (normally Democratic)		
Kansas		
Nebraska		
New Hampshire (one-party Republican)		
Oregon		
Vermont (one-party Republican)		
Group III: Two-Party States	14	31
A. Democratic-leaning two-party states	8	17
Colorado		
Connecticut		
Maine (normally Republican)		
North Dakota (normally Republican)		
Oklahoma (one-party Democratic)		

Massachusetts
Minnesota (normally Republican)
Missouri (normally Democratic)
Montana
Nevada (normally Democratic)
New Jersey (two-party Republican)

Pennsylvania (normally
   Republican)
Rhode Island (normally Democratic)
South Dakota (normally Republican)
Washington (two-party-evenly
   divided)
West Virginia (normally Democratic)
Wisconsin (normally Republican)

8

B. Republican-leaning two-party states

Idaho (two-party Democratic)
Indiana (two-party Democratic)
Iowa (normally Republican)
New York (two-party Democratic)

Ohio (two-party Democratic)
Virginia (one-party Democratic)
Utah (normally Democratic)
Wyoming (two-party-evenly
   divided)

3

3

C. Evenly divided two-party states

Alaska (none)
California (normally Republican)
Delaware (two-party Republican)
Illinois

Michigan (two-party
   Republican)
New Mexico (normally
   Democratic)

3

6

Sources: Compiled from statistics in Tables 4-11 through 4-13.

Note: For definitions of classification terms and additional information on method, see the text. When a state has changed categories from the 1930-1950 system to the present classification above, the previous designation appears next to the state in parentheses. As an example, Maine is listed in the present classification as a Democratic-leaning two-party state, but from 1930-1950 was classed as a normally Republican state.

elected Republican Winthrop Rockefeller to the governorship. Since Rockefeller's demise, the GOP has virtually collapsed at all levels in Arkansas. South Carolina might appear to have a somewhat competitive Republican party since the state is represented by one Republican (Strom Thurmond) in the U.S. Senate and elected a GOP governor, James Edwards, in 1974. But Thurmond is a former Democrat, and Edwards' election was a fluke (see Chapter 2). The competition in South Carolina, as in much of the Old Confederacy, is only skin-deep.

The Republicans have never had a political bastion to compare with the South, and the only two states to be earlier classed solely in their dominion, Vermont and New Hampshire, have moved on to the next level of competition, as normally Republican states. New Hampshire is no longer knee-jerk Republican and is now represented by two Democratic U.S. senators. While a Democrat has occasionally won the governorship, the state clearly likes to keep a Republican in the statehouse, even if he is as conservative as Meldrim Thomson. Vermont's recent history parallels her neighboring New England state, and she has elected Democrats to both the U.S. Senate and the governorship of late, but the old tradition dies hard. While no longer rock-ribbed Republican, Vermont can still normally be found in the GOP column.

Arizona has changed politically about as much as any state and has gone almost full circle from normally Democratic to normally Republican. The GOP trend that began in the early 1950s with Barry Goldwater's election to the U.S. Senate and Howard Pyle's elevation to the governorship has accelerated through the years, fed by the vast in-migration of the post-World War II era. Democrats are not shut out, though, and recently have done better in winning statewide posts (if only because of GOP intraparty quarrelling). Kansas, Oregon, and Nebraska have all stayed put in the normally Republican category despite infrequent Democratic binges.

North Carolina, Tennessee, and Florida have become sufficiently competitive to be transferred out of their previous one-party classification. Florida has had a Republican governor, a Republican U.S. senator, and several GOP congressmen since 1950, but the strong showing of Democrats since 1970 reveals its inherent tendencies. Yet a Republican win can never be ruled out of the question. The evaluations of North Carolina and Tennessee yield similar conclusions. Both states have had at least one Republican senator and governor but, all things being equal, the Democrats will still have the edge. Kentucky and Maryland have also flirted with Republicans from time to time, but no steady courtship has emerged. Yet it would be rare today to find either state without at least one major Republican officeholder.

Hawaii is an interesting case, since it is the only non-Southern or Border state to vote fairly consistently Democratic. The ethnic and racial composition of the island state's population is the root cause, but Republicans are not exluded from office there. The GOP won the governorship once and held a U.S. Senate seat for three terms. Presidentially, Richard Nixon carried the state in 1972, and Jimmy Carter only won it with great difficulty four years later.

The two-party group registers the only gains recorded for any group, with expansions of all three subcategories. The Democratic-leaning two-party states more than doubled their number, from 8 to 17. Oklahoma jumped the farthest to arrive at this designation, but there is little question that the formerly one-party state is no longer merely an extension of the "Solid South." Two successive Republican governors were elected there, and both of them were later elected to the U.S. Senate as well. Of all the Southern and Border states, only Virginia joined Oklahoma in voting against Georgian Jimmy Carter for president in 1976. The state still leans Democratic on the gubernatorial level, however, as an examination of the elections of the last two decades indicates.

Missouri is another Border state that can be persuaded to vote Republican at the state level, as the GOP's Governor Christopher Bond and U.S. Senator John Danforth happily discovered. Yet the fact that Bond was ousted in a 1976 reelection bid even as Danforth was victorious underlines both the competitive nature and Democratic leanings of the "Show Me" state. Republican gubernatorial candidates have also performed surprisingly well in West Virginia since 1950, with control of the governor's chair being split almost evenly with the Democrats. Yet the heavily Democratic character of politics in the state argues against any other categorization. Like Missouri and West Virginia, Nevada and Rhode Island were once normally Democratic but are now far more competitive on the statewide level. GOP governors and senators have represented both states in recent years, even though the political base continues to have a Democratic cast.

Two once strongly Republican states, Maine and South Dakota, have gradually been converted to two-party competition with a slight Democratic tilt. The party-building efforts of George McGovern in South Dakota and Edmund Muskie in Maine were responsible for the conversions, and Democratic candidates for offices at all levels have benefitted. South Dakota's sister state to the North has marched to the same tune of late. Wisconsin and Minnesota, politically twin Midwestern states, have moved along with their favored progressivism as it has been transfused from the Republican to the Democratic party. New Jersey and Pennsylvania have joined their fellow Northeastern states of Massachusetts and Connecticut in the Democratic-leaning column, although all four states are fiercely competitive, with Democrats and Republicans trading major posts almost every election. Washington state, on the other side of America, has also edged Democratic in races for most statewide posts. The governorship has been a singular exception, but with the retirement of Dan Evans it is probably safe to include it among the Democratic-leaning two-party states.

All of the eight competitive states judged Republican-leaning are new entrants, most of which were formerly included on the Democratic side of the ledger. Idaho, Indiana, Ohio, and New York have been competitive for some time, but leaned Democratic in the 1930-1950 period. Democrats still do quite well from time to time in all of them, but Idaho, Indiana, and Ohio have a firm and detectable bias in recent years to the GOP in statewide races. New York may well join its Northeastern neighbors by the time the next "snapshot" of party competition is taken, but the enduring vitality of progressive Republicanism on the state level, at least until the last few years, prevents another classification for the present. Iowa has come as far as any of the farm belt states in party competition over the last quarter-century. Both parties closely contest offices at all levels. Democrats have generally had the better of their rivals when the broad sweep of posts is considered, but for now the underlying trend is still slightly Republican. Nevertheless, this is a state that could also change subcategories within the near future.

Aristocratic Virginia and Western-style Utah might be thought to have little in common politically. To the contrary, a deep-seated cultural conservatism makes twins of this electoral "odd couple." The conservatism springs from alien founts. Virginia is a state heavy with history whose customs and traditionalism encourage her citizens to look to the past as much as to the future. The hidebound attitudes of Utahns stem from a religious link with Mormonism. It would not be far from the mark to characterize Utah as the "church-state," for the ideas and dogma of the Mormon church pervade politics and government there. (There is also a hardy Mormon influence in Idaho.) As the national Democratic party began to adopt social and ideological positions unacceptable to the philosophy and lifestyles of a majority of Virginians and Utahns, these two states gradually embraced the more compatible policies of the progressive-purged new Republicanism. The attachment to the GOP is not ironclad; it is more rational than emotional or habitual. Democrats are still competitive statewide, although it is normally the moderate-to-conservative Democrats who wind up in the winner's circle. Virginia, incidentally, jumped further than any other state on the scale of party competition by moving from one-party Democratic to Republican-leaning two-party. Such a shift is not accomplished effortlessly, and the Old Dominion has been in political flux as a consequence and has suffered many complicating Independent candidacies, party-switchings, and other ailments associated with full-scale party realignment.

The last subgroup of two-party states, those evenly divided by party, has also experienced growth. The new wilderness state of Alaska has been added, and two states earlier classified as Republican-leaning competitive states, Delaware and Michigan, have become used to contests that are tossups between the parties. The gubernatorial results, especially in Delaware, are usually quite close. California, though categorized with Delaware, rarely has cliffhangers, but the state has little hesitation about switching parties and often swings wildly from one election to the next. Modern California's volatility is legendary; its old "normally Republican" character has been permanently altered by the millions of new residents from across the country who have settled there since World War II. Yet another Western state, New Mexico, cut its moorings with the Democratic party to become a closely contested battleground after 1950. New Mexico nourishes her reputation as a national "bellweather" state, but some tarnish developed after President Ford grabbed the state's electoral votes in 1976. Of the three evenly divided states from 1930 to 1950, only Illinois survives. Wyoming and Washington now tip to the Republicans and Democrats, respectively, while maintaining a competitive complexion.

The changes in party competition in the states have been numerous and varied, but the trend is heavily in the direction of more intense electoral combat. As the foregoing analysis has proven, former Governor Harold Stassen of Minnesota was quite accurate in claiming: "The whole country is becoming more two-party . . . that's the major political trend of the last twenty years."[50] A summary depiction of the competitive classifications just made for 1951 to 1975, as contrasted to those for 1930 to 1950, can be found in Figures 4-4 and 4-5.

The agents originating the trend to party competitiveness include the

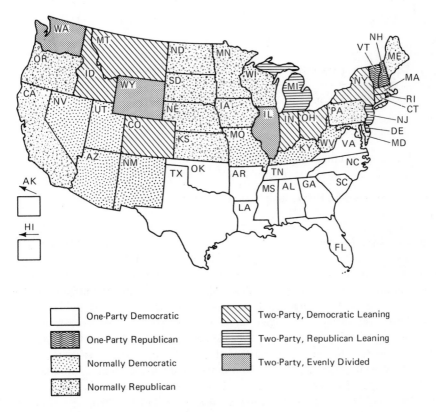

	One-Party Democratic		Two-Party, Democratic Leaning
	One-Party Republican		Two-Party, Republican Leaning
	Normally Democratic		Two-Party, Evenly Divided
	Normally Republican		

Source: Compiled from Statistics in Tables 4-10 through 4-13.

Figure 4-4. Party Competition in the American States, 1930-1950

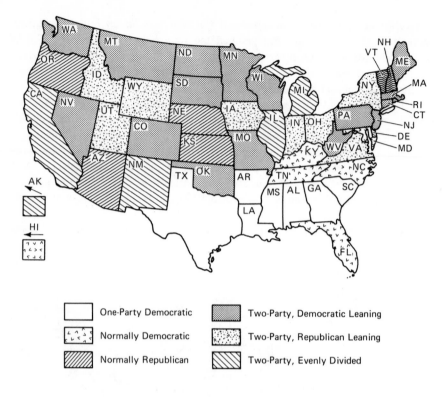

One-Party Democratic

Normally Democratic

Normally Republican

Two-Party, Democratic Leaning

Two-Party, Republican Leaning

Two-Party, Evenly Divided

Source: Compiled from statistics in Table 4-14.

Note: There were no one-party Republican states in this time period.

Figure 4-5. Party Competition in the American States, 1951-1975

decline of sectionalism and the growth of urbanization and industrialization. Duane Lockard saw the "rapid erosion" of sectionalism as inevitable, and with it the one-partyism that it helped to spawn.[51] Sectionalism's recession and party competition's spread are the results of the nationalization and homogenization of American politics that has been a steady development over the last several decades. Television has played an enormous role in this process, and the increasing mobility of people between states and regions has also been vital. The migration that has been a consistent theme of American life accelerated after World War II.[52] Demographers have catalogued vast population movements to the West, to all urban areas from South to North, and more recently from urban centers and the North to suburbia, rural regions, and the "Sunbelt" stretching from the Southeast to the West.

There appears to be a link between industrialization and urbanization, and party competitiveness, too. Thomas R. Dye found that a state's social and economic traits help to explain its politics.[53] States with high levels of family income, adult education, urbanism, and industrialization tend to have more vigorous electoral battles between parties. The rapid urbanization of America, then, has contributed to the quickened pace of party competition.

At the outset of this study's examination of party competition, the argument was made that vigorous two-party competition is desirable since it probably results in more capable persons being nominated by the parties and elected to governorships. No hard and fast proof of such a proposition is available, but some evidence in support can be presented by an examination of the outstanding governors produced by the states. Of the total of 45 governors from 1950 to 1975 who came from one-party states, 15 (or 33.3 percent) had earlier been distinguished as "outstanding." The percentage of outstanding governors in the more competitive, normally Democratic or Republican states was slightly higher (34.2 percent). Fully 40 percent of the governors from two-party states, however, were labelled "outstanding," and the highest proportion of exceptional governors by far (46.9 percent) was found in the most competitive states of all, the two-party evenly divided ones.

Better governors, then, probably were elected in two-party states, and the experience of many once uncompetitive states (including Iowa, Maine, Missouri, New Mexico, North Dakota, and Virginia) suggests that as party competitiveness increased so did the quality of their chief executives. In Jack Walker's study of innovation in the states, nine of the ten states determined to be the most creative were two-party states.[54] More resourceful government, guided by outstanding governors, is a likelier prospect in more states than ever before with the demise of widespread one-party hegemony.

Independent Voting

The increase in party competition can also be attributed in part to the general loosening of party ties in the electorate. Ticket-splitting, whereby a voter casts his ballot simultaneously for a Democrat for one office and a Republican for another post, has become widespread in virtually all states.[55] In 1968, for example, Arkansas voted for the Independent presidential candidacy of George Wallace at the same time she was electing Republican Winthrop Rockefeller as governor and returning Democrat J. William Fulbright to the U.S. Senate. In 1972 Virginia found herself with a Republican governor, an Independent lieutenant governor, and a Democratic attorney general, which is quite a collection in her three statewide elective posts.

These cases are hardly anomalies. It has become common in every region to find states voting for a presidential candidate of one party while electing a governor of the opposite party, or simultaneously delivering mandates to a governor and a U.S. senator of different parties. Table 4-15 compares guber-

Table 4-15
Joint Election of Governors and Senators, by Party, 1950-1975

Party of Governor-elect	Party of Senator-elect	Election Year Period		
		1950-1959 No. (% of Grand Total)	1960-1969 No. (% of Grand Total)	1970-1975 No. (% of Grand Total)
D	D	48	35	25
R	R	42	21	5
Subtotal		90 (76.9)	56 (53.9)	30 (51.7)
D	R	12	21	16
R	D	15	27	11[a]
Subtotal		27 (23.1)	48 (46.1)	28[b] (48.3)
Grand Total		117 (100.0)	104 (100.0)	58 (100.0)

D = Democrat, R = Republican

Sources: Compiled from Richard M. Scammon (ed.), *America Votes*, Vol. 8 (Washington, D.C.: Governmental Affairs Institute, Congressional Quarterly, Inc., 1968); and Michael Barone, Grant Ujifusa, and Douglas Matthews, *The Almanac of American Politics, 1972 [1974, 1976]* (New York: E.P. Dutton, 1972, 1974, 1976).

Note: Gubernatorial and senatorial elections do not always coincide, since term lengths vary. (A governor serves either two or four years in a regular term, while a U.S. senator's term is six years in length.) All simultaneous elections for governor and senator, including special elections for either or both offices, are included in this tabulation. No figures could be included for the states of Kentucky, Louisiana, Mississippi, New Jersey, and Virginia since their gubernatorial elections are always held on days or years different from their senatorial elections.

[a]This figure includes the 1974 New Hampshire election, when a Republican governor was elected but in a disputed result that later was returned to the state's electorate, the Democrat was declared the winner of the seat by 10 votes. (The Democrat, John Durkin, was reelected in the special election that followed.)

[b]The subtotal includes the 1970 election in New York, when the Republican candidate was elected governor and the Conservative party candidate was elected to the U.S. Senate.

natorial and senatorial elections by party from 1950 to 1975, for instance. The percentage of cross-party joint elections has consistently grown through the decades, from 23.1 percent in the 1950s to 46.1 percent in the 1960s and 48.3 percent in the first half of the 1970s. In 1950 the number of Republican pairs was almost equal to the Democratic tally, but the fact that many more pairs of Democrats than Republicans are being elected today attests to shrinking GOP fortunes and the rise of Democrats at the state level over the past twenty-five years.

Most of the split-ticket attention has centered on the "coattail effect" of presidential elections. According to this concept, an electorally strong presidential nominee can carry his party's gubernatorial nominee to victory since many voters who have begun to pull the party's lever at the top of the ticket will supposedly continue to pull it in state (and local) contests. Straight-ticket voting from the statehouse to the White House has drastically declined, as Table 4-16 indicates. The percentage of coinciding state votes for president and governor has dropped steadily from a monolithic 93.1 percent in the late nineteenth century to but 56 percent from 1960 to 1972 (approaching the 50-50 proportion of pure chance).

Table 4-17 affords a closer look at the presidential elections from 1952 to 1976. More than three-quarters of the governorships followed the presidential lead in 1952, and Eisenhower provided significant coattails not only for governorships but also congressional seats. A tailor had been at work by 1956, however, and Eisenhower's reelection triumph was clearly a personal victory that could not mask a Democratic resurgence at the state level. Since that time no Republican presidential nominee has flexed much muscle in gubernatorial contests. In 1932 Franklin Roosevelt won 28 of the 33 states holding gubernatorial elections that year, and in 25 of the 28 states Democratic governors were elected. In 1968 Richard Nixon carried 17 of the 21 states with governor's contests, but just 10 GOP candidates emerged with statehouse victories. In 1972 the count was even worse: only 7 of 18 Nixon states with gubernatorial elections gave their nod to Republican state chief executives.

A greater proportion of presidential-gubernatorial results coincide when Democrats win the presidency because Democrats have the competitive edge at the state level in a majority of the states, but this fact in itself belies the existence of long coattails since Democrats perform well in gubernatorial

Table 4-16
The "Coattail Effect" of Presidents on Gubernatorial Elections, 1880-1972

Period[a]	Percent with Coinciding Party Results for Governor and President	Percent with Different Party Results for Governor and President
1880-1892	93.1	6.9
1896-1908	89.5	11.5
1912-1924	81.2	18.8
1928-1940	77.8	22.2
1944-1956	75.5	24.5
1960-1972	56.0	44.0

Sources: Data for the years 1880-1948 are taken from V.O. Key, Jr., *American State Politics: An Introduction* (New York: Alfred A. Knopf, 1956), p. 49. Data for the years 1952-1972 are culled from Table 4-17.

[a]Each time period includes four presidential elections.

Table 4-17

The "Coattail Effect" of Presidents on Gubernatorial Elections, 1952-1976

Party of Presidential Candidate Carrying State	Party of Governor Elected in State	Election Year												
		1952 No.	(% of Grand Total)	1956 No.	(% of Grand Total)	1960 No.	(% of Grand Total)	1964 No.	(% of Grand Total)	1968 No.	(% of Grand Total)	1972 No.	(% of Grand Total)	1976 No.	(% of Grand Total)
D	D	3		3		7		16		1		0		5	
	R	20		14		10		0		10		7		4	
Subtotal		23	(76.7)	17	(54.9)	17	(63.0)	16	(64.0)	11	(52.4)	7	(35.3)	9	(64.3)
R	R	0		0		5		8		2		0		1	
	D	7		14		5		1		7		11		4	
Subtotal		7	(23.3)	14	(45.1)	10	(37.0)	9	(36.0)	9	(42.8)	11	(64.7)	5	(35.7)
Grand Total		30	(100.0)	31	(100.0)	27	(100.0)	25	(100.0)	21[a]	(100.0)	18	(100.0)	14	(100.0)

D = Democrat; R = Republican

Sources: Compiled from Richard M. Scammon (ed.), *America Votes*, Vols. 6, 8 (Washington: Governmental Affairs Institute, Congressional Quarterly, Inc., 1964, 1968); and Michael Barone, Grant Ujifusa, and Douglas Matthews, *The Almanac of American Politics, 1974* (New York: E.P. Dutton, 1974).

Note: A varying number of states held their gubernatorial elections simultaneous with the presidential election in each year surveyed. Term length changes, special elections, and other factors caused the variance. Even though Louisiana has held its gubernatorial elections in the same year as the presidential election, the dates of each election have differed. Thus, Louisiana is not included in this table's tabulations.

[a] Grand total includes one state (Arkansas) that gave its electoral votes to Independent presidential candidate George C. Wallace, but elected a Republican governor.

elections whether their national ticket is successful or not. In the modern structure of politics, it is at least as accurate to postulate the existence of "reverse coattails" where a strong gubernatorial candidate assists his party's weaker presidential nominee. Politicians at the national level have long accepted the validity of this notion. Democratic presidential candidate Al Smith convinced Franklin Roosevelt to run for governor of New York in 1928 to strengthen his presidential bid in the Empire State and Roosevelt used Herbert Lehman to the same end in 1936. Forty years later Democrat Jimmy Carter, who won very narrowly nationally, tried to piggy-back to the presidency in states with potent Democratic gubernatorial standardbearers. (Most of the victorious Democratic candidates for governor in 1976 ran far ahead of Carter.) Even when the party's presidential nominee loses in a landslide (as Republican Barry Goldwater did in 1964 and Democrat George McGovern did in 1972), governors of the same party can manage to win. Governor George Romney of Michigan, for example, outpolled his fellow Republican Goldwater by almost 1.4 million votes to win reelection in 1964. Eleven Democrats duplicated the feat in 1972 to win governorships while Nixon was sweeping their states.

The coattail effect, then, has not only declined but has really lapsed into meaninglessness. Even as this was occurring, states were gradually insulating their politics from any coattail effect that did exist by moving the date of state elections from presidential years to the off-year congressional contests. In 1952 thirty states elected their governors in presidential years, but by 1976 the number had declined to fourteen. (One more state, Illinois, has approved a shift to off-year elections beginning in 1978.) In all, thirty-two states now schedule all their gubernatorial elections at the same time as off-year congressional elections. Five more states insulate state races further, setting them in odd-numbered years.[56] The shifts of election dates have usually taken place when states converted from two-year to four-year gubernatorial terms, although in two instances (Florida and Illinois), states already having a four-year term for the governor created a special one-time-only term of two years in order to make the switch.

Most academicians and practitioners in the field of state government and politics have applauded this election scheduling shuffle. The National Municipal League's "Model State Constitution" actually recommends the election of governors in odd-numbered years when no federal officials at all are chosen.[57] Some politicians undoubtedly have supported moving the election date to eliminate any prospect of coattails, but the states were far more concerned with focussing greater interest on state issues and candidates. Too often the platforms and pronouncements of gubernatorial aspirants, however crucial to the quality of life and government in the states, have been lost in the glare surrounding tumultuous presidential contests, and the state issues have been relegated to the back pages of the newspapers to the detriment of the citizenry.

Scheduling elections in off-years or odd-numbered years makes sense. The candidates are given greater opportunities to present their wares, and the voters have a better chance to evaluate the candidates and their programs wisely and unencumbered by the distractions and complexities of presidential politics. It is not that national issues and events would be entirely ignored in these circumstances, for that would be objectionable from several standpoints. Rather, the effect of national affairs would be less potent and overriding and less likely to eclipse state issues. As V.O. Key surmised: "Competitive states with off-year elections are by no means untouched by the great fluctuations in party strength nationally; they are simply less closely articulated with the national tides than are those close states whose local campaigns coincide with the commotion generated by a presidential election."[58]

Some have claimed that the near-demise of simultaneous presidential-gubernatorial elections has harmed the party structure by disjoining and fragmenting the party nomination and election process at the national and state levels. This statement is doubted since state parties have always been almost wholly autonomous entities. E.E. Schattschneider claimed that state party autonomy was so prominent that ". . . decentralization of power is by all odds the most important single characteristic of the American major party; more than anything else this trait distinguishes it from all others. Indeed once this truth is understood, nearly everything else about American parties is greatly illuminated."[59]

A case can certainly be made that more capable governors have emerged with surer mandates with the decline of coattails and the election shifts to nonpresidential years. The characters, experiences, and programs of the gubernatorial nominees themselves are given greater scrutiny and are the main determinants of election outcomes. A strong presidential nominee can no longer conceal the weaknesses of his party's gubernatorial nominees, and a weak party standardbearer can no longer obscure the better qualities of his compatriots on the state level.

The trend to ticket-splitting, however, can present new difficulties to a governor by permitting opposition control of one or both houses of the legislature more frequently. Gubernatorial elections no less than their presidential counterparts have exhibited coattail effects in earlier years,[60] but like the other coattails, these have grown shorter of late. Decline of gubernatorial coattails in and of itself inevitably reduces the influence wielded by any chief executive among the elected legislators of his own party, since their fates are less closely tied to his. Opposition control of even one house of the legislature can add innumerable headaches to the governor's job.

From 1931 to 1952 about two-thirds of the states had a governor with both houses of the legislature of the same party at least two-thirds of the time.[61] Table 4-18 indicates the extent of the drop-off since then. Governors and legislators were usually party compatible in the 1950s, with 68.1 percent of the governors securing majorities in both legislative houses. Republicans were more

Table 4-18
The "Coattail Effect" of Governors on State Legislative Elections, 1950-1975

Party of Newly-Elected Governor	Governor's Party Elects a Majority of	Years Surveyed[a]						Totals	
		1950-1960		1961-1970		1971-1975			
		%	(No.)	%	(No.)	%	(No.)	%	(No.)
Democratic	Both houses	64.5	(69)	62.8	(54)	70.5	(31)	65.0	(154)
	One house	14.0	(15)	12.8	(11)	9.1	(4)	12.6	(30)
	Neither house	21.5	(23)	24.4	(21)	20.4	(9)	22.4	(53)
	Totals	100.0	(107)	100.0	(86)	100.0	(44)	100.0	(237)
Republican	Both houses	72.9	(59)	52.1	(37)	26.7	(4)	59.9	(100)
	One house	8.6	(7)	9.9	(7)	6.6	(1)	9.0	(15)
	Neither house	18.5	(15)	38.0	(27)	66.7	(10)	31.1	(52)
	Totals	100.0	(81)	100.0	(71)	100.0	(15)	100.0	(167)
Overall	Both houses	68.1	(128)	58.0	(91)	59.3	(35)	62.9	(254)
	One house	11.7	(22)	11.5	(18)	8.5	(5)	11.1	(45)
	Neither house	20.2	(38)	30.5	(48)	32.2	(19)	26.0	(105)
	Totals	100.0	(188)	100.0	(157)	100.0	(59)	100.0	(404)

Sources: Compiled from Council of State Governments, *The Book of the States, 1950 [-1975]* (Chicago and Lexington, Ky.: Council of State Governments, 1950-1975); Congressional Quarterly, Inc., *Congressional Quarterly Almanac, 1970 [1972]* (Washington, D.C.: Congressional Quarterly, Inc., 1970, 1972); and Michael Barone, Grant Ujifusa, and Douglas Matthews, *The Almanac of American Politics, 1976* (New York: E.P. Dutton, 1975).

Note: Only state legislative elections held simultaneously with the election of a governor were included in the tabulation. Special elections for governor have been included. In some states part or all of one state house (usually the upper one) is not elected simultaneously with the governor. Thus it is more difficult in some states and, indeed, impossible in others for a governor to carry in a party majority in this house if it had been controlled before the election by the opposition party.

[a]Nebraska, which has a nonpartisan, unicameral legislature, is not counted. Minnesota had a nonpartisan legislature until recent years and therefore is not counted in the totals of the first two decades. The 1974 election in Maine, where an Independent was elected governor, is not counted. (In that election, a Republican state senate and a Democratic house of representatives was elected.) Elections in Alaska and Hawaii did not commence until statehood in 1959, and they are counted from that year forward.

often in this position than Democrats, which thus reflects the greater success of Democrats in winning the governorship in GOP-leaning states. By the 1960s the percentage of fully compatible governors and legislatures had shrunk to 58 percent, and this figure increased only slightly in the first half of the 1970s. In the last few years, more governors than ever (32.2 percent) have been elected while carrying neither house. Party positions have reversed since the 1950s, with Republicans (reflecting the frailty of their party at the grassroots) finding full executive-legislative compatibility only 26.7 percent of the time. Democrats, conversely, expanded their control of both houses to an all-time high for the period surveyed (70.5 percent).

V.O. Key and Corinne Silverman attributed split party control of the state executive and legislative branches to malapportionment of the legislatures by contending that ". . . only infrequently does the electorate deliberately choose to place the executive and legislature in the hands of opposing parties, despite the prevailing impression to the contrary . . . withal, this type of electoral decision . . . stems in far higher degree from factors of institutional design (i.e., malapportionment) than from deliberate electoral choice."[62] Since the Supreme Court rulings of the 1960s have thoroughly eliminated legislative malapportionment, and there does not appear to be any other institutional cause, the reason for recent party split control must be precisely the opposite of that given by Key and Silverman. Deliberate electoral choice, through massive ticket splitting, appears to be responsible. The same phenomenon was observed on the national level from 1969 to 1977 when eight years of Republican presidential rule was accompanied by uninterrupted Democratic control of Congress.

If ticket splitting is the causal agent of divided party control, then what factors have produced the new party-independent voting behavior? Briefly, these factors would include the growth of more issue-oriented politics, a blurring of the distinctions between the two major parties, the perceived failure of the parties to carry out their platforms, a decrease in the effectiveness of the local party structure, the influence of television, the effect of broader-based education and higher education levels, and the development of campaign financing that is wholly independent of the party.[63]

Some political scientists have rightly pointed out that ballot structure affects the degree of ticket splitting considerably, with provision for a straight-party ballot measurably increasing the proportion of straight-party ballots cast.[64] A decrease in the number of states with this provision might have assisted independent voting habits, but since twenty-seven states had a straight-party ballot option in 1950 and exactly the same number had it in 1975, that particular institutional mechanism has not contributed to the recorded growth of ticket splitting.[65] Rather, the mushrooming phenomenon of ticket splitting has stemmed from the emergence of a new kind of voter as a result of the factors mentioned above. The authors of the landmark study, *The American Voter* (1960), characterized independent voters as the dregs of the electorate: "Far from being more attentive, interested, and informed, Independents tend as a group to be somewhat less involved in politics. They have somewhat poorer knowledge of the issues, their image of the candidate is fainter, their interest in the campaign is less, their concern over the outcome is relatively slight. . . ."[66]

Contrast that description with the one devised by Walter De Vries and Lance Tarrance more than a decade later after an in-depth study:

Our own data suggests [sic] that the ticket-splitter is slightly younger, somewhat more educated, somewhat more white-collar, and more suburban than the typical middle-class voter. In addition, the ticket-splitter tends to consume more media output about politics and is more active politically than the straight Democrat (but less than the straight Republican).[67]

As paradoxical as it may seem, the party system has become far more competitive even as its structure was being undermined and weakened by a voter who did not respond as readily as before to party labels. The governors, as political and party actors, have had to respond and adapt to this development. Claiming that issues, not political organizations, matter to the modern electorate, former Governor Richard Hughes saw that today's gubernatorial candidate ". . . has to work harder and address the issues more carefully."[68] Candidates for governor, added other chief executives, are less partisan on the campaign trail and openly woo Independents and members of the other major party.

Not just campaigning but the administration of state government after a candidate has won the governorship has been affected by voter independence, thereby encouraging chief executives to extend their nonpartisan stances to the appointments they make and the positions they take. "We ran a very, very nonpartisan administration. . . . We appointed more Democrats than Republicans," commented Ron Schmidt on the tenure of his former boss, Oregon Governor Tom McCall.[69] The loosening of party ties has meant that governors no longer live in fear of presidential coattails, but the independent trend has been liberating for them in other ways. In 1974 Republican McCall felt free to move across the Oregon border to Idaho to kick off Democratic Governor Cecil Andrus' reelection campaign. McCall did it because he considered Andrus "one heck of a good governor," but it's doubtful he would have taken the political risk if party organizations still flexed any real muscle.[70]

Interestingly, the growth of independent voting habits has not been matched by a crop of successful Independent candidates for governor. Since 1950 only one Independent, James B. Longley of Maine, has managed to win a governorship. Longley won a plurality in 1974 against lackluster Republican and Democratic candidates. An Independent gubernatorial candidate, Henry Howell, nearly won in Virginia in 1973 when he garnered 49.3 percent of the vote. Two years earlier Howell had won the lieutenant governorship as an Independent by defeating major party candidates for the post with a 40 percent plurality. Virginia, in the throes of party realignment, has experimented with Independents more than any other state since 1950 and is also represented by an Independent U.S. senator, Harry Byrd, Jr., who twice has been elected to his federal post as an Independent by solid majorities.

Surprisingly, before 1950 fruitful Independent candidacies for governor were a bit more common. The roots go deep in American history. An Anti-Masonic party infrequently defeated the Whigs and Democrats in the Northeast in the 1830s. Over the succeeding score of years, the Free Soil and the American (or "Know Nothing") parties were occasionally victorious in the same region. The Greenback party in the 1870s and 1880s and the Populist party just before the turn of the century enjoyed some success in gubernatorial politics. Between 1912 and 1920 the "People's Independent" party in Nebraska, with the help of Democrats, filled the governor's chair. In the years 1930 to 1936 the Farmer-Labor party won four consecutive gubernatorial elections in Minnesota. (The party fused in 1944 with the Democrats in a coalition that has persisted to the present day.) Insurgent Republicans who would not accept the regular party nominees elected members of their factions as nominal Independents in Oregon (1930) and North Dakota (1932). Progressives elected Independent Philip La Follette in Wisconsin in 1934 and 1936 and another Progressive candidate in 1942. (La Follette had earlier served in the governorship as a Republican.) From 1930 to 1950 there were eleven Independent gubernatorial candidacies (primarily in the farm states of the Midwest) that polled more than 10 percent of the votes.[71] The next twenty-five years recorded a slight increase to fifteen, nine of which were in Southern and Border states. (Tennessee alone accounted for four of them.) However, the percentages of their vote amount to very little, for of the 429 gubernatorial elections held from 1950 through 1975, only twenty-three (or 5.4 percent) resulted in a governor being elected with less than 50 percent of the vote, and in just seven of these twenty-three elections did the winning candidate receive less than 48 percent of the vote. Clearly, the independent emotions of voters vent themselves almost entirely within a two-party context.

Financing Campaigns

As we have just seen, the changes in the electoral system over the past quarter-century—in tenure, issues, party competitiveness, and ticket-splitting—have generally augured well for the governorship and nurtured the development of a new breed of state chief executives. One revolutionary dimension of modern politics, though, cannot be seen in a favorable light. The culprit is, of course, campaign finance. Rare is the governor who would disagree that raising the huge amounts of cash necessary to run a winning campaign is the most distasteful and arduous task of electoral politics. The nightmare of campaign financing undoubt-edly has deterred some potentially outstanding governors from candidacies, and it exacts its pound of flesh from those who are not restrained. Corrupt relationships with special interest groups often find their genesis in a campaign fund-raising squeeze. Governors are sometimes haunted throughout their terms by investigations of financing irregularities in their past campaigns. Their effectiveness and programs can suffer irreparable harm as a consequence.

The cost of running for governor today has escalated fantastically in a relatively short time. According to Coleman Ransone, the cost of an average gubernatorial campaign in 1956 was about $100,000, with a $300,000 total in heavily populated states, and these figures did not allow for "political skulldug-gery."[72] Ransone fully acknowledged that his estimates were only guesses, since the lack of auditing and verifiable reporting standards made it impossible to determine campaign costs. (Not until the Watergate scandals did this situation improve. Laws regulating contributions, expenditures, and disclosures were passed in many states in Watergate's wake.)

Despite doubts about the accuracy of earlier figures, there is little question, even allowing for inflation, that costs have skyrocketed over the years, and television is a fundamental cause. The flamboyant politics of the Deep South, the highly personalized campaigning of the Mountain West, and the polyglot pitch of the Northeast have yielded, in whole or in part, to media-centered campaigning. Even campaigns that center around gimmicks like nonstop hand-shaking (Jimmy Carter of Georgia, 1970), walking across the state (Daniel Walker of Illinois, 1972), a lunch-pail working man's campaign (Cliff Finch of Mississippi, 1975), and "sweeping clean" brooms (David Boren of Oklahoma, 1974) depend upon television to communicate the message to a mass audience. Especially in densely populated states, "You have to get your votes wholesale, not retail," as Governor Pat Brown of California put it.[73]

In 1953 gubernatorial candidate Robert Meyner of New Jersey spent just $12,000 for a twelve-hour telethon; several minutes of prime time twenty years later cost much more. However, while Thomas E. Patterson and Robert D. McClure have suggested that television does not wield the vote-swaying power often attributed to it,[74] candidates are spending fortunes on it. In the 1970 gubernatorial races the major party candidates reported expenditures of $9 million on television and radio advertisements, and since reporting standards were so loose in most states, the total was probably much higher.[75] Not many candidates have the experience and advantages of, for example, newscaster Tom McCall of Oregon, and firms that produce and package media campaigns and train the candidate in effective use of television have become essentials of the electoral art.[76] Campaign management is a major industry, and expensive new technology (in areas like polling, communications media, literature, mass mailing, telephone banks, canvassing, and voter registration) is a key component of most successful gubernatorial campaigns.[77]

Thus television and the new campaign technology have contributed the lion's share of the increase in campaign costs, but the spread of two-party competition and the growth of the independent vote are subsidiary causes. In Florida, as the Republican party emerged from political dormancy and began seriously to challenge the long-dominant Democrats, campaign expenditures multiplied.[78] The simultaneous decline of strong party organizations across the country meant that the candidate often had to develop his own organization to get out the vote and raise funds, and these tasks required major financial outlays. It was also more difficult and costly to reach the electorally essential pool of independent voters who no longer possessed the built-in cue of party identification. In sum, to paraphrase Abraham Lincoln, it took more effort and more money to find 'em and vote 'em.

Table 4-19 is an attempt to gauge the magnitude of gubernatorial campaign spending in a single election year, that of 1970. Figures are provided for every state that held a gubernatorial election, though only for major party candidates. Compiled from the files of the Citizens' Research Foundation, these expenditures can only be regarded as estimates and are not necessarily the official figures supplied by the candidates or the states. Since reporting requirements were anything but stringent at the time, the totals are probably lower than they should be.

Overall, $11.4 million was spent in party primaries and $51.4 million in general elections for governor in 1970. The expenditures vary widely from state to state by reason of differing voting age, population, party competitiveness, perceived closeness of each race, and personal wealth held by a candidate and access to other funds. Primary costs were often low because a candidate was unopposed or virtually so. In the South the primary was sometimes more expensive than the general, since the fiercest opposition came from within the party, as in George Wallace's Alabama and Jimmy Carter's Georgia, but there was also evidence of the GOP Southern reawakening in both South Carolina and Arkansas, where Democratic nominees John West and Dale Bumpers had their toughest battles in the fall (as reflected by the pattern of their expenditures).

The Rockefeller brothers, Nelson of New York and Winthrop of Arkansas, illustrate that heavy spending can both help and hurt a candidate. In 1970 Nelson Rockefeller's infusion of $6.2 million in the general election did the trick for him and reversed a long, early lead for Democrat Arthur J. Goldberg who ran a "poverty" campaign of less than a million dollars by comparison. (This was not the first time Rockefeller money had bought the governor's chair for Nelson. Michael Kramer and Sam Roberts estimated that $30 million was spent by Nelson, his brother and sisters, and his stepmother for his four New York gubernatorial campaigns and other political activities between elections. So overwhelmed was the opposition that Kramer and Roberts claim that Rockefeller's 1962, 1966, and 1970 opponents combined spent less than the gift taxes paid on the Rockefeller family's contributions.[79]) Winthrop Rockefeller in 1970 was not so politically fortunate in Arkansas as his brother was in New York, and

Table 4-19
Campaign Expenditures in the 1970 Gubernatorial Elections

State	Gubernatorial Candidates[a]	Total Expenditures[b]		Expenditures in General Election	
		Primary[c]	General	Per Vote[d]	Per Person of Voting Age[e]
Alabama	*George C. Wallace (D)	$930,000	$96,000	$ .15	$ .05
Alaska	*William Egan (D)	94,000	79,000	1.87	.42
	Keith Miller (R)	50,000	61,000	1.64	.33
Arizona	Raul Castro (D)	10,600	59,000	.29	.05
	*Jack Williams (R)	1,100	93,000	.44	.08
Arkansas	*Dale Bumpers (D)	180,000	293,679	.78	.24
	Winthrop Rockefeller (R)	60,000	1,314,162	6.66	1.07
California	Jesse Unruh (D)	474,980	904,743	.31	.07
	*Ronald Reagan (R)	917,854	2,584,779	.75	.20
Colorado	*John Love (R)	3,211	125,000	.36	.09
	Mark Hogan (D)	160	250,000	.83	.18
Connecticut	Emilio Daddario (D)	—	577,448	1.15	.30
	*Thomas J. Meskill (R)	—	513,244	.88	.27
Florida	Claude R. Kirk, Jr. (R)	407,079	382,231	.51	.08
	*Reubin Askew (D)	392,194	345,353	.35	.07
Georgia	*Jimmy Carter (D)	1,000,000	240,000	.39	.08
	Hal Suit (R)	300,000	150,000	.35	.05
Hawaii	*John A. Burns (D)	774,679	274,861	1.99	.54
	Samuel P. King (R)	281,586	560,000	5.53	1.10
Idaho	*Cecil D. Andrus (D)	4,900	56,000	.44	.13
	Don Samuelson (R)	2,300	68,000	.58	.15
Kansas	*Robert B. Docking (D)	—	260,000	.64	.18
	Kent Frizzell (R)	100,000	212,000	.64	.15

Table 4-19 (cont.)

State	Gubernatorial Candidates[a]	Total Expenditures[b] Primary[c]	Total Expenditures[b] General	Expenditures in General Election Per Vote[d]	Expenditures in General Election Per Person of Voting Age[e]
Maine	James S. Erwin (R)	12,000	109,223	.67	.17
	*Kenneth M. Curtis (D)	50	185,140	1.13	.30
Maryland	*Marvin Mandel (D)	500,000	1,073,839	1.68	.44
	C. Stanley Blair (R)	97,289	375,000	1.19	.15
Massachusetts	*Francis W. Sargent (R)	313,734	690,000	.65	.19
	Kevin H. White (D)	187,084	500,000	.63	.14
Michigan	*William G. Milliken (R)	1,800	600,000	.45	.11
	Sander Levin (D)	230,000	445,000	.34	.08
Minnesota	*Wendell Anderson (D)	58	502,595	.68	.22
	Douglas Head (R)	50	449,461	.72	.19
Nebraska	Norbert Tiemann (R)	133,399	43,000	.21	.05
	*J.J. Exon (D)	28,927	31,000	.12	.03
Nevada	*Mike O'Callaghan (D)	36,000	130,000	1.84	.40
	Ed Fike (R)	31,000	158,000	2.45	.49
New Hampshire	*Walter R. Peterson, Jr. (R)	30,215	48,868	.48	.10
	Roger J. Crowley, Jr. (D)	22,996	19,000	.19	.04
New Mexico	*Bruce King (D)	23,962	42,000	.28	.07
	Peter V. Domenici (R)	20,000	90,000	.67	.15
New York	*Nelson A. Rockefeller (R)	584,800	6,210,627	1.97	.53
	Arthur J. Goldberg (D)	432,000	850,000	.38	.07
Ohio	*John J. Gilligan (D)	123,581	1,419,686	.82	.22
	Roger Cloud (R)	391,983	492,300	.36	.08
Oklahoma	*David Hall (D)	96,000	207,888	.61	.13
	Dewey Bartlett (R)	500	288,262	.86	.17
Oregon	*Tom McCall (R)	43,229	203,509	.55	.15
	Robert W. Straub (D)	19,917	113,268	.38	.08
Pennsylvania	*Milton J. Shapp (D)	1,100,000	1,603,005	.78	.21
	Raymond J. Broderick (R)	144,000	767,040		

State	Candidate				
Rhode Island	*Frank Licht (D)	11,000	350,000	2.02	.57
	Herbert F. DeSimone (R)	–	300,000	1.75	.49
South Carolina	*John C. West (D)	400	500,000	2.00	.32
	Albert W. Watson (R)	250	450,000	2.03	.29
South Dakota	*Richard F. Kneip (D)	1,700	49,000	.37	.12
	Frank Farrar (R)	19,000	94,000	.87	.23
Tennessee	John J. Hooker, Jr. (D)	304,000	306,000	.60	.12
	*Winfield Dunn (R)	60,000	464,000	.81	.19
Texas	*Preston Smith (D)	57,044	346,000	.29	.05
	Paul W. Eggers (R)	58,681	620,000	.60	.09
Vermont	Leo O'Brien, Jr. (D)	7,417	63,000	.95	.23
	*Deane C. Davis (R)	7,162	162,000	1.85	.59
Wisconsin	*Patrick J. Lucey (D)	100,000	225,000	.31	.08
	Jack B. Olson (R)	440	369,000	.61	.14
Wyoming	John J. Rooney (D)	60	11,241	.26	.05
	*Stanley K. Hathaway (R)	–	20,343	.27	.10
Totals		$11,216,371	$51,769,803	$ .64f	$ .15f

D = Democrat; R = Republican

*Denotes election victor

Sources: Compiled from the file reports and tallies of the Citizens' Research Foundation in Princeton, N.J. Voting age population figures are from the U.S. Bureau of the Census, *Statistical Abstract of the United States: 1973*, 94th ed. (Washington D.C.: U.S. Government Printing Office, 1973), p. 32, Table No. 37.

aOnly major party candidates are included in this tabulation. States not listed did not have a gubernatorial election in 1970.

bThese figures are compilations both of officially reported expenditures and of estimates of unreported expenditures. Note that the table measures only *expenditures* of funds; a candidate's warchest may have been considerably larger or smaller than the amount actually spent.

cWhenever run-off (or second) primaries were held, expenses for both primaries were added together.

dThe expenditure totals and voting results for the *general* elections only are used to compute this column.

eIn 1970 the voting age was 21 in all but four states: Kentucky and Georgia (age 18), Alaska (age 19), and Hawaii (age 20). The voting age populations as of 1970 are used here. (The voting age was lowered to 18 in all states effective for the 1971 elections.)

fMedian figure.

he lost badly. In fact, one of the principal causes of his defeat was the controversy created by his campaign expenditure of $1.4 million in a tiny state. His victorious rival, Dale Bumpers, incurred expenses of under a half-million dollars.

Winthrop Rockefeller was clearly the exception to the general rule that winners spend more—a lot more—than losers. Out of the 11 million-dollar candidates in 1970, 9 ended up in the winner's circle: George Wallace (D-Alabama), Ronald Reagan (R-California), Jimmy Carter (D-Georgia), John Burns (D-Hawaii), Marvin Mandel (D-Maryland), Francis Sargent (R-Massachusetts), Nelson Rockefeller (R-New York), John Gilligan (D-Ohio), and Milton Shapp (D-Pennsylvania). (Reagan's opponent, Democrat Jesse Unruh, also ran a million-dollar campaign, but Reagan outspent him by three to one.) Further, 21 of the 34 gubernatorial winners (61.8 percent) in 1970 spent more in the general election than the major party candidate they defeated. Yet large sums of money cannot insure election. In 6 of the 7 races where a challenger succeeded in beating the incumbent, the incumbent had made a larger financial outlay. Nevertheless, a well-heeled candidacy is an advantage that few gubernatorial aspirants would refuse if given the choice.

The expenditure per vote can serve as a measure of the productivity of a candidate's campaign dollar, and this data is also found in Table 4-19. The figures range from Democrat J.J. Exon's miniscule 12¢ per vote in his successful Nebraska bid to an incredible $6.66 per vote by Winthrop Rockefeller. Republican Samuel King of Hawaii did not really spend outlandishly, but got so few votes for his efforts that his per-vote total was $5.53. Other high spending races by this calculation were those in Maryland, Nevada, Rhode Island, South Carolina, Vermont, and Alaska. The last case is especially understandable in view of the state's size and the inaccessibility of some voters. Nelson Rockefeller's total is less outstanding when the votes he received are considered; even though he spent five times more in total dollar figures than Winthrop, his per-vote figure is less than a third of his brother's.

Low-spending candidates, who were either unopposed or poorly financed, included George Wallace (D-Alabama), Raul Castro (D-Arizona), Jesse Unruh (D-California), and Roger Crowley (D-New Hampshire). Judging from the election results, Democrat Preston Smith of Texas, who won only narrowly with a 29¢ per-vote expenditure, and Norbert Tiemann of Nebraska, who was actually unseated while spending just 21¢ per vote, were too overconfident in their reelection bids. The median per-vote figure for all 1970 gubernatorial contests was 64¢, which is close to double the 33¢ per-vote cost calculated for twelve general elections for governor between 1964 and 1968.[80]

The mushrooming of campaign costs is clearly apparent, but when all the above per-vote costs are examined in another perspective, they seem much less outrageous. The last column in Table 4-19 measures a candidate's expenditure in terms of the population of voting age, which is of course the group every nominee addresses. On this scale 23 of the 67 spent 10¢ or less to influence each potential vote, and almost three-quarters of the total (50 of 67) expended less than 25¢ a voter.

Money and Politics

As reasonable as campaign costs seem on paper, they present monstrous problems for both candidates and citizens. Somehow gubernatorial aspirants are supposed to raise hundreds of thousands of dollars without entangling themselves directly or indirectly with special interest groups and without making prior commitments, overt or understood, that will compromise their tenures if they are elected. Such a feat can be done only with the greatest difficulty, if it can ever really be done at all. Even the apostles of reform in campaign financing find themselves inextricably bound to opulent lobby groups or stealthily seeking legal loopholes when they assume the mantle of gubernatorial candidate.[81]

In 1974 Georgia Democratic candidate George Busbee, the prime sponsor of his state's new campaign finance statute, welcomed the support of major banks despite their interest in a pending legislative matter and in the process cleverly avoided some of his own reform law's requirements. Texas Governor Dolph Briscoe, another candidate who had won support as a reformer, contributed a total of $645,000 in gifts and loans to his bid for another term in 1974. Pennsylvania's progressive and able Governor Milton Shapp was not immune either. The Democratic State Central Committee tried to extract several hundred thousand dollars in contributions for Shapp from state employees. A similar fund-raising scheme among laborers and contractors in the Pennsylvania Highway Department resulted in the conviction of a Democratic party official. California's Edmund G. Brown, Jr., was one of the staunchest advocates of "Proposition 9," a stringent new campaign finance law passed at the same time Brown was elected in 1974. Brown spent about $2 million just in the general election; Proposition 9, had it been in effect, would have limited him to $1.26 million.[82]

All of the above illustrations as well as dozens of others that could be cited occurred after the Watergate-induced rush to reform. Between 1972 and 1976 44 states passed new and generally better campaign finance laws.[83] The laws usually required much greater financial disclosure, of both sources and amounts of contributions. Limits on overall campaign expenditures were enacted in 35 states, and contributions by individuals and groups were capped, normally at $1,000 apiece. Other limitations that were features of some state plans were later invalidated by the Supreme Court in its January 1976 ruling, *Buckley v. Valeo*.[84] Ceilings on expenditures by the candidate himself on his own campaign were disallowed, thereby again granting personally wealthy candidates a major electoral advantage. Contributions in support of a candidate by other individuals were also freed of all restraints so long as the spending was done "independent-ly" of the candidate's knowledge.

However, even without the changes inflicted by the Supreme Court ruling, the new laws were not enough to solve the basic problem. Contribution reporting schemes are important and disclosure requirements are useful to the public in evaluating candidates, but they do not prevent the development of cozy relationships between gubernatorial candidates and special interest groups since money, no matter what the ceiling is, must still flow from interest groups to campaign war chests. Debts are incurred, whether or not they are acknowl-edged as such by the debtors or the creditors. Thus, less representative and even more corrupt government may result. What is more, the cost of campaigns can only continue to climb, escalated by inflation pressures, television costs, and expensive new campaign techniques and technologies, and trying to reduce the functional costs of running for office would be the most difficult of the solutions available to the general problem. Ceilings on contributions by individu-als and groups probably reduce the special interest influence on the governor, but they also serve to make the collection of an adequate campaign treasury an even more burdensome task. Finally, the Supreme Court's ruling could easily negate the impact of formal ceilings, and there appears to be no legal way to neutralize the Court-given advantage to wealthy candidates.

All signs thus point to public financing of gubernatorial campaigns in both primaries and general elections as the best available answer. Similar to the system operated initially for presidential candidates in 1976, a gubernatorial candidate for a major party nomination could qualify for "matching funds" (money from the public till matching each dollar raised by the candidate) after a certain number of contributions to the candidate of very limited size had been received from a set percentage of the cities and counties in the state. For the general election an equal and adequate amount of money could be offered each major party candidate from the public coffers. By accepting the money (and freeing themselves of the arduous task of fund-raising), the candidates would agree to accept no contributions from anyone else (self and family included).

There are drawbacks to public financing, naturally. Some object to the use of public tax money for this particular purpose, and the question of inclusion in the scheme for independent candidates, and under what criteria, is a thorny one. Nevertheless, from the standpoint of the governorship, the type of person elected to the office and the quality of government that results, public financing is very desirable. Talented persons deterred from running for governor by the awful specter of fund raising could be more easily enticed to serve the common weal, and all governors would be less beholden to special interests that may prevent their ministering to the real interests of their states.

A Note on Voter Turnout

Voter turnout would normally appear in any listing of electoral factors that might indicate changes in the governorship. Increased participation by voters in gubernatorial elections would suggest greater interest among citizens in state government, as well as widespread recognition of governors as officials who can affect people's lives in major ways. (More evidence of this would be provided if turnout increases for gubernatorial elections surpassed those for president or U.S. senator in the last quarter-century.) The governors themselves, and their policies, would probably benefit from a larger turnout of voters since a clearer mandate would be given. Votes can work a governor's will on recalcitrant legislators and other elected statewide officers as no other commodity.

Unfortunately severe methodological difficulties prevent useful comparisons of voter turnouts over the period 1950 to 1975. The most crippling of these problems is the simultaneous election of governors and many other political officers in all but five states. For any given election, it is impossible to separate out the voters who come to the polls primarily (or wholly) to vote for governor as opposed to U.S. representative, U.S. senator, or president.[85] To cite an example, an increase or decrease in turnout from one gubernatorial election to another may be due to a heated or an unopposed race for a nongubernatorial office. Each office filled at the polls probably adds some increment to the turnout, but this increment is both indeterminate and highly variable.

There is no way around this multicollinearity (as statisticians would classify the dilemma); only extensive attitudinal surveys on successive election days in the states could furnish even a partial answer. There are five states that elect a governor at odd times, apart from all federal offices,[86] but four of them are in the Southern and Border states, where special conditions (described in a later paragraph) disqualify their general election turnouts from serious examination. Only in New Jersey, which elects a governor in the year following each presidential contest, are gubernatorial returns over the last twenty-five years sufficiently reliable and distilled for proper analysis. While absolute increases in turnout were normally recorded from one election year to the next for each major office, participation in elections for governor increased at a greater rate than that for U.S. senator or president. The gubernatorial election of 1969 showed a 30.7 percent increase in turnout over 1953, while the 1970 nonpresidential year Senate contest marked only a 21 percent gain over 1954, and just a 24.1 percent increase in the presidential vote from 1952 to 1972 was noted.[87] It would be foolhardy, however, to suggest even a tentative conclusion from a sample of the turnout in a single state.

Simultaneous elections are by no means the only obstacles to an examination of voter turnout. In all Southern states (and some Border states), for instance, voter turnout in all general elections has spurted since the 1950s. However, the increase cannot be laid to the attractiveness of any particular office or level of government, but rather to the abolition of the poll tax and the elimination of literacy tests that helped to minimize the region's electorate for much of this century. A coordinate development has been the decline of the Democratic party primary with the growth in two-party competition, which thus provides yet another explanation for burgeoning turnout in general elections in the South. Perhaps the improved delivery of services by a new and better breed of governor has played a part in the South's November surge to the polls, but again, this is impossible to determine.

The fact that the franchise was extended to eighteen- to twenty-year-olds in 1971 further complicates any turnout analysis. Studies have indicated that young voters cast ballots much less frequently than do their elders as a result of the young's mobility, occupational patterns, loose identification with a party and lack of political information, and an unstructured social position in the community.[88] Thus the pool of potential voters was considerably expanded by the eighteen-year-old vote, but the proportion of probable voters in the electorate declined.[89] Even where the absolute turnout increased a bit after 1971, the proportional turnout usually decreased. The result is, again, that turnout varies because of a factor completely independent of the actions of governors, gubernatorial candidates, or state governments. As mentioned previously, survey data for gubernatorial elections (which could partially account for the differential in turnout between young and old so that the raw turnout figures could be appropriately adjusted) do not exist.

Finally, the most crucial determinant of turnout may not be the candidates, or the issues, or the offices at stake, but yet another electoral element that bears no relation to the governorship: the process of registering to vote. As three political scientists concluded in their study of registration's effect on voting participation: "Local differences in the turnout for elections are to a large extent related to local differences in rates of registration, and these in turn reflect to a considerable degree local differences in the rules governing, and arrangements for handling, the registering of voters."[90] For a combination of reasons, then, a study of changing voter participation in gubernatorial elections is impractical, and conclusions about the governorship drawn from the data that are available would probably be inaccurate and misleading.

In sum, just as governors are actors on a larger political stage, so are their dominions, the states. As one of the three component levels of the federal system, the states interact in ever-changing ways with governments at the national and local levels. The states' role in the federal system has been a diminished one for much of this century, and this fact can hinder even the most resourceful and energetic of governors. There are indications, however, that the stock of the states has risen, even if it is not yet blue chip. This pivotal development is the subject of the next chapter.

Notes

1. See *The Federalist*, Book II, Numbers 71 and 72. Alexander Hamilton's arguments are summarized and discussed in Byron Abernathy, *Some Persisting Questions Concerning the Constitutional State Executive* (Lawrence: Governmental Research Center, University of Kansas, 1960), pp. 80-82.

2. Coleman B. Ransone, Jr., *The Office of Governor in the United States* (University: University of Alabama Press, 1956), p. 229.

3. As quoted in Council of State Governments, *The Book of the States, 1952-1953* (Chicago, Ill.: Council of State Governments, 1952), p. 150.

4. See Leslie Lipson, *The American Governor: From Figurehead to Leader* (Chicago: University of Chicago Press, 1949), p. 49.

5. Joseph E. Kallenbach, "Constitutional Limitations on Reeligibility of National and State Chief Executive," *American Political Science Review* 46 (June 1952):454. Reprinted with permission.

6. Interview with the author, August 5, 1976, Olympia, Wash.

7. Nancy Roberts, *The Governor* (New York: McNally and Loftin, 1972), p. 44.

8. Neal R. Peirce, *The Deep South States* (New York: W.W. Norton, 1973), p. 324.

9. There is one difference, however. The 22nd Amendment sets an *absolute* limit of two terms on the president. All states with term limitations but Delaware and Missouri allow a two-term governor to be reelected after a term served by someone else intervenes.

10. Interview with the author, July 30, 1976, Trenton, N.J.

11. Correspondence with the author; governor asked not to be identified.

12. This number was reduced further in November 1977, when the voters of North Carolina gave their approval to a state constitutional amendment allowing the governor to succeed himself once.

13. Peirce, *The Deep South States*, p. 130.

14. Houston completed neither term. He resigned the Tennessee term and was popularly removed from the Texas governorship because he opposed the state's secession from the Union at the start of the Civil War.

15. Joseph Schlesinger, "The State Executive," in Herbert Jacobs and Kenneth Vines (eds.), *Politics in the American States: A Comparative Analysis* (Boston: Little, Brown, 1971), p. 237.

16. Ransone, *The Office of Governor*, p. 234.

17. Ibid.

18. Joseph E. Kallenbach, *The American Chief Executive: The Presidency and the Governorship* (New York: Harper & Row, 1966), p. 202.

19. Nine "outstanding governors" have been eliminated from this tally since they had not yet completed their first terms as of 1977. See Chapter 2 for a list and discussion of outstanding governors.

20. "Opening Address to National Governor's Conference," *State Government* 29 (August 1956):145, 162.

21. See Ira Sharkansky, *The Politics of Taxing and Spending,* (Indianapolis: Bobbs-Merrill, 1969), pp. 7-10.

22. Deil Wright and David Stephenson, "The States as Middlemen: Five Fiscal Dilemmas," *State Government* 51 (Summer 1968):104-05.

23. Richard J. Hughes, "A Moral Recommitment for New Jersey: Special

Message to the Legislature," Office of the Governor, Trenton, N.J., April 25, 1968.

24. Louis Harris, "Why the Odds are Against a Governor's Becoming President," *Public Opinion Quarterly* 4 (July 1959):370.

25. Gerald Pomper, "Governors, Money, and Votes," in Pomper (ed.), *Elections In America* (New York: Dodd, Mead, 1968), Chapter 6, pp. 126-48, 270-73.

26. Interview with the author, August 4, 1976, Portland, Ore.

27. For a detailed look at Furcolo's political collapse and the tax that brought it about, see John P. Mallan and George Blackwood, "The Tax That Beat a Governor: The Ordeal of Massachusetts," in Alan F. Westin (ed.), *The Uses of Power* (New York: Harcourt, Brace & Jovanovich, 1962), pp. 285-322.

28. The voters' perceptions of the candidates and their tax stances were not quite this clear-cut, but tax policy was clearly the primary campaign issue. See Leon Epstein, "Electoral Decision and Policy Mandate: An Empirical Example," *Public Opinion Quarterly* 28 (Winter 1964):564-67.

29. William C. Havard (ed.), *The Changing Politics of the South* (Baton Rouge: Louisiana State University Press, 1969), pp. 257-58.

30. Earl Black, "Southern Governors and Political Change: Campaign Stances on Racial Segregation and Economic Development, 1950-69," *Journal of Politics* 33 (August 1971):732.

31. Earl Black, *Southern Governors and Civil Rights* (Cambridge, Mass.: Harvard University Press, 1976), pp. vii, 290.

32. National Governors' Conference, *The State of States, 1974* (Washington, D.C.: National Governors' Conference, 1974), p. 9.

33. Ibid.

34. Advisory Commission on Intergovernmental Relations, *American Federalism: Into the Third Century* (Washington, D.C.: ACIR, 1974), p. 33.

35. National Governors' Conference, "The Governors' Messages" (mimeograph), Washington, D.C., February 1975, p. 4.

36. National Governors' Conference, *The State of the States*, p. 4.

37. Ibid., p. 13.

38. National Governors' Conference, "The Governors' Messages," p. 4.

39. Interview with the author, September 13, 1976, Washington, D.C.

40. V.O. Key, Jr., *Southern Politics* (New York: Alfred A. Knopf, 1949), pp. 46-52, 101-05, 303-04.

41. Ransone, *The Office of Governor*, pp. 12-94.

42. Samuel R. Solomon, "United States Governors, 1940-1950," *National Municipal Review* 41 (April 1952):193.

43. The fifteenth strong Republican state, Washington, elected a Democratic governor in 1976.

44. Some of the more important attempts that provided the background for the analysis in this study are: Paul T. David, *Party Strength in the United*

States, 1872-1970 (Charlottesville: University Press of Virginia, 1972); V.O. Key, Jr., *American State Politics: An Introduction* (New York: Alfred A. Knopf, 1956), pp. 98-99; V.O. Key, Jr., *Politics, Parties and Pressure Groups*, 5th ed. (New York: Thomas Y. Crowell, 1964), pp. 314-15; Duane Lockard, *The Politics of State and Local Government* (New York: Macmillan, 1963), pp. 174-81; David G. Pfeiffer, "The Measurement of Inter-Party Competition and Systematic Stability," *American Political Science Review* 61 (1967):457-67; Austin Ranney, "Parties in State Politics," in Jacob and Vines, *Politics in the American States*, pp. 84-91; Austin Ranney and Willmore Rendall, *Democracy and the American Party System* (New York: Harcourt, Brace, and World, 1956), Chapter VII; Ransone, *The Office of Governor*, Chapters I-IV; Joseph A. Schlesinger, "A Two-Dimensional Scheme for Classifying the States According to Degree of Interparty Competition, *American Political Science Review* 49 (1955):1120-46; and Joseph A. Schlesinger, "The Structure of Competition for Office in the American States," *Behavioral Science* 5 (1960):197-217. See also the bibliography in David, ibid., pp. 79-81.

45. Correspondence with the author, July 22, 1976.

46. See the author's *The Democratic Party Primary in Virginia Tantamount to Election No Longer* (Charlottesville: University Press of Virginia, 1977).

47. See Ransone, *The Office of Governor*, pp. 38-72.

48. See ibid., pp. 73-94.

49. Ranney in Jacob and Vines, *Politics in the American States*, p. 87.

50. Interview with the author, 24 August, 1976, Philadelphia, Pa.

51. Lockard, *The Politics of State and Local Government*, pp. 201-02.

52. Ranney and Rendall, *Democracy and the American Party System*, p. 118.

53. See Thomas R. Dye, *Politics, Economics and the Public: Policy Outcomes in the American States* (Chicago: Rand-McNally, 1966). Dye's conclusions are confirmed in an independent analysis by Richard E. Dawson and James Robinson, "Inter-Party Competition, Economic Variables, and Welfare Policies in the American States," *Journal of Politics* 25 (1963):265-89.

54. Jack L. Walker, "The Diffusion of Innovations among the American States," *American Political Science Review* 63 (September 1969):883. The ten states scoring highest on Walker's innovative scale were New York, Massachusetts, California, New Jersey, Michigan, Connecticut, Pennsylvania, Oregon, Colorado and Wisconsin. Only Oregon is not judged to be two-party competitive as of 1975.

55. See Walter De Vries and Lance Tarrance, *The Ticket-Splitter: A New Force in American Politics* (Grand Rapids, Mich.: William B. Eerdmans, 1972).

56. These states are Virginia and New Jersey (elections in November of the year following presidential elections), Mississippi and Kentucky (elections in November of the year before presidential elections), and Louisiana (elections in October of the year prior to presidential elections).

57. National Municipal League, Committee on State Government, *Model State Constitution with Explanatory Articles* (New York: National Municipal League, 1948), p. 66.

58. Key, *American State Politics*, p. 48.

59. E.E. Schattschneider, *Party Government* (New York: Holt, Rinehart, and Winston, 1942), p. 129.

60. Lockard, *The Politics of State and Local Government*, pp. 167-69.

61. V.O. Key, Jr., and Corinne Silverman, "Party and Separation of Powers: A Panorama of Practice in the States," in Frank Munger (ed.), *American State Politics: Readings for Comparative Analysis* (New York: Thomas Y. Crowell, 1966), p. 444, Table 1.

62. Ibid., pp. 457-58.

63. For a detailed discussion of each of these factors, see the author's *Aftermath of Armageddon: An Analysis of the 1973 Virginia Gubernatorial Election* (Charlottesville: Institute of Government, University of Virginia, 1975), pp. 92-110.

64. Angus Campbell and Warren E. Miller, "The Motivational Bases of Straight and Split Ticket Voting," *American Political Science Review* 51 (June 1957):293-312.

65. There was some movement over the twenty-five-year period, however, as five states added and five states dropped the straight-party ballot option. Obviously, no net change resulted.

66. Angus Campbell et al., *The American Voter: An Abridgement* (New York: John Wiley and Sons, 1964), p. 83.

67. De Vries and Tarrance, *The Ticket-Splitter*, p. 61.

68. Interview with the author, July 30, 1976, Trenton, N.J.

69. Interview with the author, August 4, 1976, Portland, Ore.

70. Interview with the author, August 4, 1976, Portland, Ore.

71. Ransone, *The Office of Governor*, pp. 52-56.

72. Ibid., pp. 105-06.

73. Telephone interview with the author, August 8, 1976.

74. Thomas E. Patterson and Robert D. McClure, *The Unseeing Eye: The Myth of Television Power in National Politics* (New York: Putman, 1976).

75. As quoted from *The New York Times*, June 18, 1971, in Thad L. Beyle and J. Oliver Williams (eds.), *The American Governor in Behavioral Perspective* (New York: Harper & Row, 1972), p. 3.

76. See Stanley Kelley, Jr., *Professional Public Relations and Political Power* (Baltimore: Johns Hopkins Press, 1956); and Joseph Napolitan, *The Election Game and How to Win It* (New York: Doubleday, 1972).

77. See Dan Nimmo, *The Political Persuaders: The Techniques of Modern Election Campaigns* (Englewood Cliffs, N.J.: Prentice-Hall, 1970); Paul Van Riper, *Handbook of Practical Politics*, 3rd ed. (New York: Harper & Row, 1967); and William T. Murphy, Jr., and Edward Schneier, *Vote Power* (New York: Anchor Press/Doubleday, 1974).

78. Elston Roady and Carl D. McMurray, *Republican Campaign Financing in Florida, 1963-1967* (Princeton, N.J.: Citizens' Research Foundation, Study No. 15, 1969), p. 36, Table 8.

79. See Michael Kramer and Sam Roberts, *"I Never Wanted to be Vice-President of Anything!": An Investigative Biography of Nelson Rockefeller* (New York: Basic Books, 1976).

80. David Adamany, *Campaign Finance in America* (Belmont, Calif.: Wadsworth, 1972), pp. 36-38, Table 2.6.

81. All of the cases cited in the following paragraphs are taken from the articles comprising Herbert E. Alexander (ed.), *Campaign Money: Reform and Reality in the States* (New York: The Free Press, 1976).

82. Still, Brown's spending was hardly exceptional, and indeed a bit under average recent expenditures for statewide offices in California. See John R. Owens, *Trends in Campaign Spending in California, 1958-1970: Tests of Factors Influencing Costs* (Princeton, N.J.: Citizens' Research Foundation, Study No. 22, 1973), especially pp. 56-59, 63, Tables 14, 15, and 17.

83. Alexander, *Campaign Money*, pp. 1-6.

84. Ibid., p. 6.

85. Even in those states that elect a governor in nonpresidential years, all U.S. representatives and usually one U.S. senator are elected simultaneously with the governor.

86. See note 56.

87. The election years selected were dictated by the U.S. Senate contests, since the last Senate election in New Jersey held in a nonpresidential year occurred in 1970. The gubernatorial and presidential election years noted are those nearest chronologically to the Senate years. This is not to say, however, that the various years are equivalents since political conditions differ considerably from one year to the next. Still, given many constraints, these are the best comparisons that can be made.

88. See Seymour Martin Lipset, *Political Man* (New York: Doubleday, 1960), pp. 202, 209-11; and Angus Campbell et al., *The American Voter* (New York: John Wiley and Sons, 1960), pp. 496-97.

89. The "potential electorate" consists of the entire population legally entitled to vote. Turnout should always be measured as the percentage of the potential, rather than the registered, electorate since registration figures have been notoriously inaccurate (or fraudulent) in many regions of the United States for much of the country's history. Some states also purge their voting rolls periodically, thereby eliminating many thousands of voters who have not cast a ballot in a certain number of years. A researcher who relies on official registration totals, then, can find that his turnout percentages will sometimes fluctuate solely because of the purges. By contrast, the potential electorate for any state can be calculated easily and accurately from official U.S. Census Bureau publications.

90. See Stanley Kelley, Jr., Richard E. Ayres, and William G. Bowen, "Registration and Voting: Putting First Things First," *American Political Science Review* 61 (June 1967):359-79.

5 The States and Federalism: New Partnerships

Let's stop fooling ourselves. We don't have sovereign states anymore. All we have are a bunch of provinces. . . . We are becoming conveyor belts for policies signed, sealed and delivered in Washington.[1]

—Anonymous state governor

In the last four years I've seen the beginnings of change and, I guess, I'm a little reluctant to leave office now since I see that things are beginning to come back our way.[2]

—Governor Daniel J. Evans of Washington

For more than a decade after the Revolutionary War had been won, the United States of America was little more than a loose confederation of nearly autonomous states. The national government was clearly subjugated in a system of states' sovereignty. Although some of their authority was yielded in 1789 in recognition of the necessity of an energized central government, the states retained a decisive power edge in the federal configuration. Less than two centuries later America had come full circle. Government in Washington ruled the federal roost—a product of the gradual accumulation by circumstances and intent of responsibility and authority in a wide range of fields.[3] Anticipating the situation alleged by the first governor quoted above, Leonard D. White predicted in 1953: "If present trends continue for another quarter-century, the states may be left hollow shells, operating primarily as the field districts of federal departments. . . ."[4]

At the third level of federalism, local government, the states found themselves eclipsed and despised even though basic control of localities rested with the states. Cities and urban counties in particular, after years of neglect and acrimonious dealing with their states, turned to Washington for solace. Very recently, the pendulum of power has begun to move back a bit from national to state governments. At the same time states and their localities at last found common ground. The states have formed new and still tentative partnerships above and below them in the federal system to their benefit and that of their governors, as the following analysis will show.

States' Rights and States' Wrongs

The national income tax, the Great Depression, and foreign crisis were all partially responsible for the decline of the states in this century. In essence,

171

however, nothing was as pivotal as the states' own lack of will to meet challenges. The states complained that the national government had "preempted" them in the tax field, but there is no evidence to suggest that the states would have adopted the income tax if Washington had not in 1913.[5] The charge that the national government had also encroached upon the prerogatives of the states in policy and functional fields also reverberated from shore to shore from the New Deal onwards, but again, the implication was that the states would have taken action themselves in the same policy fields.[6] More likely, little or nothing would have been done in most states had the national government "returned" the "stolen" fields to the states.

It is not unfair to say that state inaction, even abdication, led to much of the growth of the national government in this century. The states had themselves to blame for a good deal of their federal troubles. As Adlai Stevenson once remarked, "There would be less talk about states' rights if there had been fewer states' wrongs." This subject was one on which he and his two-time presidential rival agreed. President Dwight Eisenhower, in an address to the 1957 National Governors' Conference, condemned the growth of national power at the expense of the states, but chided the governors for allowing it to happen:

Every state failure to meet a pressing public need has created the opportunity, developed the excuse, and fed the temptation for the National Government to poach on the States' preserves. . . . Opposed though I am to needless Federal expansion, since 1953 I have found it necessary to urge Federal action in some areas traditionally reserved to the states. In each instance State inaction, or inadequate action, coupled with undeniable national need, has forced emergency federal intervention.[7]

Fortunately, the federal system is constituted so that none of its components can entirely wither away.[8] Constitutional provisions of the electoral college, senatorial representation, allotment of lower house representation, and the amendment process all depend on the states. The political parties, ingrained American institutions despite their extraconstitutional nature, are essentially state-based units. State presidential primaries have become the most important nominating method for the nation's highest office. The states also have a great deal of autonomy even at their lowest point; one has only to catalogue the legislative products of a single year's state assemblies to recognize this. Writing in 1949 at the nadir of state influence, Harold Laski believed: "It is unquestionable that an American state, even when it is as small as Delaware in area or as small as Nevada in population, has nevertheless, an initiative in law-making to which no English county, and, still less, any French department, can pretend."[9]

It is easy to ignore the significance of many seemingly mundane activities of states as well. Highways, sanitation, water maintenance, and control of food quality have little glamor, no matter how well they are accomplished. Yet, as Ira Sharkansky points out: "It is only after a trip to an exotic part of the world—or after the occasional failure in an American water system—that we think of state programs for licensing and inspection."[10] Further, while the states are rarely credited for an exemplary performance in major fields like higher education, about seven of every ten college students attend state-sponsored and supported institutions.[11]

While increased mobility has undoubtedly reduced the average citizen's emotive loyalties to his state, these feelings are still strong enough to register in most regions of the country. James Madison's contention that ". . . the first and most natural attachments of the people will be to the governments of their respective states" remains valid.[12] This attachment is a cardinal reason why logical schemes to reshape and diminish the number of states, which pop up occasionally, are doomed to fail even though they may very well produce better size and population balances and promote fiscal economies.[13]

The states, too, are vehicles for the expression of diversity, culturally, economically, and politically. Mass communications and other nationalizing trends have tied Americans closer together, but homogenization has not occurred. The United States is a polyglot nation-continent, and differentiation is far more than a luxury. The varying traditions of the states, and the communities that comprise them, are valuable in themselves since they permit the venting and exhibition of divergent backgrounds and desires. Vice President Nelson Rockefeller, long-time governor of one of the most socially variegated states, ascribed the states' vitality to the fact that they ". . . are able to adapt to the tremendous variety that this country has."[14]

This diversity is a link to another fundamental governmental concept in America: the diffusion of power. The national government, in theory, promotes the national interest, but just as the Founding Fathers insisted, the tyranny of the majority is an evil that pragmatically cannot be ignored. The states can provide an important check on national power, on the condition they themselves are vigorous enough to meet the challenge. For most of this century they have not been sufficiently vigorous, but the transformation of the states already described in this study—the result of a stronger governorship, a reapportioned legislature, widespread constitutional revision, large-scale reorganization, and the spread of two-party competition, among other factors—has energized the states and enabled them to compete for authority and responsibility with the national government.

Their quest has been strengthened by Washington's own actions.[15] In the disillusioning aftermath of many Great Society programs, the limitations of the national government were exposed. Many well-intentioned policies had met failure not because they were intrinsically misdirected but because their standards had been nationalized. Decentralization—community control—was the missing element. With the realization that the states and the localities would probably be more successful in administering the same programs, and with the knowledge that the transformed states and their leaders were more capable and willing than ever before to undertake new programs and duties, the national government began to reverse the federal power flow with the historic first steps of revenue sharing and block grants.

Revenue Sharing and Block Grants

A classic and recurrent political hypocrisy in this century was the righteously indignant states' rights governor, railing about national interference with state prerogatives while holding out his hand for Washington's booty. After such a stemwinding speech by Alabama Governor Braxton Comer to a 1908 conference of state chief executives, President Theodore Roosevelt remarked: "We are greatly indebted to Governor Comer for his speech protesting against centralization. Governor, I do not understand that you object to the National Government appropriating money to clear out the Muscle Shoals?"[16]

Now that the states possess and have demonstrated the will to take action, perhaps governors can more easily complain about their federal brethren. From an objective viewpoint, there is indeed much to complain about. In a 1976 report prepared for the Office of Management and Budget in the White House, governors cited thirty-five current illustrations of their problems with the federal bureaucracy.[17] Prominent among them were a lack of coordination among federal departments that resulted in contradictory regulations, heavy and often ridiculously duplicative paperwork requirements on states participating in national programs, and unreasonable administrative delays.

Few would fault the governors for their frustrations, for as virtually anyone with experience in Washington government can attest, dealing with the federal bureaucracy is akin to punching a giant marshmallow. Consider these comments made by governors in the course of interviews or correspondence:

The principal problem is finding out who's doing it to you. . . . How do you find the guy way down in the federal administration who's really making the decision? Now I can go talk to a cabinet member, and he's always affable and we sit down in the office with a cup of coffee while I pour out my woes with the department and he promises to look into it. But what I really need to do is get together with the guy who's going to make that decision.[18]

It comes down to nitpicking regulatory overkill. . . . The rules and regulations written to carry out legislative intent . . . in many, many cases go far beyond the legislative intent and, in some cases, even destroy it.[19]

The biggest problem is that the federal government makes policy without any idea of the practical impact at the state level, particularly financial, so that the result of a new program is often the opposite of that desired. For example, to "help improve child care and get mothers off welfare" the federal government raised day care staffing requirements beyond the financial reach of the states. The result: day care costs went up from $5.00 per day to $15. This leads to putting mothers back on welfare, or mothers who continue to work take children from licensed facilities and place them in cheaper unlicensed ones.[20]

The states were hamstrung most seriously by the primary instrument of federal assistance, the categorical grant-in-aid. In the 1972-73 fiscal year the states received $27 billion in categorical grants, almost 24 percent of their total revenue, which they could hardly afford to do without.[21] However, categorical grants are a quarter carrot and three-quarters stick, encumbered as they are with a multitude of rules and regulations. Most grants are specifically targeted for a policy area or subarea and must be expended entirely there. The states are usually required to match a certain percentage of the grant with their own money without gaining any control over its use. The federal administrative rules that accompany the grant are often so specific that the states are reduced to mere conduits. Frank Smallwood, a professor-turned-state senator in Vermont, gave these impressions of the categorical grant scheme:

Paradoxically, one of our major financial problems resulted from the fact that Vermont received a sizable bundle of federal grants. This meant, however, that we became locked in to matching-fund programs, and we were also overwhelmed by a tangle of federal regulations that made it impossible for us to breathe in many areas. . . . if we refused to accept the federal regulations, we lost our federal grants—which we couldn't afford to lose, because we didn't have sufficient revenues to cover our own programs. The states are really caught in the middle . . . I think the area of federal-state coercion represented the single most frustrating aspect of my entire legislative experience in Montpelier. I'm not so sure that you should never look a gift horse in the mouth.[22]

Some governors have been able to surmount the obstacles and use federal grants-in-aid to strengthen their own political and administrative positions and those of their states by skillful use of grant funds and manipulation of constituent groups.[23] A survey by the Advisory Commission on Intergovernmental Relations indicated that a moderate amount of gubernatorial control over the grant process (at least at the early stages) exists in the states,[24] but most governors would surely agree with their colleague, Thomas Salmon of Vermont, who insisted: "Categorical grants heavily laden with rules, regulations and mindless red tape directly impair governors in their governance."[25]

Washington was eventually convinced, for reasons outlined earlier, that the grant-in-aid was often not the best approach, and with that concession the New Federalism began in the early 1970s.[26] While steps were taken to standardize and fund nationally social welfare payments to the aged, blind, and disabled (with the blessing of financially hard-pressed governors), the main thrust of the new approach was decentralization, and general revenue sharing and "block grants" were the tools.

General revenue-sharing was proposed in Washington as early as 1963, but it was not considered a priority item by the Johnson Administration.[27] A key Democratic group, the big-city mayors, opposed the program since they were fearful of state control of the money; they naturally much preferred to do business with a sympathetic Washington government than with the state administrations and rural-dominated legislatures neglectful of or hostile to urban needs. The National Governors' Conference, however, pushed hard for the proposals and eventually was joined by local government organizations less fearful of more responsive state governments, after the guarantee of some grant of money directly from the federal government without a state intermediary. One governor, Nelson Rockefeller of New York, was particularly instrumental in the adoption of revenue sharing. After securing the endorsement of his proposals by Republican governors, Rockefeller fought hard for the idea at the White House. President Nixon made a specific proposal to Congress for $16 billion in revenue-sharing funds in 1971, and just prior to the 1972 presidential election, after intense battles and extensive revisions of the plan in both House and Senate, revenue sharing was passed and signed into law.

This first act provided for payments of $30.1 billion between 1972 and 1976 to all 50 states and 38,000 local communities to be allocated to each governmental unit by a complicated weighting system based on population, tax burden, and other factors. The money, which had relatively few strings attached, was the antithesis of the categorical grant-in-aid. States were permitted to spend their allotments on anything they desired except that the revenue-sharing funds could not be used to match other federal grants and the states were required to maintain the same level of aid as before to their local governments from nonrevenue-sharing money.

In late 1976 the Congress passed and the president signed a renewal and reform of revenue sharing.[28] The program was extended at least through 1980, the funding mechanism was changed from a trust fund to guaranteed entitlement financing, and the authorization levels were increased to $6.65 billion per year (with a possible rise to $6.85 billion after 1977). Importantly, the provision barring use of revenue-sharing monies as matching funds for other grants was abolished.

Revenue sharing, in terms of dollars, is the largest domestic aid bill ever enacted, and in 1975 comprised 14.3 percent of the estimated total federal aid to state and local governments.[29] While revenue sharing amounts to only 2 to 6.5 percent of the general fund budgets in the states, the consequences of the program's discontinuance would be very serious.[30] Personal income taxes would have to rise from 5 to 27 percent over their current levels, or if sales taxes were to substitute, a 4 to 20 percent increase would be necessary. Severe program cuts might be necessary as well. If education was chosen to carry the burden, for example, school aid would have to be reduced from 4 to 12 percent, or higher education tuition hiked by 59 to 131 percent.

Revenue sharing is hardly a faultless program. Due to its newness and the natural reluctance of Congress and the president to permit funds they have raised to be spent by others, states and localities have been unsure that they could count on revenue sharing in the future. Thus, they utilized the money for nonrecurrent capital improvements and expenses (like highways, public buildings, and so forth) instead of operating expenses for social welfare problems, which might be considered more deserving recipients. Another of revenue sharing's shortcomings is its distribution to every locality, regardless of need. Some additional selectivity would be advisable. Still, the program has proved to be a major advance for the states and has garnered the strong support of the public.[31] Evaluations of revenue sharing have been positive and heartening from several perspectives. One team of researchers from The Brookings Institution, for instance, reported that in about one-half of all jurisdictions surveyed, revenue sharing was resulting in the involvement of more groups in the policy-making process and that additional progress on this front was to be expected.[32]

The second tool of New Federalism, the block grant, may prove even more important in the long run than revenue sharing.[33] Under the block grant concept, states receive federal money to use in broad policy areas with very few strings attached. Block grants, accounting for about a tenth of total federal assistance to state and local governments in 1975, have been established in the fields of community development, manpower, law enforcement, social services, and health. All but one of these (law enforcement) originated in a merger of separate categorical grants. By 1975 block grants totalled over $5 billion after a remarkably rapid growth. (There were no block grants at all only a decade earlier.) Besides strengthening states and localities in the federal system, the concept helps to overcome some of the often overwhelming bureaucratic problems described earlier. President Ford offered this accurate evaluation of one block grant program to a 1976 gathering of governors:

I am encouraged by the way states and localities are responding to the challenge of balanced Federalism. Behind the block grant concept is the conviction that you can do a better job in many ways than the Federal government. Under one such block grant, the Community Development Program: Federal regulations which a community must follow have decreased from 2,600 pages under the categorical programs to 25 pages for the block grant program; a community need only file one application, consisting of 50 pages, rather than the previous average of five applications consisting of 1,400 pages; processing and approval of a community development block grant application averaged 49 days, although under the categorical urban renewal program, processing took over two years.[34]

The rise of revenue sharing and block grants has signalled a lessening of the importance of the troublesome categorical grants-in-aid. While categorical grants comprised fully 98 percent of all federal aid to state and local governments in 1966, only about three-quarters of the 1975 total could be found in that category.[35] Note that these grants continue to account for the lion's share of the federal aid despite the significant reduction that has occurred, but the deep-rooting of revenue sharing and the block grant concept—providing state and local performance keeps on approaching promise in policy areas—will likely mean further whittling of the categorical grants proportion.

The States' Growth

The major changes in federalism have not just transpired in Washington and flowed from top to bottom. "Everyone says that all the growth in power, program, and prestige has been with the federal government. But I think that's a lot of baloney," proclaims former Pennsylvania Governor William Scranton. "State governments have had at least as much progressive growth in the last few decades as the federal government."[36]

The statistics for the past two decades prove Scranton correct. In 1972, for instance, combined state and local expenditures for domestic services was close to $160 billion, or a 349 percent increase over the 1956 level, which is a rise far in excess of inflation.[37] Total spending by the national government that same year amounted to $246.5 billion, but only $145.3 billion was spent on domestic services (defense and foreign affairs accounted for the difference).[38] Thus state and local governments spent about $15 billion more than Washington on domestic needs. From 1954 to 1974 the state-local sector's total expenditures grew from 7.4 percent to 11.6 percent of the Gross National Product.[39] General civilian government employment, comprising 14.6 percent of the U.S. labor force, is only one-fifth national government.[40] Fully 4 out of 5 government employees are found at the state and local levels. From 1955 to 1973 state-local governmental employment jumped by 119.5 percent compared to just 17.1 percent at the national level (and 35.8 percent in the private sector).

Not only in employment but in revenues collected and expended, and by other measures, state government has grown more rapidly than either its national or local counterparts.[41] Just in the 1973 fiscal year, the states spent $90 billion from their own sources on domestic services (education, welfare, health, transportation, and so forth); in 1954 only $15.8 billion was so expended by the states.[42] This startling boost has not condemned the states to fiscal disaster as is commonly supposed. Despite New York's crisis and a severe economic slump, only four states in 1974 saw their expenditures exceed their revenues.[43] This essential fiscal soundness has resulted from the step-up of revenues at a pace that at least equals expenditures. Total state expenditures in 1965 amounted to $46.6 billion, and the comparable figure in 1974 was $132.1 billion.[44] At the same time total revenues rose from $48.8 billion to $140.8 billion to more than match the spending surge.

These data imply a coordinate tax swell whose political impact on the governor has already been documented (see Chapter 4). An equally significant repercussion of this tax swell has been the diversification and consequent strengthening of the state-local revenue base.[45] In contrast to the base prevailing in the early 1950s, consisting largely of revenue from property taxes and special fees, six groups of taxes and aids carried the revenue load in 1976. Each of these (income tax; sales and gross receipts tax; federal aid; property tax; utility, liquor store, and insurance trust revenue; and charges and miscellaneous fees) burdened their fair share, with none exceeding a fifth of total revenue and none providing less than a tenth. The most substantial revenue diversification on the state level has come about because of the income and sales taxes.[46] In 1957 income taxes comprised only 9.5 percent of total tax receipts, but by 1973 23 percent was derived from that source. Revenues from state sales taxes rose from just $3 billion in 1950 to more than $15 billion in 1972.

Federal aid has been a vital source of revenues for the states and localities, so much so that one researcher refers to them as Washington "clients" who stand in line and lobby like any other constituency.[47] The states fully recognize the financial gravity of the national aid commitment. Between 1964 and 1969 almost one-half of the governors instituted a state liaison office in Washington, and nine of the ten most populous states have a full-time office well-staffed by the governor's "ambassadors."[48] Yet, in spite of the additions of revenue sharing and block grants to the federal aid repertoire, Washington's financial assistance to the states and localities has declined as a percentage of state-local expenditures in the 1970s.[49] Federal aid has of course increased in absolute dollars, but not at the same swift rate at which states and localities have been expanding their own fiscal capacities. As the National Governors' Conference concludes, "States and cities are taking on an increasing share of government program responsibilities from their own resources."[50]

The states have added to their weight in the federal system in other ways. One crucial state advance at the expense of the national government was made by courtesy of the Supreme Court. In a June 24, 1976 landmark decision the Court struck down the 1974 Fair Labor Standards Act Amendments in a suit brought by the National Governors' Conference and the National League of Cities (in conjunction with 20 states and 4 cities).[51] The amendments in question would have extended national minimum wage and maximum hour provisions to all nonsupervisory state and local employees. In effect, the state charged that the amendments would have substantially transferred personnel policy over their own employees to the national level. The Court's decision, which overruled its 1968 finding on the same subject,[52] marked the first time in four decades that a major piece of congressional economic legislation had been declared unconstitutional.[53]

The National Governors' Association

Liaison offices offer governors the opportunity to speak as individuals, but the National Governors' Association (until 1977 called the National Governors' Conference),[54] headquartered in Washington, D.C., gives the state chief executives the chance for a unified voice in federal matters that affect most or all of them, as well as interstate cooperation and exchange of ideas. The Governors' Conference was initiated by a call from a U.S. president. Theodore Roosevelt convened the first session of thirty-four governors at the White House on May 13, 1908, and declared the occasion a significant one since it was "... the first time in our history the chief executives of the States separately, and of the States together forming the Nation, have met...."[55] The president was very much in charge of the conference and skillfully used the governors to lobby for his natural resources legislation. (Roosevelt's handpicked but steward-like successor, William Howard Taft, characteristically encouraged the governors to meet separately, which they did annually from 1910 onwards.)

Roosevelt was not the originator of the idea of a Governors' Conference. Rather, William George Jordan, former editor of the *Saturday Evening Post*, first urged the formation of a "House of Governors," which he foresaw as an activist body on the national level. Until quite recently, Jordan would have been disappointed. Following are some representative comments on the National Governors' Conference by governors who served prior to 1966:

I got pretty disgusted with it. Everyone was posturing to get a resolution passed when it didn't matter a damn one way or the other. ... the Governors' Conference got nothing done by debating resolutions.[56]

I finally concluded that [the Conference's] basic significance was as a place where governors could meet each other. ... I thought it was used by people who were seeking the national political spotlight. ... Not too much serious business came out of the Conference. What can fifty governors really do?[57]

You've got fifty independent governors. ... None of them are going to surrender any of their authority to the Governors' Conference. So you really don't accomplish very much except to know other governors. ... The resolutions are absolutely meaningless.[58]

With due respect to those who worked hard on the Governors' Conference through the years, there was not very much to show for all the effort. Barely half the membership ever showed at the annual meetings (which tended to be heavily social) until after World War II, and conservatives dominated the progressives who hoped for a more activist role. The record contains many heated discussions about social security, deficit spending, and states' rights, but the hot air was the most notable product of it all. The governors usually could not reach a consensus on specifics and were often only half-hearted in their requests for the "return" of certain programs to the states since the costs would have been so great to the states. As Don Haider surmises, "If Conference-supported resolutions on key issues of federal-state relations are taken as benchmarks for evaluating the governors' national influence during the 1940s and 1950s, the ledger would record few if any victories and nearly all defeats."[59]

The structure of the Governors' Conference could not fairly be faulted for the organization's troubles. The constitution was brief and easily amendable. Full and regional meetings were held annually, with interim authority vested in an executive committee of governors. Bipartisanship was structurally maintained, with the conference chairmanship alternating between the two major parties while a majority of the executive committee was required to belong to the party opposite that of the current chairman. Prospective presidential candidates were traditionally excluded from the chairmanship. Finally, since all governors voted for each conference chairman, the party caucus did not necessarily get its choice of "spokesman." The Conference has been a good deal political, as might be expected from an organization of fifty successful politicians, although there are actually separate affiliated groups of each party's governors that meet annually for partisan purposes. Party groups often use their forums to screen presidential candidates or push one of their own number for a national party nomination, and Franklin Roosevelt, Thomas E. Dewey, Nelson Rockefeller, and Ronald Reagan, among others, used the "nonpartisan" conferences for political promotion prior to their presidential bids. Eisenhower supporters, led by Sherman Adams of New Hampshire, used the 1951 Governors' Conference to boost their favorite's candidacy. Republican governors (including William Scranton, Nelson Rockefeller, George Romney, Mark Hatfield, and John Volpe) used the 1964 Governors' Conference to quite a different end: opposition to the Barry Goldwater bandwagon. Democratic chief executives (Jimmy Carter prominent among them) followed suit in 1972 to attempt George McGovern's derailment.

The selection of a chairman has hardly been as perfunctory as the conference's by-laws would imply. Brevard Crihfield, executive director of the Council of State Governments and intimately connected with the conference until 1974, described a bit of the politics that intruded:

John Bailey, the Democratic national chairman for four or five years, personally picked who the Republicans could have for chairman when it was their turn. On the other side of it, back in the 1950s, the Northern and Western Republicans and the Southern Democrats would team up to make sure that a Northern liberal Democrat could never be chairman. "Soapy" Williams of Michigan was shafted that way.[60]

If structure was not the root of the conference's difficulties, neither was politics. The Governors' Conference, its image and output, was a product of its membership, but as the group of governors grew more capable and directed, this change was reflected in the conference. Just as the signs of change appeared in the governors in the 1960s, so too did the conference begin the process of invigoration. The governors' shift from criticism of current national programs to requests for further federal aid culminated in the 1965 adoption of a revenue-sharing schema for advocacy. Symbolically, the governors added "National" to the title of the Governors' Conference, thereby emphasizing their new focus, and while the Great Society was swirling about them, the governors realized that a complete restructuring of their conference would be essential if they were ever to exercise influence in Washington. Such a reorganization study was authorized in 1965.

The alterations came fast and furious thereafter. At a special interim meeting in 1966 the governors established an Office for Federal-State Relations in Washington, under the auspices of the Council of State Governments. This unprecedented full-time governors' lobby was funded by annual appropriations from the individual states. By the end of 1967 the governors' lobby was fully operational and joined the ranks of similar but already well-established organizations for mayors and county officials.[61]

The National Governors' Conference also constituted its first permanent standing committees, with all governors serving on at least one. The committees centered on policy fields, like transportation, education, and labor, and received foundation financial support. The membership participated more actively in formulating conference policy than ever before, and these efforts were augmented by the addition in 1968 of a second annual meeting held at mid-winter in Washington and usually attended by most major national government officials. Governors used this opportunity to lobby extensively on Capitol Hill, at the White House, and in the channels of the federal bureaucracy. As the Conference revved its lobbying motor, it shed its long-time sponsor, the Council of State Governments, which constitutionally could not engage in lobbying—the final disaffiliation came in 1975—and the conference's own staff was augmented in number and in quality.[62]

A critical step was the creation of a well-endowed "Center for Policy Analysis" in 1974 to serve as the "think tank" for the National Governors' Conference. In its first years of operation the center provided the governors with professional research on energy, the economy, health care, medical insurance, policy management, and other fields.[63] In the energy arena, for instance, the center worked with the conference's Committee on National Resources and Environmental Management (chaired by Governor Thomas Salmon of Vermont) to formulate energy policy from the governors' perspective. Through their efforts, an energy office was organized in every state, and the views of the governors were incorporated into the national energy program. The center gives the governors the heretofore unavailable advantage of formulating their own policy options, instead of merely reacting to those proposed by the national government.

Another step of some importance was taken by the National Governors' Conference in June 1975 when the development of a "Hall of the States" in Washington, D.C., was authorized. Until that time the Washington headquarters of the various states and state lobby groups had been scattered throughout the city, which hampered communications and effectiveness. The December 1976 opening of the hall, located just 1,500 feet from the U.S. Capitol, changed the situation considerably. The building's site, coupled with the promise of better coordination of state efforts and decreased costs for central services, attracted virtually all major state organizations. By mid-1977 forty-four states and associations had leased space in the hall. Representatives of these groups meet with the Governors' Conference weekly to plan jointly Capitol Hill strategy.

When the governors convened for their 1977 annual meeting, they took stock of the conference's ever-increasing tempo of activity, and decided to rename the Governors' Conference. Henceforth, the governors decreed, the group would be known as the National Governors' Association since the term "association" was thought to reflect more accurately the full-time, continuous work of the organization.

The comments of more recent governors present a happy contrast to those of their pre-1966 predecessors. Governors serving in the 1970s, in particular, are pleased and excited by the Association's advances and anxious for the operations to be expanded still further:

Great headway has been made, and the conference is on a solid footing. It's now a working organization, not just a meeting organization ... [and it's] gained credibility.[64]

I am satisfied with the National Governors' Conference and hope that its activities will expand. I feel it can serve as a spokesman for the governors on a national level ... as well as provide some valuable research.[65]

Good progress has been made, with better personnel and funding now, research task forces, and a central Washington office. ... If there's any dissatisfaction, it's only that I'm so eager to see more progress made.[66]

The conference meetings in recent years have reflected the new seriousness of purpose in the organization and the heavy emphasis on socializing has been shoved off center stage by the press of substantive matters. Nevertheless, there is ample room for further progress in the National Governors' Association. While the number of its lobbyists (6) equals or exceeds the lobbying staff of all other state-local organizations but the National Association of Counties, the Association's resources from dues are the smallest of all.[67]

Built-in problems have also hampered the organization in some respects, for when an association hosts fifty prima donnas, the inevitable frictions, conflicting ambitions, and jealousies can make it a laborious task to operate the group harmoniously or to develop a consensus on a policy issue. When the actors in such an organization are individually prominent and can command attention on a national scale by themselves, that organization is bound to be distracted and impeded by the machinations of its principals. State-local lobbies with larger memberships, where each member is less conspicuous and well-known, have much less difficulty creating a consensus or taking a forceful stand, even though they have more constituents to please. The U.S. Conference of Mayors is one such group. Cohesion there is aided by the singularity of big-city problems, wherever the cities might be located. The characteristics of states vary far more widely, by contrast, and policy agreements by governors are concluded more arduously. Nevertheless, a former president of the U.S. Conference of Mayors, Moon Landrieu of New Orleans, while noting that the governors would never "develop the solidarity of mayors," saw that "the governors are forging a more effective group than they ever have in the past."[68]

Whether it has been helping to secure revenue-sharing and its extension, or successfully lobbying for the temporary suspension of matching requirements on highway trust funds, or convincing the Department of Justice to withdraw exorbitantly expensive regulations on data processing equipment, the National Governors' Association in the last five years has been making the governors' voice heard on the national level and proving that the governors' collective influence is substantial.[69] Most importantly of all, the Governors' Association has institutionalized a role for the state chief executives on the national level, and enabled them to affect federal aid and regulations that directly influence their ability to perform their job well.

When former Governor Jimmy Carter met with the Democratic governors at the July 1976 meeting of the National Governors' Conference, he accepted their unanimous presidential endorsement with the promise that he would "re-establish a partnership that recognizes the independence of the states and the role of the governors in shaping major legislation, the federal budget, and rules and regulations before the final decision is made. I intend to re-establish a close, continuing, and cooperative relationship between the statehouse and the White House."[70] It will not be that simple, of course, but the National Governors' Association can now insure that the governors will not have to rely on promises alone.

States and Their Localities

"I debated the mayor of San Juan on the relative roles of the state and local governments, and he was so critical of state governments," reported Governor Tom McCall. "I said, 'Well, what do you think the state governments ought to do?' and he snapped at me, 'Roads and agriculture, period!' "[71] The open hostility between states and localities was virtually the rule almost until the dawning of the 1970s. Cities and urban counties, especially, were rightly resentful that states had so much control over their activities—and the states rarely hesitated to use their clamps—while they seemed to care little for the localities entrusted to them. However, the state Hatfields and the local McCoys have at last called a truce in their self-destructive feud, as they simply had to do in an era when almost three-quarters of all Americans live in a metropolitan area, and while the hatchet may not be entirely buried, it has at least been placed on a shelf out of easy reach.

Localities were not always under the thumb of their states; in the years following the Revolutionary War, the right to local self-government was widely accepted as absolute, and local governments were given near autonomy.[72] Gradually, however, state supremacy became the law in spite of occasional local protests. The death blow to local sovereignty was struck by the Iowa Supreme Court in an 1868 decision later upheld by the U.S. Supreme Court. The Iowa court's finding, called "Dillon's Rule" after the judge who authored it, included this historic passage:

Municipal corporations owe their origin to, and derive their powers and rights wholly from, the legislature. It breathes into them the breath of life, without which they cannot exist. As it creates, so may it destroy. If it may destroy, it may abridge and control. Unless there is some constitutional limitation on the right, the legislature might, by a single act, if we can suppose it capable of so great a folly and so great a wrong, sweep from existence all the municipal corporations in the State and the *corporation* could not prevent it. We know of no limitation on this right so far as the corporations themselves are concerned. They are so to phrase it, the mere *tenants at will* of the legislature.[73]

"Dillon's Rule" has never been abrogated and is the prevailing guideline for state-local legal relationships today. While it is wholly the ward of the state by law, the locality has normally had more autonomy in practice.[74] In some cases outright "home rule," whereby the state cedes its supervisory responsibilities to the city, has been granted.

Most cities were not so fortunate. The earlier ills that bound the states (Neanderthal constitutions, nightmarish organizations, rural-based malapportioned legislatures, inadequate and undiversified revenue systems, and shackled governors who often exercised little leadership) bound the cities just as tightly since they were in the legal grip of the states. Because the states refused to recognize their local responsibilities, the localities in desperation formed an axis with the national government that was to become the most vibrant part of the federal organism. It was an unnatural and forced relationship, however, and a symptom of federal disorder. Roscoe Martin unhappily reckoned as late as 1965 that:

If a federal system, and specifically the American system, is to function properly all members of the partnership must be strong and vigorous. It is a central conviction of this study that this precondition to success does not now obtain in America in that the states have not been able or willing to assume their share of federal responsibilities, particularly during the last three decades, and that the national government has been compelled to develop active relations with local governments in order to make the American system operationally effective.[75]

While the national government could provide financial assistance to the cities, it could have little effect on other crucial local matters that clearly fell within the purview of the states. Through the years state inattention compounded the localities' ills. Severe limits on municipal taxing and borrowing powers, restricted annexation and unrestricted incorporation, the haphazard development of special districts, and lack of planning controls on general urban growth, all of which created chaotic local conditions in time, were unquestionably the results of state neglect.

Only a decade after Martin wrote his justified condemnation of the states, the president of the U.S. Conference of Mayors, Mayor Moon Landrieu of New Orleans could report that state-local relations had "improved substantially,"[76] and citing the "better educated" modern governor, he indicated: "Most governors today would be inclined to want to improve relationships with their localities." The governors are but one cause of the shift in attitudes, of course. The same developments that have brought about the strengthened governorship have, by and large, also produced a new state-local affinity: reapportionment, the passage of civil rights laws and the Voting Rights Act, growth of party competition, industrial mushrooming, reconstitution and reorganization in the states, and the adoption of new revenue devices, among others. Overshadowing all of these is the sheer expansion of urban-suburban areas. The metropolitan areas now predominate politically in all but a handful of states (and the old urban-rural battles have given way to a new form of metropolitan conflict: urban-suburban).[77] The new-found political muscle of urban areas is reflected in the pattern of state aid. The states are no longer misers when it comes to their localities. Next to the property tax, state grants are the largest source of local revenue, and the states provide about four times the aid given by the national government to localities.[78] Even "no strings" revenue-sharing grants to the localities by the states exceeded the national government's allocation.[79] State aid to local governments has progressed steadily from 41.7 percent of locally derived revenue as of 1954 to 57.5 percent in 1974.[80] (A little over half of this amount is for education.) States have been noticeably more responsive to local needs in the fields of land-use planning, health policy and delivery of services, housing and community development, energy policy, criminal justice, and transportation.[81]

Recent governors have been at the forefront of the reconstruction of state-local relationships. The state chief executives have variously pushed for large additional financial packages for their localities, state assumption of general assistance welfare costs, state loan programs to encourage economic development and environmental protection, and the formation of municipal bond banks to reduce the cost of local borrowing. Often at the instigation of the governor, seventeen states have created commissions to recommend changes in local-state relations since 1968, and significant reforms have been enacted as a result.[82] More than four-fifths of the states had permanent departments of urban or local affairs by 1975, whereas in 1960 similar departments existed in only two states.

In light of these auspicious developments it is not surprising to discover that a weakening of the Washington-city hall axis has occurred.[83] As the states have become more responsive, the federal system has begun to regain its equilibrium. Since states are vested with the primary responsibility and authority for their localities, it naturally follows that the states should be closest to them. The national government is further removed from the problems of cities and counties and, as the localities painfully found out with the passage of years, this distance brings hardships of its own. Mayor Landrieu summarized the shift this way:

In the past we [mayors] preferred to work through the "feds" rather than states and governors. . . . Now, however, we see the new, more cooperative attitudes among governors. There are a lot of problems with the more removed federal approach. So we'll give the states and the governors a try.[84]

It is a measure of their new-found cooperation that the states and localities have joined together to lobby the national government in a group called the "New Coalition."[85] Forged in the 1972 struggle to enact revenue sharing and staffed by the National Governors' Association, the New Coalition is a loosely organized but continuing committee of governors, state legislators, mayors, and county officials. (Some of the officers of the lobbies representing each of these groups of officeholders are automatically members of the New Coalition.) Besides the major role it played in the enactment and reenactment of revenue-sharing, the New Coalition now meets with cabinet members and other federal officials every few months to discuss the interstate programs and regulations promulgated by the national government. Welfare and Medicaid reform, in addition to regulatory revisions, have been adopted as priority items. The New Coalition is a valuable addition to the federal lobbying caucus. The organization encourages close consultation and cooperation among states and localities while the national government is informed of state and local perspectives (and pressured to incorporate those views into its programs). The Coalition also prods state and local leaders representing divergent interests to compromise and present a cohesive and unified front to the national government.

Much progress has been made by the states in meeting the legitimate needs of their localities, but much more remains to be done.[86] Détente has not yet developed into a comradely friendship, and for good reason. Some states do relatively little for their localities, while six states (California, Michigan, Minnesota, New York, Ohio, and Wisconsin) containing about a third of the country's urban residents account for about two-thirds of the "no strings" aid to local governments.[87] Almost all states have done little to move further toward substantial "home rule," and some have retained crippling limits on local borrowing. The knotty problems of jurisdictional overlap, special district multiplication, and regional cooperation have yet to attract the concentration of still other states. If the nascent return to a more natural and healthy federal balance is to be sustained, governors will have to devote more of their time and talents and more of their states' resources than ever before to their local "tenants at will."

Summing Up the New Federalism

Federalism is a complicated, tangled, snarled concept, involving as it does the interwoven relationships of tens of thousands of governmental units. Devotees of the subject have resorted to comparing it to layer cakes, marble cakes, and spaghetti in attempts to get the idea across.[88] Thus, conclusions about federalism should only be made with its dimensions in mind. A general summation of new relationships cannot begin to account for the interactions of every state, city, county, and arm of the national government. This is not to say that general patterns cannot be discerned, for they can and have been in the course of this study. The most significant of them all is that the states, responsible in good part for their own earlier federal ostracization, have started to fulfill their proper role in the federal scheme of government. The state changes that have been catalogued, from the spread of party competition to legislative reapportionment, have given the states the will to act, to cooperate, and at the same time to compete with the national government for power and responsibility.

The failure of some Great Society programs eventually convinced the national government that a greater degree of community control was necessary, and (with the added nudge of vigorous state and local lobbying efforts) revenue sharing, the largest domestic aid program in American history, was born. Block grants supplemented (and may one day surpass in importance) revenue sharing. Both programs trimmed costly bureaucratic red tape and supplanted some categorical grants-in-aid. But categorical grants still predominate in the federal aid scheme, and further expansion of block grants will be necessary before states and localities have rid themselves of the worst aspects of federalism.

The shift to states and localities is observed in other areas as well. State and local spending on domestic services and growth in public employment has outpaced the national government. A more diversified state revenue base, coupled with fundamental state fiscal soundness, has proven especially encouraging to advocates of the New Federalism. States and localities have been growing so rapidly in the public sector that federal aid as a percentage of total expenditures has actually been falling. Even the courts have been acknowledging again the existence of state prerogatives in the federal system now that the states have indicated they are responsible repositories of authority.

This responsible state attitude is detected on yet another level: their relations with localities. The old hostility stemming from many states' shameful neglect of their cities and urban counties has been giving way to cooperation with the advent of more sympathetic financial and technical treatment of localities' needs. The Washington-city hall alliance has been similarly fading as state-local mutual efforts like the New Coalition come to the fore. This restoration of a more natural federal partnership between states and their localities is a welcome innovation, but one that must be nurtured carefully—and generously—by the states.

The governors themselves have benefitted from both this new partnership and the reversal of the federal power flow, and have been asserting themselves on a national level in an unprecedented and surprisingly effective manner of late. Their vehicle has been the National Governors' Association, revolutionized from the hollow shell of yore to a bustling, professional lobby that can achieve results (and overcome the serious handicaps to effectiveness inherent in a high-powered constituency like the governors). With the association's Center for Policy Analysis, the governors can propose their own policy alternatives rather than simply react to those of others. Further strengthening of the National Governors' Association is in order, for developments at the national level are too crucial to the governors' success and the states' welfare not to insure that the governors are heard in Washington.

The best way for a governor to be heard in the nation's capital, of course, would be for the governor to become master of it! The opportunity that governors have to seek and win the presidency can also serve as a clue to the prominence and prestige of the governorship in the entire political system, and governors' quests for the ultimate prize in American politics is the subject of the concluding chapter.

Notes

1. As quoted from James L. Buckley, *If Men Were Angels: A View from the Senate* (New York: G.P. Putnam's Sons, 1975), pp. 80-81.

2. Interview with the author, August 5, 1976, Olympia, Wash.

3. See Chapter 1 for the causes of the shift.

4. Leonard D. White, *The States and the Nation* (Baton Rouge: Louisiana State University Press, 1953), p. 3.

5. See Roscoe Martin, *The Cities and the Federal System* (New York: Atherton Press, 1965), pp. 164-65.

6. Ibid.

7. President Dwight D. Eisenhower, "Address to the 1957 National Governors' Conference," in Daniel J. Elazar (ed.), *The Politics of American Federalism* (Lexington, Mass.: D.C. Heath, 1969), pp. 188-93.

8. See Ira Sharkansky, *The Maligned States: Policy Accomplishments, Problems, and Opportunities* (New York: McGraw-Hill, 1972), pp. 13-16, 30-35, 153; and Ernest S. Griffith, *The American System of Government*, 5th ed. (London: Methuen, 1976), pp. 17-21.

9. Harold J. Laski, *The American Democracy: A Commentary and an Interpretation* (London: Allen and Unwin, 1949), p. 138.

10. Sharkansky, *The Maligned States*, p. 13. See also Terry Sanford, *Storm Over the States* (New York: McGraw-Hill, 1967), Chapter 7.

11. Ibid.

12. *Federalist No. 46*, as quoted in Sharkansky, ibid., p. 2.

13. See Lee Harris, "Geographer Offers Plan to Redesign the U.S.," *The Los Angeles Times*, August 12, 1973, pp. 1, 16.

14. In an interview with Rockefeller by Martin Diamond, March 4, 1976. (Transcript provided by the Office of the Vice President, Washington, D.C.)

15. See Richard H. Leach, "A Quiet Revolution, 1933-1976," in the Council of State Governments, *The Book of the States, 1976-1977* (Lexington, Ky.: Council of State Governments, 1976), pp. 21-27.

16. Office of the President, *Proceedings of a Conference of Governors at the White House* (Washington, D.C.: U.S. Government Printing Office, 1909), p. 212.

17. National Governors' Conference, *Federal Roadblocks to Efficient State Government* (Washington, D.C.: National Governors' Conference, 1976).

18. Interview with Governor Calvin Rampton, August 3, 1976, Salt Lake City, U.

19. Interview with Governor Daniel Evans, August 5, 1976, Olympia, Wash.

20. Correspondence with a governor who did not wish to be quoted.

21. Griffith, *The American System*, p. 170.

22. Frank Smallwood, *Free and Independent* (Brattleboro, Vt.: Stephen Greene Press, 1976), pp. 148-49.

23. See Thomas J. Anton, 'State Planning, Gubernatorial Leadership, and Federal Funds: Three Case Studies," in Elazar (ed.), *The Politics of American Federalism*, pp. 88-95.

24. Advisory Commission on Intergovernmental Relations, *The States and Intergovernmental Aids* (Washington, D.C.: ACIR draft chapter, 1976), Chapter III, pp. 48-50.

25. Correspondence with the author, July 22, 1976. See also Don Haider, *When Governments Come to Washington* (New York: Free Press, 1974), p. 58.

26. See Carol S. Weissert, "Significant Developments in Federal-State Relations," in the Council of State Governments, *Book of the States 1976-1977*, pp. 577-82. See also Advisory Commission on Intergovernmental Relations, *American Federalism: Into the Third Century* (Washington, D.C.: ACIR, May 1974), p. 3.

27. For a detailed history of the enactment of revenue sharing and the conflicting interest group pressures brought to bear during debate on the issue, see D.H. Haider, *When Governments Come to Washington* (New York: The Free Press, 1974), especially pp. 64-75.

28. Advisory Commission on Intergovernmental Relations, "GRS Extended for 3-3/4 years," *Intergovernmental Perspective* 2 (Fall 1976): 4.

29. Haider, *When Governments Come to Washington*, p. 75; and Weissert, "Significant Developments," p. 577.

30. See National Governors' Conference, *Revenue-Sharing and the States: An Impact Survey* (Washington, D.C.: National Governors' Conference, February 1976). This study is the source of the figures quoted below in the same paragraph.

31. See Advisory Commission on Intergovernmental Relations, *Changing Public Attitudes on Governments and Taxes* (Washington, D.C.: ACIR, 1976). Three of every five Americans expressed support for revenue-sharing in an ACIR poll.

32. Richard P. Nathan, Allen D. Manvel, Susannah E. Calkins, et al., *Monitoring Revenue Sharing* (Washington, D.C.: The Brookings Institution, 1975), pp. 311-12.

33. Weissert, "Significant Developments," pp. 578-82.

34. President Gerald R. Ford, "Remarks to the National Governors' Conference," Office of the White House Press Secretary, Washington, D.C., mimeograph, February 23, 1976.

35. Weissert, "Significant Developments," p. 581.

36. Interview with the author, August 24, 1976, New York, N.Y.

37. National Governors' Conference, *State of the States, 1974* (Washington, D.C.: National Governors' Conference, 1974), pp. 15-16.

38. Ibid.

39. Advisory Commission on Intergovernmental Relations, *Trends in Fiscal Federalism, 1954-1974* (Washington, D.C.: ACIR, 1975), p. 2.

40. Ibid., pp. 2-3.

41. Roscoe C. Martin, *The Cities and the Federal System* (New York: Atherton Press, 1965), p. 187.

42. National Governors' Conference, *State of the States, 1974*, p. 6.

43. Council of State Governments, *The Book of the States, 1976-1977*, pp. 249-51.

44. Ibid.

45. Advisory Commission on Intergovernmental Relations, *Significant Features of Fiscal Federalism* (Washington, D.C.: ACIR, 1976), p. 3.

46. National Governors' Conference, *State of the States, 1974*, p. 12.

47. Haider, *When Governments Come to Washington*, p. 92.

48. Ibid., p. 96.

49. National Governors' Conference, *State of the States, 1974*, p. 12.

50. Ibid.

51. *National League of Cities v. Usery*, 44 U.S. *Law Week*, 4974.

52. *Wirtz v. Maryland*, 392 U.S. 183 (1968).

53. Advisory Commission on Intergovernmental Relations, "Court Strikes Down FLSA Extension to States, Cities," *Intergovernmental Perspective* 2 (Summer 1976): 2.

54. The organization's change of name came about at the annual meeting of governors in September 1977. The terms "association" and "conference" are used interchangeably in this study.

55. Office of the President, *Proceedings of a Conference of Governors at the White House*, p. 3. For a history of the Governors' Conference from inception until 1960, see Glenn E. Brooks, *When Governors Convene: The Governors' Conference and National Politics* (Baltimore: Johns Hopkins Press, 1961). Also see Haider, *When Governments Come to Washington.*

56. Interview with Governor Terry Sanford, July 21, 1976, Durham, N.C.

57. Interview with Governor Matthew Welsh, August 10, 1976, Indianapolis, Ind.

58. Telephone interview with Governor Edmund G. Brown, Sr., August 8, 1976.

59. Haider, *When Governments Come to Washington*, p. 22.

60. Interview with the author, September 21, 1976, Lexington, Ky.

61. See Haider, *When Governments Come to Washington*, pp. 26-28.

62. The most recent changes in the National Governors' Conference are described in Rochelle L. Stanfield, "The PIGs: Out of the Sty, Into Lobbying with Style," *National Journal* 8 (August 14, 1976):1134-39.

63. Some of these conference reports are listed in the bibliography.

64. Interview with Governor Robert Ray, August 31, 1976, Des Moines, Ia.

65. Correspondence with Governor Jerry Apodaca of New Mexico, July 22, 1976.

66. Interview with Governor Daniel Evans, August 5, 1976, Olympia, Wash.

67. Stanfield, "The PIGs," p. 1137. There are four major state-local lobbies besides the National Governors' Association: the National Conference of State Legislatures, the National League of Cities, the U.S. Conference of Mayors, and the National Association of Counties.

68. Interview with the author, September 7, 1976, New Orleans, La.

69. Weissert, "Significant Developments," p. 582.

70. *The Washington Post*, July 7, 1976, p. A-2.

71. Interview with the author, August 4, 1976, Portland, Ore.

72. For a history of state-city relations, see Martin, *The Cities*, especially pp. 28-33.

73. *City of Clinton v. Cedar Rapids and Missouri River Railroad Company*, 24 Iowa 455 (1868).

74. Martin, *The Cities*, pp. 29-31.

75. Ibid., p. 46.

76. Interview with Mayor Moon Landrieu, September 7, 1976, New Orleans, La.

77. Daniel J. Elazar, "The New Federalism: Can the States be Trusted?" *Public Interest* 11 (Spring 1974):91-93.

78. Council of State Governments, *Book of the States, 1976-77*, pp. 263, 592; and National Governors' Conference, *The State of the States, 1974*, pp. 16-17.

79. National Governors' Conference, ibid.

80. Advisory Commission on Intergovernmental Relations, *Trends in Fiscal Federalism, 1954-1974*, p. 2.

81. George S. Blair, "State-Local Relations in 1974-75," in Council of State Governments, *Book of the States, 1976-1977*, pp. 586-91. See also the National Governors' Conference, *States' Responsibilities to Local Governments: An Action Agenda* (Washington, D.C.: National Governors' Conference, October 1975).

82. See Vincent L. Morando, "The Reemerging Role of States in Local

Reorganization," *State Government* 58 (Summer 1975):177-82; and the Advisory Commission on Intergovernmental Relations, *State Legislative Program* (Washington, D.C.: ACIR, November 1975), pp. 43-44.

83. Haider, *When Governments Come to Washington*, p. 289.

84. Interview with the author, September 7, 1976, New Orleans, La.

85. Stanfield, "The PIGs," pp. 1138-39. Memoranda to New Coalition members supplied by the National Governors' Conference also served as source material.

86. See National Governors' Conference, *States' Responsibilities to Local Governments: An Action Agenda*; National Governors' Conference, *Proceedings of the 1975 National Governors' Conference* (Washington, D.C.: National Governors' Conference, 1975), pp. 8-10; and Troy R. Westmeyer and Wesley Westmeyer (eds.), "Cities v. States on Finance," *National Civic Review* 65 (July 1976):358-59.

87. National Governors' Conference, *Proceedings*, ibid., pp. 85-86.

88. See Deil S. Wright and David E. Stephenson, "The States as Middlemen: Five Fiscal Dilemmas," *State Government* 51 (Summer 1968):107.

6 The Governorship as Pathway to the Presidency

"The President of the United States . . . " are words written and spoken by Americans with a reverent mixture of awe, mystery, and respect not shared by most citizens of other nations toward their highest official. The presidency transcends the person who holds it, and it can emerge intact, with its lustre only faintly dimmed, even from a tenure as disastrous as that of Richard Nixon. It is not ignorant or contemptuous of the balance of separated powers to declare the presidency the nation's highest office, the central focus of attention, and the preeminent repository of the country's hopes and dreams.

Governors are serving longer terms in the statehouses, and the evidence already presented suggests that the governorship is now viewed as more than just a waystation before moving on to other posts. Still, rare is the man (and now woman) elected governor, the highest public honor awarded by a single state's electorate, who does not, if only in his heart of hearts, fancy himself in the Oval Office. It is hardly beyond the realm of possibility. Governorships are one of the four primary pathways to the presidency, and nearly all serious presidential contenders are drawn from either the statehouse, the U.S. Senate, the cabinet, or the vice presidency.[1] Circumstance and plain luck as much as any other factors determine the winners of the quadrennial party presidential sweepstakes, but access to the major party nominations is certainly influenced by a candidate's elective portfolio. Whether one is, say, a governor or a U.S. senator can have some impact on one's White House prospects. Exactly how much impact varies, as the following analysis indicates.

Gubernatorial Presidents and Politics

Incumbent governors fared very poorly in presidential competition for a startlingly lengthy period in America's early years. It was more than four score years after George Washington first took the oath of office that a sitting governor even received a major party presidential nomination. It took nine-tenths of a century before one could actually call the White House home.

At first the vice presidency seemed the standard career path to the top job, and John Adams and Thomas Jefferson moved directly from one post to the other. The secretaries of state thereafter moved to the fore, as three in succession (James Madison, James Monroe, and John Quincy Adams) took the presidential oath. Congress and the military supplied most of the chief executives after the second Adams, and the governors appeared to be a sadly neglected bunch. Actually, five early presidents had been state governors at some time in their careers (James Monroe, Martin Van Buren, John Tyler, James K. Polk, and Andrew Johnson), and this number swells to eight if Thomas Jefferson (Virginia's Revolutionary War governor), Andrew Jackson (territorial governor of Florida), and William Henry Harrison (Indiana's territorial chief) are included. None of these men, though, held governorships at the time of their nominations.

The first breakthrough for an incumbent governor came in 1868 when the chief executive of New York, Horatio Seymour, was named the Democratic national standardbearer. Seymour lost, but the governors as a group did not suffer a lasting stigma. Just two presidential elections later, in 1876, both parties nominated sitting governors for the presidency: Ohio's Rutherford B. Hayes for the Republicans and New York's Samuel Tilden for the Democrats. This time a governor had to win and, strangely enough, both did, in the most disputed presidential election in U.S. history. Tilden garnered a solid edge in the popular vote and Hayes, after some highly questionable political maneuverings (to which Hayes was not a party), was awarded an electoral college majority of one. The electoral college's choice, not the people's, took up residence on Pennsylvania Avenue.

The age of the gubernatorial presidents then began in earnest, although nongovernor chief executives were interspersed throughout the period. Elevated from the statehouse to the White House were Democrat Grover Cleveland of New York (elected 1884 and, nonconsecutively, in 1892 again), Republicans William McKinley of Ohio (in 1896 and 1900) and Theodore Roosevelt of New York (first succeeding upon McKinley's assassination and then elected in his own right in 1904), Democrat Woodrow Wilson of New Jersey (elected in 1912 and 1916), and Republican Calvin Coolidge of Massachusetts (via the vice presidency at Warren Harding's death and subsequently elected in 1924). The victory of New York's Franklin Roosevelt in 1932 marked the last time that the governorship would serve as a steppingstone to the presidency for forty-four years. Jimmy Carter of Georgia, of course, renewed the gubernatorial tradition in 1976.

Besides the successful contenders there were a half-dozen gubernatorial party nominees who lost the big prize: Samuel Tilden (D-New York, 1876), James Cox (D-Ohio, 1920), Al Smith (D-New York, 1928), Alf Landon (R-Kansas, 1936), Thomas E. Dewey (R-New York, 1948),[2] and Adlai Stevenson (D-Illinois, 1952 and 1956). Several other governors through the years have narrowly missed a major party nomination for president, including William H. Seward (R-New York, 1860), Frank Lowden (R-Illinois, 1920), and Ronald Reagan (R-California, 1976).[3]

Governors have secured more vice presidential than presidential nominations in U.S. history. Eleven men were chosen for the vice presidential party spot primarily on the basis of their gubernatorial records, and seven of them went on to win election, including since 1900 Theodore Roosevelt, Thomas R. Marshall (D-Indiana, 1912 and 1916), Calvin Coolidge, Charles W. Bryan (R-Nebraska, 1924), Spiro Agnew (R-Maryland, 1968 and 1972), and Nelson Rockefeller (R-New York, by appointment in 1974).[4] Seven other former governors were also given party vice presidential nods, but they were serving in other offices at the time.

In this century third parties, whose roots can often be traced directly to reform or protest movements in the states, have drawn heavily—almost exclusively—from gubernatorial ranks. The 1912 Progressive party ticket was composed of two governors (one current and one former), with Theodore Roosevelt for president and California's Hiram Johnson for vice president. Robert La Follette, the ex-governor of Wisconsin, headed up the Progressive party slate in 1924. Two conservative movements with Southern strongholds elevated governors to the top posts. In 1948 the Dixiecrats were led by Governor J. Strom Thurmond of South Carolina and, in the second slot, Governor Fielding Wright of Mississippi. And in 1968 former Governor George Wallace of Alabama made a run for the presidency atop the American Independent party banner.

Gubernatorial involvement in presidential politics has hardly been limited to formal candidacies. A single governor has sometimes crucially influenced the actual outcome of a presidential election.[5] The Democratic governor of New York, David B. Hill, is credited with (or blamed for) the election of Republican candidate Benjamin Harrison by denying Grover Cleveland the state's electoral votes in 1888. Gubernatorial support of Teddy Roosevelt's 1912 third-party bid was a major factor in the crushing defeat of regular Republican William Howard Taft by Democrat Woodrow Wilson. Four years later Republican Governor Hiram Johnson insured Wilson's reelection over GOP candidate Charles Evans Hughes by throwing his state of California to the progressive Democratic incumbent.

Governors have exercised considerable influence within the party conventions, too, even when the major contenders were nongovernors.[6] Their roles as delegates, delegation leaders, and convention officers have grown through the decades. In 1860 only one governor was in attendance at the major party conventions, whereas by 1956 twenty of twenty-seven Democratic governors and fifteen of twenty-one Republican governors were members of their party convention delegations. (In three-quarters of these cases the governor served as delegation chairman.)

One of the critical advantages possessed by Dwight Eisenhower in his 1952 party struggle with Robert Taft was his support by thirteen Republican governors (from states with 370 delegates) while only three governors (from states with 64 delegates) backed Taft.[7] The governors so tightly controlled their delegations that they steered about three-quarters or more of their states' delegate votes to their preferred candidates. On the Democratic side in 1952 governors generally supported the convention winner, Adlai Stevenson, although their influence was less significant than that of their brethren in the GOP. (State chief executives naturally tend to have more power within the party when it is out-of-power presidentially.)

In 1960 much of John Kennedy's key support in early stages was gubernatorial. Governor Michael DiSalle of Ohio gave Kennedy an early boost when he pledged his "favorite son" delegation to him in January 1960. Republican governors in 1964 were much less successful in securing the party nomination for one of their favorites. Even though Goldwater made his worst showings in the states controlled by GOP governors, there were too few Republican governors at the time to affect the outcome.[8] A similar situation prevailed in 1976 when most Republican chief executives backed President Ford over Ronald Reagan. Again, while they usually assisted their candidate materially in their own states, less than a third of the states then had a GOP governor.

Democratic governors have been much less effective because of the adoption of new party rules controlling the nomination process since 1972. The rules call for "full participation" by women and minority groups and have democratized the selection of delegates in states choosing by the convention, caucus, or mass meeting methods. Although the rules were weakened slightly in time for the 1976 convention, governors are still no longer able to exercise the control they once did over the selection of delegates.

The mushrooming of the direct primary system as a method of nominating delegates has also reduced gubernatorial sway in both parties. As W. Brooke Graves deduced, "The Governor's control is likely to be most effective if the delegates are selected by a state convention, less certain if all or a major portion of them are selected by district conventions, still less certain if they are elected unpledged, and least certain of all if they are chosen in a primary and pledged to a candidate."[9] Fully thirty of the fifty states now hold presidential primaries, up from just sixteen in 1960, and most choose some or all of their delegates by direct vote. The 1976 presidential conventions offer a fascinating irony as a result. The first conventions in two decades with governors as the principal stars marked the modern nadir of gubernatorial influence in presidential selection. It is interesting that neither former Governor Carter nor former Governor Reagan was the favorite of his party's gubernatorial band. To the contrary, both were clearly disliked by their statehouse contemporaries who were actively supporting their rivals. Only one Republican governor endorsed Reagan, and just two Democratic executives backed Carter before his bandwagon started to roll.

Governors and Senators: Conflicting Claims on the White House

If governors have less control than ever over the identity of the party presidential nominee, no other group really exerts any greater influence. The selection process has been too democratized for effective boss control, at least in the Democratic party. More than at any time in American history, independents run for the party nominations and independents are nominated for president. These independents cannot be evaluated by the tried and true methods of yesteryear—that is, by mere reference to the blocs and party organizations supporting them. Other more subtle factors may ultimately determine the party nominees and the groups from which they come. There are, for example, distinct presidential advantages that attend specific public offices and can govern whether bearers of a certain title are thought to be "presidential material" and seriously considered at all by the parties. The offices of vice president, governor, and senator amply illustrate the point.

Vice presidents now occupy the preeminent post in presidential politics, having been thrust into the spotlight by the Twenty-Second Amendment to the U.S. Constitution that prevents third terms for presidents, as well as the three direct successions to the presidency (Truman, Johnson, and Ford) that have occurred since 1945. Every vice president elected since 1952 has either run for or succeeded to the presidency or has figured heavily in the political speculation for the top job at some time. Richard Nixon, who came tantalizingly close to White House residency during Eisenhower's three major illnesses, lost the presidency in 1960 but finally grabbed the prize in 1968. He defeated the incumbent vice president, Hubert Humphrey, to do it. Nixon's second-in-command, Spiro Agnew, was considered to be the leading GOP prospect for 1976 until his corruption was discovered. Gerald Ford's appointed vice-president, Nelson Rockefeller, was a veteran of several previous presidential campaigns and, after his fallout with Ford, was touted for a time as a possible electoral roadblock to Ford's nomination for a full term.

The aura of the office has even managed to surround a few losing vice presidential nominees, who have capitalized on the campaign exposure to make presidential bids of their own. Edmund Muskie, because of his selection as Humphrey's 1968 Democratic running mate, was regarded as the early front-runner for the 1972 party presidential nomination. Sargent Shriver (on the McGovern ticket in 1972), Thomas Eagleton (also on the 1972 McGovern ticket), and Henry Cabot Lodge (Nixon's 1960 choice) were not so fortunate. One vice presidential loser, Goldwater's William E. Miller, lapsed into such obscurity that he took to doing television commercials on the value of a certain credit card for unrecognized persons.

The vice president is normally presumed to be the president's heir apparent and is treated as such by the news media who thereby inflate the office's image and import far beyond the position's due substantive worth. Vice presidents since Truman's Alben Barkley have been kept busier than their predecessors, and sometimes have been given plums like world tours that keep them in the public eye. At least until Carter's Walter Mondale, though, their tasks have been less than overwhelming and have often taken on the appearance of "make work" projects. Their prominence in the presidential nomination process must be attributed to the symbolic nature of their office rather than any substantive training or presidentially comparable experience afforded by their post.

Vice presidents and their advantages notwithstanding, the traditional rivalry for presidential nominations has been between governors and U.S. senators. Fair comparisons can be made for these two offices since their electoral dominions (the states) are equivalent (whereas the vice presidency and cabinet posts are national in scope). The relative weight of each state office in presidential politics can probably be ascertained in the process. It is perhaps appropriate that governors and senators are presidential antagonists since they are political competitors in the state sphere as well. The two groups do not mix well, by and large, and it is no secret among politicians that governors and senators usually do not think very much of one another. The typical representative of each office is probably oriented quite differently, because the executive nature of the governorship and the legislative nature of the U.S. Senate should, reasonably and even ideally, attract different types of persons.

Governors who become U.S. senators, we will remember, are somewhat dissatisfied with their new office and do not quite fit in (see Chapter 2). From 1945 to 1972 senators were highly successful, and governors were virtually shut out, in presidential politics.[10] Men with senatorial backgrounds captured nomination after nomination in both parties: Harry Truman, Richard Nixon, John Kennedy, Barry Goldwater, Lyndon Johnson, Hubert Humphrey, and George McGovern. The flow was interrupted by only one governor (Adlai Stevenson) and a general (Eisenhower). Governors were just as numerically wanting in the vice presidential sweepstakes, with only one governor (Spiro Agnew) securing a major party nomination for the post. In only four presidential elections since the Civil War has a governor not filled at least one of the two top spots in one of the major parties. Two of them (those of 1960 and 1964) occurred after 1945 and occurred consecutively.[11]

Why the rise of senators on the presidential front? During the era of gubernatorial presidents, governors were favored for party nominations both because of their ironclad control of state convention delegations and for their lack of close identification with divisive national issues (since without a great deal of "baggage" they could be more easily molded to fit the temper of the times). Perceptions of the gubernatorial office changed, however, and governors became less attractive to parties hungry for victory. One of the major electoral debits assigned to the governorship occurred from the executive nature of the position. Briefly, chief executives are forced to make tough decisions that legislators rarely face, and governors make them almost every day. This political fact of life was accentuated in the 1960s as governors, charged with providing for the general welfare of their citizenry, sought to raise taxes in order to meet pressing social needs. They became politically unpopular for it and, with an eroded home base, thus stood little chance of a party presidential nomination. The problems at home were so knotty and demanding as well that most governors had little time for the countrywide gallivanting necessary to successful pursuit of the party nod. The implication here is not that U.S. senators evaded the tough decisions that the governors had to make; rather, senators did not have to make them at all. Governors, as the chief executive officers, are on the firing line daily and have to grapple with problems that they alone will judge. Senators, while they may deal with "weightier" matters in terms of world moment, are among a hundred. There is a collective responsibility for what is produced or not produced; no single senator carries the onus alone.

The fact that decision making itself is qualitatively different for governors and senators is another derivative of the divergent executive and legislative roots of their offices. Governors are apt to issue rapid-fire verdicts, for the sheer volume and the urgency of a wide-ranging array of executive subjects awaiting adjudication allow them little rest. Senators, by contrast, are usually given the relative luxury of mulling over their thoughts for several weeks before they cast their votes on a major item. Within the social system of the Congress, senators are in effect responsible only for the topics enveloped by their committees. This division of labor allows senators the opportunity for specialization that is not afforded governors, and it also results in the resolution of many of the senators' voting decisions, since they are able to take their voting "cues" on issues outside the purview of the committees from fellow senators of their party or ideological bent who do serve on the relevant committees. The collective responsibility of Congress also permits skillful and nimble senators to obscure their liability for any particular action. They are aided in the pursuit of this goal by the multifaceted votes that are usually taken on an item. Senators can vote against a bill in committee and for it on the floor; for the unamended version and against the amended version; for amendments to weaken the bill, then, despite the amendments' failures, for the intact bill on the final vote, and so forth in infinite variation.

The line of responsibility in the states' executive branch, however, runs clearly to the governors, or at least that is the public perception. Even when governors have taken no part in a major or minor administrative (or legislative or judicial) decision, they must often bear the blame for mishaps. (Credit for accomplishments is usually more divided, as politicians and administrators suddenly appear out of the woodwork to take their bows.) Since governors make the tough decisions and are the focus of the public attention within each state, it is not surprising that they are better known on the average than either of their states' U.S. senators.[12] For the very same reasons, governors are usually more unpopular than senators. In 1970 a polling firm found that in almost all of twenty states surveyed, the governor was disliked by a greater portion of the population than either senator, regardless of similar or conflicting affiliations or whether either governor or senator was up for reelection.[13]

While the recognition factor for senators may be lower on the average than for governors, nationally it will probably far surpass that of the governors if they are at all prominent in the Senate. It is the tremendous publicity edge held by senators that has permitted them to leapfrog the governors in the presidential preliminaries and to become well-known across the country even when bested at home. The news media, especially television, have concentrated heavily on the nation's capital, and as reporter David Broder observed, "Men of any importance in the Senate—and many of compelling unimportance—can become famed in the land simply by making themselves available to the gents with the tape recorders and the cameras."[14] Even big-state governors, who can command some national media attention, cannot compete with senators because they are not often in Washington, the site chosen by the media for the concentration of communications facilities. Some senator can always be found to fill a three-minute open slot on the *CBS Evening News*. If the Shah of Iran cancels out on *Meet the Press* at the last minute, a senator or two can be scouted up without much difficulty. This type of Washington news monopoly has been partly the result of convenience and laziness on the part of the press, but it also has reflected the judgment of the people and the press as to where the action has been in government. The decline of gubernatorial presidents was yet another price the states paid for their reluctance to meet their responsibilities.

Senators have had other built-in advantages over governors in presidential politics. Since World War II foreign policy more often than not has dominated presidential elections, as the United States lunged from one foreign adventure to another while participating in the Cold War. Governors, whose concerns are statewide and national, have rarely ventured into international politics, whereas senators have been able to develop an expertise in foreign affairs and travel widely at taxpayers' expense (sometimes even when their committee assignments have had little to do with international relations). By presidential election time, senators are familiar and conversant with major foreign policy topics while governors usually have to start from scratch. Senators also have a longer term of office (six years compared to two to four for the governor) in which to entrench themselves politically in their home state and thus alleviate the pressures posed by some political construction chores. Their term length also bestows the advantage of greater flexibility in presidential maneuvering. They can adopt an image or issues that may be good for them presidentially while being unpopular with their constituents, and still, if the presidential bid fails, have a sufficient "buffer" of time to mend their home fences.

Senators have more opportunities to run for president without relinquishing their congressional seats, which is an added advantage, and unlimited succession gives senators time to plan properly a future presidential bid (and bide their time if necessary). In addition, the salaries and staffing for senators have been far more generous than for governors, even though the purely legislative duties of senators devour much less of their time than do the executive duties of governors. Congress is out-of-session for several months each year and operates on a four-day work week when it is in session. Congressmen are not idle by any means during breaks and recesses, but their time is much more flexible and permits, for example, a great deal more travel to build political organizations in states across the country prior to a presidential bid. By contrast, governors truly have full-time jobs and are not only expected but required to be in their own states, if only because of the press of business, virtually all the time. In 1976, for instance, when Governor Jerry Brown left California to campaign in three state primaries (in Maryland, Oregon, and Nevada) he was called to task and roundly criticized in his state for his absence. No senator or congressman campaigning against him (or running in years past, for that matter) had been similarly missed and rebuked.

By now the reader is probably convinced that governors are out of the presidential running, that rational governors have long since packed away their presidential dreams in an abandoned hope chest. Yet in 1976 a former big-state governor very nearly defeated his party's incumbent president for the Republican nomination, and a little-known ex-governor from a small Deep South state beat a gaggle of congressmen to the Democratic throne and, ultimately, to the White House. (Carter's closest rival was, in fact, another governor, Brown of California.) It is not that the logic that gave the competitive edge to senators was faulty or no sturdier than a house of cards. Instead the suppositions upon which the logic was erected have been altered, modified by some of the same events that have recently transformed the governorship and state administration. The differing natures of the executive and legislative jobs have certainly been maintained, and governors still make tough decisions in a manner unmatched by senators, but their decisions have been eased and the aftermaths made less politically disastrous for governors with the abatement of the tax issue squeeze (see Chapter 4). With politically more secure home bases, governors are thus becoming more attractive to their parties as potential presidential nominees. Senators continue to hold the tenure advantage, but the gap has been narrowed considerably by the extension of virtually all governors' terms from two to four years, the addition of successive term provisions for governors, and the shift of gubernatorial elections to nonpresidential years—all of which afford governors some of the same political benefits enumerated earlier for senators as a result of their term structure. Gubernatorial salaries and staffing have also been fortified in most cases to the point of equivalency or beyond (see Chapter 3).

With the Indochina war concluded and tensions reduced with both the Soviet Union and the People's Republic of China, foreign policy assumed a lesser role in 1976 presidential politics than in any election for decades, especially since the campaign was conducted in the midst of a serious recession. This deemphasis on foreign affairs redounded to the governors' favor, but even if international relations had been more prominent, governors would not have been quite as helpless and uninformed as in years past. The growing impact of foreign trade and investment on state economies has prodded governors to step into the international sphere. In 1970 only three states had an overseas office; by 1975 sixteen states had opened at least one.[15] In 1974 alone twenty-eight states sponsored trade and investment missions abroad.[16] These missions are often led by governors, who use them not only to further industrial development in their states but also to augment their contacts and knowledge of international relations. Jimmy Carter employed these tactics in the years prior to his presidential bid. Like Carter other governors have served on various governmental and private commissions whose subject matter is foreign policy. Carter's vehicle was the "Trilateral Commission" formed to encourage closer cooperation and consultation among the United States, Western Europe, and Japan. It was through his service on this commission that Carter met most of the men he later chose to be his major foreign policy advisers, including Secretary of State Cyrus Vance and National Security Adviser Zbigniew Brzezinski.

The 1976 election also showed that the advantage of senators in the media can be overrated. An obscure former governor from a small state, by demonstrating his campaign talents and organizational abilities, was able to capture sufficient press exposure to eclipse an entire cast of Washington political characters in a matter of a few months. Columnist James Kilpatrick prophetically suggested long before the Carter phenomenon that,

The media, especially television, can now produce a recognition factor so rapidly that if a Governor comes along who has the capacity for leadership, the charisma, the appeal . . . I believe that in a year of good work and national exposure, such a Governor could gain the kind of reputation that would permit him to launch into a presidential primary campaign with some reasonable hope of success.[17]

Thanks to the news media, the theory that only a big-state governor could successfully make a bid for a party presidential nomination anymore was debunked in 1976,[18] and, hopefully, the media will begin to give governors and states their fair share of coverage in nonelection years as well, now that federal power is generally acknowledged to be flowing to the states. If this change occurs, gubernatorial presidential aspirants will have less catching up to do in the future. Some print journalists, David Broder and Neal Peirce foremost among them, have been doing their best to change the old habits of their colleagues, but television news has been much slower in adapting to remodelled federal realities.

The fact that one governor prevailed and other governors performed so well in 1976 presidential politics has been repeatedly attributed to the electoral environment created by Watergate. This scandal-charged atmosphere, it has been supposed, was solely responsible for creating the conditions that permitted Jimmy Carter to win and Ronald Reagan and Jerry Brown to run so strongly. Watergate certainly was not an asset to Washington-based candidates, but as the foregoing analysis has attempted to show, the reemergence of governors is the outgrowth of many factors. Since Watergate is not wholly responsible for the new success of gubernatorial presidential candidates, the phenomenon is not likely to fade with the bad taste created by the scandal. Governors of the new, better breed will continue to make themselves felt at the presidential level, just as they have done in state politics and government. The commanding performances turned in by governors in 1976 have thrust state chief executives back into the presidential spotlight, and voters and party activists alike will remember to include governors in future political forecasts, thereby ending their exclusionary obsession with U.S. senators. Even the governors themselves may be emboldened to strike out on more presidential quests, now that they realize the ventures are not doomed from the start. The prediction here is not that governors will be dominating presidential politics for "X" number of decades, but that governors once again will be amply considered along with vice presidents and senators when presidential years come around. Carter's performance in office may have some effect on the success of future White House bids by governors, but his record would have to be catastrophic for the gubernatorial ranks to be permanently branded.

One further note on governors in presidential politics is necessary. Modern state executives are so tied to their work and the proper administration of states requires such constant devotion that it is becoming increasingly difficult for sitting governors to seek the presidency. Former Governor Frank Sargent of Massachusetts declared bluntly: "There is no possibility a sitting governor today could go all out and run for president."[19] Former Governor Robert Meyner of New Jersey, who has observed the mushrooming gubernatorial workload in his industrial state, agreed: "I don't think a governor with the responsibilities he has today can run for president and do justice to his work."[20] The 1976 experience tended to confirm their observations. Carter and Reagan, as former governors, could campaign full-time while Brown, a sitting governor, delayed his entry and was unable to make a total commitment to his presidential bid because of his incumbent duties. This suggests a change in the old pattern of gubernatorial succession to the presidency. In earlier years incumbent governors who had held office only a few years were generally the ones chosen to be the parties' standardbearers.[21] Now it appears that former governors (but those out of office just recently) have the advantage since they can meet the heavy demands of modern campaigning (and can more than match senators' scheduling flexibility).

Now that the rise of governors in recent presidential politics at the expense of U.S. senators has been catalogued, it might be profitable to consider briefly the relative merits of each post as preparation for the Oval Office. Since this is a study of governors, the reader might reasonably suspect a bias if the argument was weighted heavily to the governorship as the most auspicious pathway to the presidency. Yet it is hard to find scholars and political observers who quarrel with that assessment.

Elbridge Gerry of Massachusetts actually suggested at the 1787 Constitutional Convention that the national president should be appointed by the state governors since they knew best what qualities an executive should possess.[22] Historian Wilfred E. Binkley may not have gone quite that far, but he insisted that the historical record strongly suggested a correlation between successful presidencies and prior gubernatorial experience.[23] Calling the governorship "an incomparable executive apprenticeship," Binkley compared the gubernatorial and nongubernatorial presidents from the end of the Civil War to 1945. The contrast of the former group (Rutherford Hayes, Grover Cleveland, William McKinley, Theodore Roosevelt, Woodrow Wilson, Calvin Coolidge, and Franklin Roosevelt) to the latter (U.S. Grant, James Garfield, Benjamin Harrison, William Howard Taft, Warren Harding, and Herbert Hoover) was so ". . . striking . . . that it might be mistaken for a deliberate attempt to catalogue the less happy choices of the American electorate for the presidency" among the nongubernatorial chief executives. Binkley treated the senator-presidents with special scorn. By his count in 1958, not one of six "great" nor the four "near great" presidents had served a full Senate term, but three of eleven "average," three of the six "below average," and one of two "failure" presidents had been senators. By contrast, more than half the combined "great" and "near great" group had served as governor.

The governorship and the presidency certainly require compatible executive talents, whereas the executive and management skills of senators are very much subordinate to their legislative gifts as determinants of their success. There is overlap, of course; persuasive ability and familiarity with the work of government are two examples. Yet is it not normal and proper to fill a job with a person who has been the most thoroughly trained of the candidates available in the skills it requires? Looking to the earlier listing of outstanding governors, there were superior state chief executives in each party who could have made more capable presidents than any of the nongovernors who served in the White House from 1952 to 1976. As much has been acknowledged by political professionals through the years. In 1960 Russell Baker, for instance, reported: "It is worth noting in passing the number of Democratic professionals who believe that, if [Nelson] Rockefeller had been a Democrat, the party would have rejected all its Senate contenders this year and stampeded . . . to the governor of New York."[24] The failings of two of our recent presidents, Lyndon Johnson and Richard Nixon, went far beyond their lack of executive expertise, but Gerald Ford offers an excellent illustration of the executive-legislative dichotomy. Ford's sole pre-presidential experience in public life before his brief tenure as vice president had been his long-time service as a congressman. He was trained in the byways and the folkways of the legislature, which more than adequately kept him abreast of governmental policy but did not confer upon him any executive skills. The dynamism, decisiveness, forceful leadership, and sheer sense of movement that characterize a trained executive were absent in the man, as knowledgeable and well-intentioned as he was. Thus Americans turned elsewhere for leadership in 1976, and it was to an executive—more particularly, a recent state governor—that they turned.

Goodbye, Good-Time Charlie

The inventory of change is now complete, and the transformation of the American governor—from near omnipotent colonial to emasculated "cypher" to the modern new breed—is now apparent. How far the state chief executive has come since one politician told Alexis de Tocqueville, "The Governor counts for absolutely nothing and is only paid 1,200 dollars"![25]

While governors are still an elite corps of white, male lawyers and businessmen, they are slowly becoming more heterogeneous; women have established toeholds, and blacks are a step away from governorships. Religion is no longer much of a bar to election, and Catholic and Jewish chief executives are more numerous than ever. Informal candidacy requirements like marital status are no longer so absolute. The new governors are younger and better educated, and the break with the past is perhaps most striking in the South. The preparation in public office that governors receive prior to their elections is more thorough and appropriate. The governorship has become so attractive that a goodly number of congressmen have been enticed to leave their Washington haven for a crack at the statehouse. Former governors have found recently that their talents are in greater demand by voters and presidents alike, and the postgubernatorial federal administrative, judicial, and elective posts have generally been more prestigious than before.

The governors' bailiwick, state government, has been heavily overhauled of late. Constitutional revision and reorganization has proceeded at a pace that is nothing short of astounding. Thanks to this rapid, basic transformation of the structure of state government, modern governors work in a much less inhibiting administrative environment that is only marred by the persistence of a cluster of other statewide elective offices not directly under the governors' control. The decline of patronage is judged a boon that has liberated chief executives from a time-consuming, outmoded, and frustrating chore. In the place of patronage, governors have gained appointive powers where it really matters—at the top levels of state government. Gubernatorial staff and salaries have been generously augmented, as have those of lieutenant governors. The holders of the second highest state post, with the addition of more substantial duties, are being better trained for the top job that many of them will eventually win. Their relationship with the governors is given greater assurance of harmony by the institution of team election of governor and lieutenant governor. Meanwhile the strengthening of the executive budget and other planning and management tools have consolidated the control of chief executive over state administration (even granting them a bit more leverage over the other statewide elected officers). Legislatively, the near-invincible veto power of governors has been enlarged, while reapportionment has meant that governors and state legislatures now represent the same constituencies and have more compatible outlooks and orientations as a result. No development has been more crucial to the strengthening of the governors and the states.

The political transition matches the transformation of state institutional practices. Two-party competition that has spread throughout the country exhibited tremendous growth in the past quarter-century and has encouraged the nomination of more capable persons for governorships. Those nominees who are elected are able to hold their office longer and to make a greater impact by the extension of term length from two to four years with the possibility of a consecutive reelection. Experience in recent years has indicated that governors are indeed fulfilling their tenure potential, and thereby devoting more of their career and talents to the job. Governors today are electorally less threatened by the tax issue since most of the wrenching tax decisions have already been made by courageous predecessors. With the major sales and income taxing tools already at hand, there will likely be fewer "tax-loss" governors in the future, even though tax increases to meet legitimate needs are inevitable. Another favorable electoral trend is that fewer governors are being defeated because of political and administrative incompetency. The growth of ticket splitting and independent voting (coupled with numerous reschedulings of gubernatorial elections to nonpresidential years) has insulated statehouse candidates from the nefarious effects of presidential coattails. Better governors with surer mandates have resulted, now that state issues are not so easily lost in the shuffle. However, one destructive side effect of ticket splitting can, in certain circumstances, cripple a governor's program: split party control of the legislature. Yet this electoral evil pales in comparison with the wretched system of campaign fund raising, a condition which can probably be corrected only by campaign financing derived from the public treasury.

Federally, the shift has been to the states. Now that states have awakened to their responsibilities and the national government has realized that it cannot accomplish its duties without their help, the states have been able to assume their proper federal role. It is not that the states are threatening to eclipse the federal government by any means; rather, a constructive partnership based on cooperation as much as conflict is developing. Revenue sharing and block grants, enacted by the national government, are significant innovations in federalism; not only have they supplanted some categorical grants-in-aid, which are much less desirable from the states' perspective but they have also helped to override masses of bureaucratic red tape.

The parallel expansion of program and activity on the state level, which continued even in the midst of a severe recession, has also been noted.[26] A more diversified revenue base, combined with massive spending increases in domestic services and employment, has altered the states' fiscal pattern to such an extent that federal aid, while increasing, accounts for a reduced proportion of state revenues. This situation also holds true on the local level, where old and justifiable hostilities with the statehouse have been giving way to more state aid and cooperative federal ventures like the New Coalition. However, the Washington-city hall axis will continue to weaken only if the new-found state responsiveness to localities endures and redoubles.

One of the reasons for recent state advances on the federal level has been the exceptional development of the National Governors' Association from nonentity to professional lobby group. By effectively representing the governors' viewpoints and advocating for the states, the association has institutionalized a gubernatorial contribution to federal policy making. Its Center for Policy Analysis lets the governors move a giant step beyond merely reacting to the proposals of others. The National Governors' Association will never be as unified or, consequently, as potent as some other governmental lobby groups, but it nevertheless performs an essential and long-overdue mission for the governors.

The national influence of governors has grown in other ways as well. While state chief executives have less influence in their parties' convention choices for national chief executive (due to the mushrooming primary system of nomination and revisions in party rules), they have been able to exert a greater claim on the White House itself and have dethroned senators from their long-favored position in the process. The reemerging prominence of governors in presidential politics is really a culmination of the changes that have fused to beget a new breed of governor. Even the concentration of news communications facilities in Washington is an insurmountable hurdle no more. Governors, while they will not dominate presidential politics to the exclusion of other officials, are no longer shut out of the Oval Office. They—especially former governors—will be considered at party nomination time because they have managed to even out the previously overwhelming advantages possessed by U.S. senators. Since the executive skills bestowed by the governorship are more compatible with the talents necessary for an effective presidency, better governance may well result.

The governor's resurrection, presidentially and in the states, was a feat not easily accomplished, a product of the intricate interweaving of the social, political, economic, and institutional forces that wrought urbanization, the civil rights revolution, the spread of two-party competition, and reapportionment. The resultant new breed of governor has had, and will continue to have, enormous significance for government on all levels in the United States. Good-time Charlie could command little respect at home or beyond his state's boundaries; more importantly, he could not accomplish very much for his people, shackled by his own inadequacies and those of his state government. Good-time Charlie is gone. In Arkansas and Arizona, North Dakota and New Mexico, Oklahoma and Oregon, and in most states across the country, concerned, capable, accomplished persons have been elected in his stead. The register of their state achievements irrefutably demonstrates that Good-time Charlie is not missed.

Notes

1. William R. Keech and Donald Matthews, *The Party's Choice*, Studies in Presidential Selection No. 7 (Washington, D.C.: The Brookings Institution, 1976), pp. 18-19.

2. Dewey also ran for president in 1944 as the Republican nominee, but had not yet served as a governor.

3. See Ralph G. Plumb, *Our American Governors* (Manitowoc, Wisc.: Manitowoc Printing and Lithographing Corp., 1956), pp. 35-36.

4. Joseph E. Kallenbach, "Governors and the Presidency," *Michigan Alumnus Quarterly Review* 60 (Spring 1954):238; also Plumb, ibid., pp. 32-34.

5. Kallenbach, ibid., pp. 238-39.

6. See Paul T. David, "The Role of Governors at the National Party Conventions," *State Government* 33 (Spring 1960):103-10.

7. Keech and Matthews, *The Party's Choice*, pp. 179-81.

8. Ibid., pp. 195-96.

9. See W. Brooke Graves, *American Governmental Relations: Their Origins, Historical Development and Current Status* (New York: Scribner's, 1964), pp. 237-40.

10. See Louis Harris, "Why the Odds are Against a Governor's Becoming President," *Public Opinion Quarterly* 4 (July 1959):361-70; Russell Baker, "Best Road to the White House—Which?" *New York Times Magazine*, November 27, 1960; and David Broder, "What's the Best Road to the White House?" *New York Times Magazine*, September 23, 1963.

11. The others were in 1880 and 1908.

12. See poll results summarized in Chapter 1.

13. James Clotfelter and William R. Hamilton, "Electing a Governor in the Seventies," in Thad L. Beyle and J. Oliver Williams (eds.), *The American Governor in Behavioral Perspective* (New York: Harper & Row, 1972), p. 32.

14. David Broder, *The Party's Over: The Failure of Politics in America* (New York: Harper & Row, 1972), p. 91.

15. James Harwell, "The States' Growing International Role," *State Government* 58 (Winter 1975):2-5.

16. Ibid.

17. National Governors' Conference, *Meet the Governors* (Lexington, Ky.: Council of State Governments, 1973), p. 9.

18. Keech and Matthews, *The Party's Choice*, pp. 24-25.

19. Interview with the author, October 16, 1976, Staffordshire, England.

20. Interview with the author, July 29, 1976, Newark, N.J.

21. See Joseph Schlesinger, "The Governor's Place in American Politics," *Public Administration Review* 30 (January 1970):4. About 80 percent of governors who have received party presidential or vice presidential nominations have served four years or less.

22. Kallenbach, "Governors and the Presidency," p. 235.

23. Wilfred E. Binkley, *President and Congress* (New York: Alfred A. Knopf, 1947), pp. 297-98; and Blakley, *The Man in the White House* (Baltimore: Johns Hopkins Press, 1958), pp. 92-93.

24. Baker, "Best Road to the White House," p. 124.

25. Alexis de Tocqueville, *Journey to America*, J.P. Mayer (ed.) (London: Faber and Faber, 1959), p. 94.

26. See Neal Peirce, "The States: Innovative Solutions to the Recession," *The Washington Post*, February 27, 1976, p. A-25.

Appendixes

Appendix A
Interviews, Research,
Correspondence

Interviews

Governors

Terry Sanford
(D-N.C., 1961-1965)
Duke University
Durham, N.C.
July 21, 1976

Robert Meyner
(D-N.J., 1954-1962)
Newark, N.J.
July 29, 1976

Richard J. Hughes
(D-N.J., 1962-1970)
Supreme Court of New Jersey
Trenton, N.J.
July 30, 1976

Edmund G. Brown, Sr.
(D-Calif., 1959-1967)
Beverly Hills, Calif.
August 2, 1976[a]

Calvin Rampton
(D-Utah, 1965-1977)
Governor's Office
Salt Lake City, Utah
August 3, 1976

Tom McCall
(R-Ore., 1967-1975)
Portland, Oregon
August 4, 1976

Daniel J. Evans
(R-Wash., 1965-1977)
Olympia, Wash.
August 5, 1976

G. Mennen Williams
(D-Mich., 1949-1961)
Supreme Court of Michigan
Detroit, Mich.
August 6, 1976

Matthew Welsh
(D-Ind., 1961-1965)
Indianapolis, Ind.
August 10, 1976

William Scranton
(R-Penn., 1962-1966)
United Nations
New York, N.Y.
August 24, 1976

Harold Stassen
(R-Minn., 1938-1943)
Philadelphia, Penn.
August 24, 1976

Robert D. Ray
(R-Iowa, 1969–)
Governor's Office
Des Moines, Iowa
August 31, 1976

---

[a]Continued by telephone on August 8, 1976.

Reubin Askew
(D-Fla., 1971–)
Governor's Office
Tallahassee, Fla.
September 8, 1976

George Romney
(R-Mich., 1963-1969)
Bloomfield Hills, Mich.
September 23, 1976

John J. Gilligan
(D-Ohio, 1971-1975)
Keele, Staffordshire, England
October 16, 1976[b]

Francis W. Sargent
(R-Mass., 1969-1975)
Keele, Staffordshire, England
October 16, 1976[b]

Scott Matheson
(D-Utah, 1977–)
Salt Lake City, Utah
August 2, 1976, and
Washington, D.C.
January 20, 1977

Others

Ron Schmidt, former Administrative Assistant to Governor Tom McCall, Portland, Ore., August 4, 1976

David Oman, Press Secretary to Governor Robert Ray, Des Moines, Ia., August 31, 1976

Mayor Moon Landrieu (D-New Orleans), President of the U.S. Conference of Mayors (1975-76), Mayor's Office, New Orleans, La., September 7, 1976

Paul Schnitt, Press Secretary to Governor Reubin Askew, Tallahassee, Fla., September 8, 1976

Neal Peirce, author and columnist, *The National Journal*, Washington, D.C., September 13, 1976

Terry Smith, Staff Director, Executive Management and Fiscal Affairs, National Governors' Conference, Washington, D.C., September 16, 1976

Brevard Crihfield, Executive Director, Council of State Governments, Lexington, Ky., September 21, 1976

---

[b]Interviewed at a conference entitled, "American Politics Today," sponsored by the David Bruce Centre, University of Keele.

217

James Reichley, White House Consultant and former Legislative Secretary to Governor William Scranton, Washington, D.C., September 14, 1976

Research

Democratic National Convention, New York, N.Y., July 12-15, 1975

Republican National Convention, Kansas City, Mo., August 16-20, 1976

Citizens' Research Foundation, Princeton, N.J.

The National Journal, Washington, D.C.

Advisory Commission on Intergovernmental Relations, Washington, D.C.

National Governors' Conference, Washington, D.C.

Council of State Governments, Lexington, Ky.

Library of Congress, Washington, D.C.

The National Governors' Conference (Annual Meeting), Detroit, Mich., September 7-9, 1977

Correspondence—Governors

Jerry Apodaca
(D-N.M., 1975–)

Francis W. Sargent
(R—Mass., 1969-1975)

Thomas Salmon
(D-Vt., 1973-1977)

John J. Gilligan
(D—Ohio, 1971-1975)

Milton Shapp
(D-Penn., 1971–)

David Boren
(D—Okla., 1975–)

George Leader
(D-Penn., 1955-1959)

Interview Questions for Governors

The following prepared questions were asked in most interviews with governors. These particular questions were designed for former governors; incumbents were asked a slightly different set. In addition, specialized questions were prepared for each interviewee based on his background and gubernatorial experiences. No two interviews were exactly alike, and this outline of questions is meant only to suggest the scope of most interviews.

Section A. Outstanding Governors

1. Which governor or governors in your state over the past quarter-century have been the most outstanding in your opinion? Why? Who have been the least outstanding? Why?
2. Within your party, who have been the most outstanding governors in the nation in the past quarter-century—including those currently serving? Why? Who have been the least outstanding? Why?
3. Within the other party, who have been the most outstanding governors in the nation in the past few years—including those currently serving? Why? Who have been the least outstanding? Why?
4. What do you think of the so-called "new breed" of governors—those who shun the ceremonies of office?
5. Overall, how would you rate the type of person being elected governor today throughout the nation with the kind elected two decades ago—better, worse, or about the same?

Section B. Power of the Governor

1. Has the power of the governor increased, decreased, or stayed the same in the last couple of decades in your state? If an increase or decrease, how and why?
2. Would you like to see the office of governor strengthened further? If so, how?
3. Did you have difficulties during your term with the other constitutionally elected state officers? If so, please describe. Have there been or are there any efforts to reduce the number or powers of the other officers? Have you or do you support such efforts? Why or why not?
4. Did you feel you had sufficient power or control over the state's executive branch—including the departments, commissions, and boards? How has this situation changed, if at all, since you left the governor's office?
5. Do you favor or oppose a limit on the number of consecutive terms a governor may serve? Why?
6. Have the governor's patronage powers been strengthened, weakened, or remained about the same in the last couple of decades? If a change, what effect has this had on the governor? How important was patronage to you—and how important is it to today's governor—in maintaining control?

7. Has the office of lieutenant governor been strengthened in your state? If so, has this proved of any help to the governor? If not, would you like to see it strengthened?

8. Has Watergate and its aftermath had any appreciable effect on the governor's executive powers at the state level? Has the state legislature attempted to place any controls on the governor similar to those enacted by Congress to restrain the president?

9. How do you see the office of governor developing in the next decade or so?

Section C. Federal Relations

1. Has the power of the governor (and the power position of the state) vis-à-vis the federal government increased, decreased, or stayed the same in the last couple of decades? If increased or decreased how and why? How does this differ from your conception of the governor's role at the time you served in the office?

2. What kinds of problems did you have in dealing with the federal government?

3. How do you see the relationship between the states and the federal government developing in the next decade or so?

4. How would you evaluate the evolution of the National Governors' Conference? Should the NGC's present scope of activities be contracted or expanded?

5. How has the relationship between the governor and the state, and the localities, changed over the past decade or so? Has the state become more or less powerful with respect to the localities, or has the power relationship stayed about the same?

6. Have state governments proven more sympathetic and helpful to their cities over the last decade than the preceding one?

7. In what policy areas have the states "grabbed the ball" and taken significant action on the problems of the cities?

8. In which states or areas of the country have state governments done the most or been most sympathetic to the problems of their cities?

9. How do you see the relationship between the states and their localities developing in the next decade or so?

Section D. Issues

1. What was the key issue, or issues, that first helped you to win the governorship? What were your main opponent(s)'s primary issues in that first campaign?

2. In your subsequent reelection campaign(s) (if any), what were your key

issues and those of your oponent(s)? How have the issues, and the candidates' use of them, changed since your time in office?

3. Hypothetically, what action or actions would a governor take that would most insure his reelection? His defeat for re-election?
4. What was the greatest single problem you faced during your term?
5. What do you consider to be the single most important of your accomplishments in office? Other significant accomplishments? Greatest single failing? Other important failings?

Section E. Career and Personal

1. Did your background in [business, political offices, etc.] prepare you well to serve as governor? In your opinion, what might be the ideal background for a governor—a set of certain political offices, a particular business occupation, or what?
2. What did you plan or hope to do once your governorship was completed?
3. How much would it matter to the electorate in your state if a candidate for governor today was divorced? single? a woman? black? How has this changed since the time you were in office?
4. Almost all governors in the past 25 years have been either lawyers or businessmen. They have been overwhelmingly white, male, and middle aged. Is there a need for a greater diversification in the people who serve as governor or does this not matter a great deal?

Section F. Politics

1. Would you say that your state now has two strongly competitive parties? Which party has the edge? How has the party competition changed over the past decades?
2. All in all, would you say it's easier or more difficult for an incumbent governor to get reelected today than, say, 25 years ago? Why?
3. Has the trend of ticket splitting and independent voting among the electorate changed the way in which a gubernatorial candidate campaigns for office? If so, how? Has this trend changed the way a governor conducts himself in office? If so, how?
4. What were the most effective campaign techniques you used in running for governor? Were there any especially effective techniques used by your opponent(s) or other gubernatorial contenders through the years? Could you describe the changes in campaign techniques that have taken place since you first ran for governor?
5. Has voter turnout and interest in elections for state offices in this state been

increasing, decreasing, or staying about the same in the past decade? If a change, why?

6. What is the method of nomination for the governorship in this state? Are you satisfied with this process or would you prefer another method?

7. This year for the very first time in two decades we are seeing governors superseding U.S. senators and vice presidents at the top of the national party decks in the presidential contests. Why do you think governors have reemerged so strongly as presidential candidates? Do you think this trend will continue in future presidential contests?

Appendix B
Governors of the
States, 1950-1975

Alabama

James E. Folsom	D	1947-1951, 1955-1959
Gordon Persons	D	1951-1955
John Patterson	D	1959-1963
George C. Wallace	D	1963-1967, 1971–
Lurleen B. Wallace	D	1967-1968
Albert P. Brewer[a]	D	1968-1971

Alaska

William A. Egan	D	1959-1966, 1970-1974
Walter J. Hickel	R	1966-1969
Keith H. Miller[a]	R	1969-1970
Jay Hammond	R	1974–

Arizona

Dan E. Garvey[a]	D	1948-1951
Howard Pyle	R	1951-1955
Ernest W. McFarland	D	1955-1959
Paul Fannin	R	1959-1965
Samuel P. Goddard, Jr.	D	1965-1967
Jack Williams	R	1967-1975
Raul H. Castro	D	1975-1977
[Wes Bolin] [a]	[D]	[1977-1978]
[Bruce Babbitt] [a]	[D]	[1978-]

Arkansas[g]

Sid S. McMath	D	1949-1953
Francis Cherry	D	1953-1955
Orval E. Faubus	D	1955-1967
Winthrop Rockefeller	R	1967-1971
Dale Bumpers	D	1971-1975
David Pryor	D	1975–

California

Earl Warren	R	1943-1953
Goodwin J. Knight[a]	R	1953-1959
Edmund G. Brown, Sr.	D	1959-1967
Ronald Reagan	R	1967-1975
Edmund G. Brown, Jr.	D	1975–

Colorado

Lee Knous	D	1947-1950
Walter Johnson	D	1950-1951
Dan Thorton	R	1951-1955
Edwin C. Johnson[c]	D	1955-1957
Steven L.R. McNichols	D	1957-1963
John A. Love	R	1963-1973
John D. Vanderhoof[a]	R	1973-1975
Richard Lamm	D	1975–

Connecticut

Chester Bowles	D	1949-1951
John Lodge	R	1951-1955
Abraham A. Ribicoff	D	1955-1961
John Dempsey[a]	D	1961-1971
Thomas J. Meskill	R	1971-1975
Ella Grasso	D	1975–

Delaware[g]

Elbert N. Carvel	D	1949-1953, 1961-1965
J. Caleb Boggs	R	1953-1960
Charles L. Terry, Jr.	D	1965-1969
Russell W. Peterson	R	1969-1973
Sherman W. Tribbitt	D	1973-1977
[Pierre S. "Pete" DuPont]	[R]	[1977–]

Florida

Fuller Warren	D	1949-1953
Dan McCarty	D	1953
Charley E. Johns[a]	D	1953-1955
LeRoy Collins[b]	D	1955-1961
Farris Bryant	D	1961-1965
Haydon Burns	D	1965-1967
Claude R. Kirk, Jr.	R	1967-1971
Reubin O.D. Askew	D	1971–

Georgia

Herman Talmadge[b]	D	1949-1955
S. Marvin Griffin	D	1955-1959
S. Ernest Vandiver	D	1959-1963
Carl E. Sanders	D	1963-1967
Lester G. Maddox	D	1967-1971
Jimmy Carter	D	1971-1975
George Busbee	D	1975–

Hawaii

William F. Quinn[f]	R	1959-1962
John A. Burns	D	1962-1975
George Ariyoshi	D	1975–

Idaho

C.A. Robins	R	1947-1951
Len Jordan	R	1951-1955
Robert E. Smylie	R	1955-1967
Don Samuelson	R	1967-1971
Cecil D. Andrus	D	1971-1977
[John Evans] [a]	[D]	[1977–]

Illinois

Adlai E. Stevenson	D	1949-1953
William G. Stratton	R	1953-1961
Otto Kerner	D	1961-1968
Samuel H. Shapiro[b]	D	1968-1969
Richard B. Ogilvie	R	1969-1973
Daniel Walker	D	1973-1977
[James Thompson]	[R]	[1977–]

Indiana

Henry F. Schricker[c]	D	1949-1953
George N. Craig	R	1953-1957
Harold W. Handley	R	1957-1961
Matthew E. Welsh	D	1961-1965
Roger D. Branigin	D	1965-1969
Edgar D. Whitcomb	R	1969-1973
Otis R. Bowen	R	1973–

Iowa[g]

William S. Beardsley	R	1949-1954
Leo A. Hoegh	R	1955-1957
Herschel C. Loveless	D	1957-1961
Norman A. Erbe	R	1961-1963
Harold E. Hughes	D	1963-1969
Robert D. Ray	R	1969–

Kansas[g]

Frank Carlson	R	1947-1951
Edward F. Arn	R	1951-1955
Fred Hall	R	1955-1957
George Docking	D	1957-1961

John Anderson, Jr.	R	1961-1965
William H. Avery	R	1965-1967
Robert Docking	D	1967-1975
Robert F. Bennett	R	1975–

Kentucky

Earle C. Clements[a]	D	1948-1950
Lawrence W. Wetherby[a]	D	1950-1955
Albert B. Chandler[c]	D	1955-1959
Bert Combs	D	1959-1963
Edward T. Breathitt	D	1963-1967
Louie B. Nunn	R	1967-1971
Wendell H. Ford	D	1971-1974
Julian Carroll[a]	D	1974–

Louisiana

Earl K. Long[c]	D	1948-1952, 1956-1960
Robert F. Kennon	D	1952-1956
Jimmie H. Davis[c]	D	1960-1964
John J. McKeithen	D	1964-1972
Edwin W. Edwards	D	1972–

Maine[g]

Frederick G. Payne	R	1949-1952
Burton M. Cross	R	1952-1955
Edmund S. Muskie	D	1955-1959
Clinton A. Clauson	D	1959–
John H. Reed[a]	R	1959-1967
Kenneth M. Curtis	D	1967-1975
James B. Longley	I	1975–

Maryland

William Preston Lane, Jr.	D	1947-1951
Theodore R. McKeldin	R	1951-1959
J. Millard Tawes	D	1959-1967
Spiro T. Agnew	R	1967-1969
Marvin Mandel[b]	D	1969-1977
[Blair Lee III] [a]	[D]	[1977–]

Massachusetts

Paul A. Dever	D	1949-1953
Christian A. Herter	R	1953-1957
Foster Furcolo	D	1957-1961

John A. Volpe	R	1961-1963, 1965-1969
Endicott Peabody	D	1963-1965
Francis W. Sargent[a]	R	1969-1975
Michael Dukakis	D	1975–

Michigan

G. Mennen Williams	D	1949-1961
John B. Swainson	D	1961-1963
George Romney	R	1963-1969
William G. Milliken[a]	R	1969–

Minnesota[d]

Luther W. Youngdahl	R	1947-1951
C. Elmer Anderson[a]	R	1951-1955
Orville L. Freeman	D	1955-1961
Elmer L. Andersen	R	1961-1963
Karl F. Rolvaag	D	1963-1967
Harold LeVander	R	1967-1971
Wendell R. Anderson	D	1971-1977
[Rudy Perpich] [a]	[D]	[1977–]

Mississippi

Fielding L. Wright[a]	D	1946-1952
Hugh White[c]	D	1952-1956
James P. Coleman	D	1956-1960
Ross R. Barnett	D	1960-1964
Paul B. Johnson	D	1964-1968
John Bell Williams	D	1968-1972
William L. Waller	D	1972-1976
Cliff Finch	D	1976–

Missouri

Forrest Smith	D	1949-1953
Phil M. Donnelly[c]	D	1953-1957
James T. Blair, Jr.	D	1957-1961
John M. Dalton	D	1961-1965
Warren E. Hearnes	D	1965-1973
Christopher Bond	R	1973-1977
[Joseph Teasdale]	[D]	[1977–]

Montana

John W. Bonner	D	1949-1953
J. Hugo Aronson	R	1953-1961

Donald G. Nutter	R	1961-1962
Tim M. Babcock[a]	R	1962-1969
Forrest H. Anderson	D	1969-1973
Thomas L. Judge	D	1973–

Nebraska

Val Peterson	R	1947-1953
Robert B. Crosby	R	1953-1955
Victor E. Anderson	R	1955-1959
Ralph G. Brooks	D	1959-1960
Dwight W. Burney[b]	R	1960-1961
Frank B. Morrison	D	1961-1967
Norbert T. Tiemann	R	1967-1971
J. James Exon	D	1971–

Nevada

Vail Pittman[a]	D	1945-1951
Charles H. Russell	R	1951-1959
Grant Sawyer	D	1959-1967
Paul Laxalt	R	1967-1971
Mike O'Callaghan	D	1971–

New Hampshire

Sherman Adams	R	1949-1953
Hugh Gregg	R	1953-1955
Lane Dwinell	R	1955-1959
Wesley Powell	R	1959-1963
John W. King	D	1963-1969
Walter Peterson	R	1969-1973
Meldrim Thomson, Jr.	R	1973–

New Jersey

Alfred E. Driscoll	R	1947-1954
Robert B. Meyner	D	1954-1962
Richard J. Hughes	D	1962-1970
William T. Cahill	R	1970-1974
Brendan T. Byrne	D	1974–

New Mexico[g]

Thomas J. Mabry	D	1947-1951
Edwin L. Mechem	R	1951-1955, 1957-1959, 1961-1962
John Field Simms	D	1955-1957
John Burroughs	D	1959-1961

Jack M. Campbell	D	1963-1967
David F. Cargo	R	1967-1971
Bruce King	D	1971-1975
Jerry Apodaca	D	1975–
New York		
Thomas E. Dewey	R	1942-1955
Averell Harriman	D	1955-1959
Nelson A. Rockefeller	R	1959-1973
Malcolm Wilson[a]	R	1973-1975
Hugh Carey	D	1975–
North Carolina		
W. Kerr Scott	D	1949-1953
William B. Umstead	D	1953-1954
Luther H. Hodges, Sr.[a]	D	1954-1961
Terry Sanford	D	1961-1965
Dan K. Moore	D	1965-1969
Robert W. Scott	D	1969-1973
James E. Holshouser, Jr.	R	1973-1977
[James Hunt]	[D]	[1977–]
North Dakota		
Fred G. Aandahl	R	1945-1951
C. Norman Brunsdale	R	1951-1957
John E. Davis	R	1957-1961
William L. Guy	D	1961-1973
Arthur A. Link	D	1973–
Ohio[g]		
Frank J. Lausche[c]	D	1949-1957
C. William O'Neill	R	1957-1959
Michael V. DiSalle	D	1959-1963
James A. Rhodes	R	1963-1971, 1975–
John J. Gilligan	D	1971-1975
Oklahoma[g]		
Roy J. Turner	D	1947-1951
Johnston Murray	D	1951-1955
Raymond Gary	D	1955-1959
J. Howard Edmondson	D	1959-1963
Henry Bellmon	R	1963-1967
Dewey F. Bartlett	R	1967-1971

David Hall	D	1971-1975
David Boren	D	1975–

Oregon

Douglas McKay[b]	R	1949-1952
Paul L. Patterson	R	1952-1956
Elmo Smith[a]	R	1956-1957
Robert D. Holmes[b]	D	1957-1959
Mark O. Hatfield	R	1959-1967
Tom McCall	R	1967-1975
Robert Straub	D	1975–

Pennsylvania

James H. Duff	R	1947-1951
John S. Fine	R	1951-1955
George M. Leader	D	1955-1959
David L. Lawrence	D	1959-1963
William W. Scranton	R	1963-1967
Raymond P. Shafer	R	1967-1971
Milton J. Shapp	D	1971–

Rhode Island[g]

John O. Pastore[a]	D	1945-1951
Dennis J. Roberts	D	1951-1959
Christopher Del Sesto	R	1959-1961
John A. Notte, Jr.	D	1961-1963
John H. Chafee	R	1963-1969
Frank Licht	D	1969-1973
Philip W. Noel	D	1973-1977
[J. Joseph Garrahy]	[D]	[1977–]

South Carolina

J. Strom Thurmond	D	1947-1951
James F. Byrnes	D	1951-1955
George Bell Timmerman, Jr.	D	1955-1959
Ernest F. Hollings	D	1959-1963
Donald S. Russell	D	1963-1965
Robert E. McNair[a]	D	1965-1971
John C. West	D	1971-1975
James B. Edwards	R	1975–

South Dakota

George T. Mickelson	R	1947-1951
Sigurd Anderson	R	1951-1955

Joe J. Foss	R	1955-1959
Ralph Herseth	D	1959-1961
Archie Gubbrud	R	1961-1965
Nils A. Boe	R	1965-1969
Frank L. Farrar	R	1969-1971
Richard F. Kneip	D	1971–

Tennessee

Gordon Browning[c]	D	1949-1953
Frank G. Clement	D	1953-1959, 1963-1967
Buford Ellington	D	1959-1963, 1967-1971
Winfield Dunn	R	1971-1975
Ray Blanton	D	1975–

Texas

Allan Shivers[a]	D	1949-1957
Price Daniel	D	1957-1963
John B. Connally	D	1963-1969
Preston Smith	D	1969-1973
Dolph Briscoe	D	1973–

Utah

J. Bracken Lee	R	1949-1957
George D. Clyde	R	1957-1965
Calvin L. Rampton	D	1965-1977
[Scott M. Matheson]	[D]	[1977–]

Vermont[g]

Harold J. Arthur[a]	R	1950-1951
Lee E. Emerson	R	1951-1955
Joseph Blaine Johnson	R	1955-1959
Robert T. Stafford	R	1959-1961
F. Ray Keyser, Jr.	R	1961-1963
Philip H. Hoff	D	1963-1969
Deane C. Davis	R	1969-1973
Thomas P. Salmon	D	1973-1977
[Richard A. Snelling]	[R]	[1977–]

Virginia

John S. Battle	D	1950-1954
Thomas B. Stanley	D	1954-1958
J. Lindsay Almond, Jr.	D	1958-1962
Albertis S. Harrison, Jr.	D	1962-1966
Mills E. Godwin, Jr.[e]	D	1966-1970, 1974-1978

Linwood Holton	R	1970-1974
[John N. Dalton]	[R]	[1978–]

Washington

Arthur B. Langlie[c]	R	1949-1957
Albert D. Rosellini	D	1957-1965
Daniel J. Evans	R	1965-1977
[Dixy Lee Ray]	[D]	[1977–]

West Virginia

Okey L. Patteson	D	1949-1953
William C. Marland	D	1953-1957
Cecil H. Underwood	R	1957-1961
William W. Barron	D	1961-1965
Hulett C. Smith	D	1965-1969
Arch A. Moore	R	1969-1977
[John D. "Jay" Rockefeller IV]	[D]	[1977–]

Wisconsin

Oscar Rennebohm[a]	R	1947-1951
Walter J. Kohler, Jr.	R	1951-1957
Vernon W. Thomson	R	1957-1959
Gaylord A. Nelson	D	1959-1963
John W. Reynolds	D	1963-1965
Warren P. Knowles	R	1965-1971
Patrick J. Lucey	D	1971-1977
[Martin J. Schreiber] [a]	[D]	[1977–]

Wyoming

Arthur G. Crane[a]	R	1949-1951
Frank A. Barrett	R	1951-1953
C.J. Rogers[a]	R	1953-1955
Milward L. Simpson	R	1955-1959
J.J. Hickey	D	1959-1961
Jack R. Gage[a]	D	1961-1963
Clifford P. Hansen	R	1963-1967
Stanley K. Hathaway	R	1967-1975
Ed Herschler	D	1975–

Sources: Compiled from various issues of *The Book of the States* (Council of State Governments, Chicago, Ill., and Lexington, Ky., 1942-1975); and Michael Barone, Grant Ujifusa, and Douglas Matthews, *The Almanac of American Politics, 1976* (New York: E.P. Dutton, 1975). Information on "interim" governors listed below in footnote g is from Congressional Quarterly, Inc., *Guide to U.S. Elections* (Washington, D.C.: Congressional Quarterly, Inc. 1975).

Note: Governors first elected or succeeding to office since 1975 are listed in brackets, but were not included in the study; if the term of an incumbent began before 1950, the full dates of tenure are nonetheless listed; and for Alaska and Hawaii, only the popularly elected governors after 1959 are listed.

[a]Succeeded to the governorship due to the death, resignation, or disability of the incumbent.

[b]Initially elected to the governorship by the state legislature or the people in midterm due to the death, resignation, or disability of the term's original incumbent.

[c]Had also served part or all of a previous term as governor, before the years noted in this table.

[d]The Democratic party is called the Democratic-Farmer-Labor (DFL) party in Minnesota.

[e]Godwin ran and was elected as a Democrat for his first term, and as a Republican for his second term.

[f]Quinn had served from 1957-1959 as the presidentially appointed governor of the territory of Hawaii.

[g]Each of these nine states has had at least one "interim" governor who held office for just a few days or weeks between a change of administrations. Usually the cause of succession was the election of the incumbent governor to the U.S. Senate, whose members take the oath of office shortly after New Year's Day. Since most state gubernatorial terms do not officially commence until the second week in January, the incumbent governor (and senator-elect) is forced to resign shortly before the end of his term. The lieutenant governor or designated officer then becomes governor until the newly elected administration legally takes office. These "interim" governors are not included in this table nor in any of the tabular material that appears in the text. The rule of thumb for exclusion was simply this: Any succession that occurred after a November general election immediately preceding a January change of state administrations was not counted for the purposes of this study. The "interim" governors, the dates of their terms, and the reason for their successions are listed below:

Arkansas
Bob Riley (D), Jan. 3-14, 1975: Gov. Dale Bumpers elected to U.S. Senate.
Delaware
David P. Buckson (R), Dec. 30, 1960-Jan. 17, 1961: Gov. Caleb Boggs elected to U.S. Senate.
Iowa
Leo Elthon (R), Nov. 22, 1954-Jan. 13, 1955: Retiring Gov. William S. Beardsley died in office.
Robert D. Fulton (D), Jan. 1-16, 1969: Gov. Harold Hughes elected to U.S. Senate.
Kansas
Frank L. Hagaman (R), Nov. 28, 1950-Jan. 8, 1951: Gov. Frank Carlson elected to U.S. Senate.
John McCuish (R), Jan. 3-14, 1957: Gov. Fred Hall resigned to take judgeship.
Maine
Robert N. Haskell (R), Jan. 3-8, 1959: Gov. Edmund Muskie elected to U.S. Senate.
New Mexico
Tom Bolack (R), Nov. 30, 1962-Jan. 1, 1963: Gov. Edwin L. Mechem appointed himself to vacancy in U.S. Senate.
Ohio
John W. Brown (R), Jan. 3-14, 1957: Gov. Frank J. Lausche elected to U.S. Senate.
Oklahoma
George P. Nigh (D), Jan. 6-14, 1963: Gov. J. Howard Edmondson appointed himself to vacancy in U.S. Senate.
Rhode Island
John S. McKiernan (D), Dec. 19, 1950-Jan. 2, 1951: Gov. John O. Pastore elected to U.S. Senate.

All of these "interim" governors succeeded to the office from the lieutenant governorship, with the exception of Maine's Robert Haskell who was president of the state senate.

Bibliography

Bibliographical Essay

The study of state government and politics has long been eclipsed by a singular concentration on the politics of Washington, D.C. Political scientists have preferred to analyze the federal government's governors for two primary reasons. For one, the elements of the federal system were believed to be more "interesting" and "glamorous" than the activities of stick-in-the-mud state governments with cadres of hack politicians, regressive legislatures, and programs no more exciting than highways and irrigation. For another, it was much easier; statistics on the presidency, Congress, and the federal bureaucracy have been collected for decades in centralized sources. Even when the information was not readily available, it could be gotten with considerably less difficulty than comparative data on fifty states strung out over thousands of miles.

As the foregoing study has hopefully proved, the first reason for ignoring the states is no longer a valid one. There has clearly been a renaissance in state government, and it could be argued that most programmatic innovations now find their root there. Political scientists have responded to some degree, and thanks to the efforts of several organizations, the number of publications on states and their governors has mushroomed—even though the comparative data is still relatively hard to gather.

Resource Organizations

Any topical investigation in the field of state government almost inevitably leads to one or more of three organizations: the Council of State Governments (CSG), the Advisory Commission on Intergovernmental Relations (ACIR), and the National Governors' Association (NCA).[a] The CSG, formerly located in Chicago but now situated at Iron Work's Pike, Lexington, Ky., is the organization that most comprehensively covers state government. Created by the states in 1933 and supported financially by them, the CSG has long served as an information and research source for state agencies and officials. The headquarters library has a wealth of data—some of which are unique—on almost all aspects of state government, and the staff is most helpful in satisfying requests. The CSG also publishes biennially the standard reference work on the states, *The Book of The States*, an invaluable starting point for any investigation. Three more of the organization's publications are also research essentials: *State Government* (published quarterly), *State Government News* (published monthly), and *Suggested State Legislation* (published annually).

---

[a]Until 1977 the organization was called the National Governor's Conference. The name was changed by the governors at their annual meeting in 1977. The term "association" was thought to reflect more accurately the full-time activity of the organization.

The ACIR was created by Congress in 1959 and charged with the oversight of "federalism." The organization monitors the relationships among national, state, and local governments, and makes recommendations on intergovernmental matters. Probably no other group produces so much documentation and so many reports on the structure and functioning of all three layers of government. The changing fiscal pattern is the subject of much of their research. The ACIR reports (many of which are mentioned in this essay) are professionally done and the data is reliable if not always distilled.

The NGA was first organized in 1908, but was a loosely organized entity until after World War II. Long affiliated with the CSG, little published research was produced by the NGA itself. Then, coincident with the election of a new breed of activist governors in the late 1960s and early 1970s, the NGA came alive (and eventually became an independent organization). The focus of the Association turned to lobbying the national government and an energetic staff began churning out a great deal of material both supporting the positions taken by the governors at their gatherings and suggesting actions in policy areas from energy to health care. The Center for Policy Research and Analysis was set up in 1974 as a division of the NGA, and all signs point to a continuance of the new interest in research on state and federal-state issues. Like those of the CSG and ACIR, the research products of the NGA are of high quality, though one must always be aware of the significant bias toward governors and states that is inevitably present.

Several other reference books complement the materials produced by the CSG, ACIR, and NGA. The Census Bureau's many publications summarizing the decennial census are certainly among them, as are the Bureau's *Census of Governments*, the *County and City Data Book*, and the *Statistical Abstract of The United States*.

The Governorship

Up-to-date comprehensive works on the governorship itself unfortunately cannot be found. The material exists, but in "bits and pieces." The most recent original work which dwells on the governorship is Joseph Kallenbach, *The American Chief Executive: The Presidency and The Governorship* (1966). Two other works of this nature are still circulated, although dated: Leslie Lipson, *The American Governor: From Figurehead to Leader* (1949); and, the best-known work in the field, Coleman Ransone, Jr., *The Office of Governor in the United States* (1956). (Ransone is currently working on a revised edition.) Previous to his book on the governorship throughout the nation, Ransone had published *The Office of Governor in The South* (1951). Both of his studies stress the public and administrative roles of sitting governors.

The career backgrounds and personal characteristics of governors were examined exhaustively by Joseph A. Schlesinger in *How They Became Governor: A Study of Comparative State Politics, 1870-1950* (1957). Schlesinger later expanded, elaborated and theorized on gubernatorial career patterns in *Ambition in Politics: Political Careers in The United States* (1966). The methodology used to compile the career section of my study was drawn directly from Schlesinger. The necessary personal characteristics could usually be found in Marquis, Inc., *Who's Who in America*; Paul A. Theis and Edmund L. Henshaw, Jr., *Who's Who in American Politics* (published biennially since 1967); and Michael Barone et al., *The Almanac of American Politics* (published biennially since 1972).

While there has been a scarcity of full-length books on the American governorship, a number of scholarly articles have been written in recent years. Some of the better ones are drawn together in Thad Beyle, *The American Governor in Behavioral Perspective* (1972). A "Symposium on the American Governorship in the 1970s" was organized for the January 1970 issue of *Public Administration Review*, and several excellent articles were included. Finally, Samuel P. Solomon has reviewed each decade's governors from the 1940s through the 1960s in three articles published in the *National Civic Review* (formerly *National Municipal Review*).

Sometimes it is difficult to locate even the most basic facts about governors and their terms of office. Fortunately this information has now been collected by the Council of State Governments in a publication called, *The Governors of The States, 1900-1974* (1974). Some data on governors prior to 1900 can be found in William Welch Hunt, *The Book of Governors* (1935). Information for currently serving governors on background, public offices held, and terms of office is readily available in a periodic pamphlet published by the Council of State Governments. The provisions of state constitutions concerning governors are summarized in Bennett M. Rich, *State Constitutions: The Governor* (1960), published by the National Municipal League but in need of revision to account for the dramatic changes of the last decade and a half.

What governors themselves are saying is certainly of interest and value. Annually in an issue of the CSG's *State Government* magazine, the governors' "state of the state" messages are analyzed. The National Governors' Conference in 1976 presented an extended version of this in a monograph, *Constraint and Concern: The Governors' State of The State Messages.* A rather unique, if thin, volume is *A Governor's Notes* (1961), written by Governor G. Mennen Williams (D-Michigan, 1949-1961). In it Williams discusses randomly some of the problems that confronted him as he attempted to govern one of the nation's largest states. Former Governor Luther H. Hodges (D-North Carolina, 1954-1961) also put his perspectives to paper as he finished his term in *Businessman in the Statehouse: Six Years as Governor of North Carolina* (1962).

Several dozen governors provided guidance to the NGA in the design of *The*

Critical Hundred Days: A Handbook for the New Governor (1975), which is a revealing and insightful look at the herculean tasks that face a new governor. In prescribing what an incoming governor should do and what he should avoid, the booklet manages to convey the flavor of the successes and failures of previous governors. The importance of selecting a good staff is particularly stressed in the *Handbook*, and Donald R. Sprengel examines the staffing aspect more closely in *Gubernatorial Staffs: Function and Political Profiles* (1969). Many times the quality and orientation of the staff can tell a good deal about the governor, in addition to helping determine the fate of any administration.

Generalizations about fifty governors who serve in such diverse states are risky, and often it is more useful to study the development of a single state's governorship. One of the best and most rewarding such studies is Duane Lockard, *The New Jersey Governor: A Study in Political Power* (1964). Another less-cohesive example is Paul Fannin et al., *Office of Governor in Arizona* (1964). To a researcher's chagrin there exists no single study of the governorship in most states. However, public documents available through the governor's office and the state printing office can tell at least part of the story.

The National Governors' Association in and of itself has a fascinating history. The verbatim proceedings of all the annual conferences are available from the CSG and NGA. In 1961 an interesting but inadequate study was published by Glenn Brooks, *When Governors Convene*, which tended to be overly optimistic about the impact the NGA was having. A more perceptive modern account of the governors' collective clout can be found in Rochelle L. Stanfield, "The PIGs: Out of the Sty, Into Lobbying with Style" in the *National Journal* (1976). ("PIGs," let me hasten to add, refers not to the governors but to Public Interest Groups!)

The quadrennial search for a president sometimes leads to a statehouse. Journalists have perhaps been more concerned with this aspect of the governorship than have scholars, and there are several excellent presentations by reporters on the topic, including David S. Broder, "What's the Best Road to the White House?" (1963) and Russell Baker, "Best Road to the White House—Which?" (1960). Both of these articles appeared in the *New York Times Magazine.* Louis Harris added a national pollster's interpretation in his *Public Opinion Quarterly* article, "Why the Odds Are Against A Governor's Becoming President" (1959). Scholars have not entirely ignored the subject; both Paul T. David, "The Role of Governors at The National Party Conventions" (*State Government*, 1960) and William R. Keech and Donald R. Matthews, *The Party's Choice* (1976) recount instances where governors were crucial in determining party presidential nominees.

Lieutenant Governors

The lieutenant governorship in the states suffers the same scourge as the office of vice president at the national level. Both are ignored for the same reason they are significant: Standby equipment rarely attracts attention until it is needed. Yet lieutenant governors have been given increasingly important assignments of late in some states and have been accorded more than scant coverage in published materials. The CSG surveyed all the states and summarized the data in *The Lieutenant Governor: The Office and Its Powers* (1973). The findings indicated the progress and upgrading that had occurred since an earlier researcher, R.F. Patterson, had examined the office in 1944. One state's lieutenant governors are analyzed in detail by Thomas R. Morris in *Virginia's Lieutenant Governors: The Office and The Person* (1970). The National Conference of Lieutenant Governors, a CSG-affiliated organization, annually publishes biographical sketches and portraits of the incumbent officeholders.

A subject that vitally concerns lieutenant governors, that of succession to the governorship in the event of the governor's death, resignation, or disability, is discussed in the CSG booklet, *Issues in Gubernatorial Succession* (1969). No less important is the transition that occurs during a scheduled change of governors at the end of a term. Another CSG publication, *Gubernatorial Transition in the States* (1968, revised 1972), summarizes state practices and suggests revisions. Some of the political and administrative problems that often accompany transitions are depicted in Thad Beyle and Oliver Williams, *New Governor in North Carolina* (1969).

State Politics

Politics in the American states, collectively and individually, has received more attention from academics than virtually any other sector of state government. The first major study in the contemporary era was V.O. Key's *American State Politics* (1957), which, like so much of Key's work, set high standards indeed for succeeding studies. Duane Lockard's *The Politics of State and Local Government* (1963) provided a lucid description of the politics of the 38,000 subnational governments in the United States. Kenneth Jacob and Herbert Vines produced a useful compendium of articles in their *Politics in the American States: A Comparative Analysis* (1971). Capsuled analysis of the current political conditions in each state is found in Michael Barone et al., *The Almanac of American Politics* (published biennially since 1972).

Regional approaches to state politics may be the best form of analysis since meaningless national generalizations can be avoided while a comparative framework is retained. Once again V.O. Key, Jr., provides the model with *Southern Politics* (1949). Two recent attempts to update Key failed to match his style and perceptiveness, but did provide much useful analysis of altered Southern political patterns: William C. Havard (ed.), *The Changing Politics of the South* (1969); and Jack Bass and Walter DeVries, *The Transformation of Southern Politics* (1976). Neal Peirce's series of seven books on regional politics in the states (*People, Politics, and Power . . .*) has been widely acclaimed and justly so.

Like John Gunther, Peirce manages to integrate smoothly the history, politics, and government of each state with its geographical and regional characteristics, with memorable vignettes of the state's people and leaders woven in for good measure. (Peirce is now authoring a much-needed syndicated newspaper column on state and local government.)

Other important and reliable regional political books include: Duane Lockard, *New England State Politics* (1959); John F. Fenton, *Midwest Politics* (1966) and *Politics in The Border States* (1974); Frank H. Jonas (ed.), *Politics in The American West* (1969); A. James Reichley, *States in Crisis: Politics in Ten American States, 1950-1962* (1964); Ira Sharkansky, *Regionalism in American Politics* (1970); and Andrew M. Scott and Earle Wallace, *Politics U.S.A.: Cases on the American Democratic Process* (1974).

Many books and articles on politics in individual states are listed in the bibliography. Among the most noteworthy are Joseph P. Harris, *California Politics* (1967); Allan P. Sindler, *Huey Long's Louisiana* (1956); G. Theodore Mitau, *Politics in Minnesota* (1960); Warren Moscow, *Politics in the Empire State* (1948); and Robert H. Connery and Gerald Benjamin, *Governing New York State: The Rockefeller Years* (1974).

Securing dependable information and voting statistics on state elections is not a simple task. The most thorough and investigated description of the issues in each gubernatorial and U.S. Senate campaign is published in a series in *The Congressional Quarterly Weekly* beginning about a month before election day. *The Washington Post* and *The New York Times* usually contain between them one fairly detailed preelection report on any state election; however, postelection analysis is much poorer and more sporadic. The weekly news magazines, with the possible exception of *U.S. News and World Report*, were little better.

Researchers should be cautioned against the use of any election statistics from news sources, since the final, official results—which sometimes differ significantly from the crude precinct totals calculated on a rushed election night—are only released a month or more after most elections. The official results can be found within a few weeks after the election in *The Congressional Quarterly Weekly*, and they are preserved in the annual *Congressional Quarterly Almanac* as well. The Congressional Quarterly has also compiled the voluminous *Guide to U.S. Elections* (1975), which contains most general election statistics for state races in this century (and Southern Democratic primaries, too). Official election tabulations and other information can also be found in Richard H. Scammon (ed.), *America Votes,* Volume 1-10 (1956-1972); and Edward Franklin Cox, *State and National Voting in Federal Elections, 1910-1970* (1972).

The financing of candidates has been the object of intense scrutiny in the wake of the Watergate scandals, and state campaigns have often matched or exceeded the corruption exposed on the national level. The Citizens' Research Foundation (CRF) of Princeton, N.J., is dedicated to the examination and reform of campaign finance, and the Foundation's director, Herbert Alexander, has edited a searching and well-documented account of money in state elections, *Campaign Money: Reform and Reality in the States* (1976). The CRF has published a series of pamphlets on the financing of specific state races, the titles of which are contained in the bibliography. The Federal Election Commission in Washington, D.C., is the central clearinghouse for all data on the financing of congressional and presidential campaigns, but unfortunately (yet typically) no comparable repository exists for states. What information has been systematical-ly collected is found at the CRF. Three other campaign finance studies have included a significant amount of state data: David Adamany, *Financing Politics* (1969) and *Campaign Finance in America* (1972); and Gerald M. Pomper, "Governors, Money, and Votes" in his *Elections in America* (1968).

State Government

An even-balanced critique of the states is provided by Terry Sanford, former governor of North Carolina (D, 1961-1965) and now president of Duke University, in *Storm Over The States* (1967). Ira Sharkansky, who has less of a stake in defending state governments than Sanford, somewhat surprisingly extols them to a greater degree in *The Maligned States: Policy Accomplishments, Problems, and Opportunities* (1972). (Perhaps the five years that elapsed between the publication of Sanford's book and Sharkansky's gave the latter more to be optimistic about.) The National Governors' Association offers an overly laudatory exposition, *The State of The States* (1974). The positive side is again presented in the NGA's *Innovations in State Government: Messages from The Governors* (1974), which catalogues many of the genuinely exciting programs that are being undertaken by the states.

The Citizens' Conference on State Legislatures (now called Legis 50) provides an in-depth, state-by-state look at the glaring failures of the legislative branches of state governments in *The Sometime Governments: A Critical Study of The 50 American Legislatures* (1971). It should be noted that significant improvements in many state legislatures have been made since this study was published. Indeed, many of the changes came about as a direct consequence of its publication, and Legis 50 has commendably worked with legislators in state capitols across the country to effect reforms. (Printed memoranda and other documents available from Legis 50 record the major and minor alterations that have occurred.)

The Council of State Governments has conducted many studies in the less glamorous but essential field of state administration. Reorganization of the governmental structure, which virtually all states have accomplished to some degree in the last decade, is examined in the CSG's *Reorganization in the States* (1972). Neal Peirce's article in *National Journal Reports*, "Structural Reform of Bureaucracy Grows Rapidly" (1975), is both an update and a companion piece.

Constitutional revision is an equally important topic, and the details are given in a booklet written by Albert L. Sturm under the aegis of the CSG, *Trends in State Constitution-Making, 1966-1972* (1973). The managerial functions of state governments are reviewed in the CSG's *Central Management in the States* (1970) and more recently in the NGC's *The States, Governors, and Policy Management* (1975). The all-important budgeting process is thoroughly dissected by S. Kenneth Howard for the CSG in *Changing State Budgeting* (1973). Subsidiary data in tabular displays are found in *Budgeting by the States* (1967) and *Budgeting Processes in the State* (1975), both of which are CSG publications.

The ACIR provides an annual summary of *State Actions*, and both the ACIR's *State Legislative Program* (published periodically) and the CSG's *Suggested State Legislation* (published annually) suggest proper directions and provide food for thought for state leaders.

Federalism

The changing relationship between federal, state, and local governments is the specific research charge of the ACIR, and a myriad of reports issues forth from the organization, including annual reassessments of federalism and surveys of public attitudes. The bibliography contains a complete list of the available materials. If the ACIR does not have certain data on federalism, the chances are the data are not collected anywhere.

There are other worthwhile sources, however. An NGA publication in 1975, *States' Responsibilities to Local Governments: An Action Agenda*, is particularly good, and another study published a year later, *Revenue Sharing and the States: An Impact Survey*, is also useful.

The number of books and monographs on federalism is quite large; thus only a few basic reference works need be mentioned here. W. Brooke Graves published an exhaustive tome in 1964, *American Intergovernmental Relations: Their Origins, Historical Development, and Current Status*, but of course a great deal has changed since. Daniel J. Elazar has also written extensively on the subject. His *American Federalism: A View from the States* (1966) starts to account for the onslaught of the Great Society programs, and his reader, *Politics of American Federalism* (1969), continues this examination. Donald H. Haider fruitfully concentrates on the Washington lobbying efforts of state and local governments in *When Governments Come to Washington* (1974). Finally, a noteworthy effort commissioned by The Brookings Institution attempts to evaluate the progress of revenue sharing. This study, *Monitoring Revenue-Sharing*, was written by Richard P. Nathan and associates in 1975.

Bibliography

Books and Monographs

Abernathy, Byron R. *Some Persisting Questions Concerning the Constitutional State Executive.* Lawrence: Governmental Research Center, University of Kansas, 1960.

Adamany, David. *Financing Politics.* Madison: University of Wisconsin Press, 1969.

_____. *Campaign Finance in America.* Belmont, Calif.: Wadsworth, 1972.

Adrian, Charles R. *Governing Our Fifty States and Their Communities.* New York: McGraw-Hill, 1963.

Alexander, Herbert E. (ed.), *Campaign Money: Reform and Reality in the States.* New York: The Free Press, 1976.

Allen, David J. *New Governor in Indiana: The Challenge of Executive Power.* Bloomington: Indiana University, Institute of Public Administration, 1965.

Allen, Robert S. (ed.). *Our Sovereign State.* New York: Vanguard Press, 1949.

Anderson, Patrick. *The President's Men.* New York: Doubleday, 1968.

Anderson, William, Clara Penniman, and Edward W. Weidner. *Government in the Fifty States.* New York: Holt, Rinehart, and Winston, 1960.

Baker, Ray Stannard. *Woodrow Wilson, Life and Letters: Youth, 1856-1890.* London: William Heinemann, 1928.

Barone, Michael, Grant Ujifusa, and Douglas Matthews. *The Almanac of American Politics: 1972 [1974, 1976].* New York: E.P. Dutton, 1972, 1973, 1975.

Bass, Jack, and Water DeVries. *The Transformation of Southern Politics: Social Change and Political Consequence Since 1945.* New York: Basic Books, 1976.

Bellach, Bernard. *Franklin D. Roosevelt as Governor of New York.* New York: Columbia University Press, 1955.

Berman, David R. *State and Local Politics.* Boston: Holbrook Press, 1975.

Beyle, Thad L., and J. Oliver Williams. *New Governor in North Carolina: Politics and Administration of Transition.* Chapel Hill: Department of Political Science, University of North Carolina, 1969.

_____ (eds.). *The American Governor in Behavioral Perspective.* New York: Harper & Row, 1972.

Binkley, Wilfred E. *President and Congress.* New York: Alfred A. Knopf, 1947.

_____. *The Man in the White House.* Baltimore: Johns Hopkins Press, 1958.

Black, Earl. *Southern Governors and Civil Rights.* Cambridge, Mass.: Harvard University Press, 1976.

Bone, Hugh A. *American Politics and the Party System,* 5th ed. New York: McGraw-Hill, 1975.

Broder, David S. *The Party's Over: The Failure of Politics in America.* New York: Harper & Row, 1972.

Brogan, D.W. *An Introduction to American Politics.* London: Hamish Hamilton, 1954.

Brooks, Glenn E. *When Governors Convene: The Governors' Conference and National Politics.* Baltimore: Johns Hopkins Press, 1961.

Bryce, James. *The American Commonwealth,* 2 vols. London: MacMillan, 1888.

Buckley, James L. *If Men Were Angels: A View from the Senate.* New York: G.P. Putnam's Sons, 1975.

Buechner, John C. *State Government in the Twentieth Century.* Boston: Houghton Mifflin, 1967.

Campbell, Angus, P.E. Converse, W.E. Miller, and D.E. Stokes. *The American Voter.* New York: John Wiley and Sons, 1960.

_____. *Elections and the Political Order.* New York: John Wiley and Sons, 1966.

Chamberlain, Joseph P. *Legislative Processes, National and State.* London: D. Appleton-Century, 1936.

Connery, Robert H., and Gerald Benjamin. *Governing New York State: The Rockefeller Years.* New York: The Academy of Political Science, 1974.

Cox, Edward Franklin. *State and National Voting in Federal Elections, 1910-1970.* Hamden, Conn.: The Shoe String Press, 1972.

Crew, Robert E., Jr. (ed.). *State Politics.* Belmont, Calif.: Wadsworth, 1968.

David, Paul T. *Party Strength in the United States, 1872-1970.* Charlottesville: University Press of Virginia, 1972.

Davis, J. William. *There Shall Also Be a Lieutenant Governor.* Austin: Institute of Public Affairs, The University of Texas, 1967.

Dye, Thomas R. *Politics, Economics and the Public: Policy Outcomes in the American States.* Chicago: Rand-McNally, 1966.

Elazar, Daniel J. *American Federalism: A View from the States.* New York: Thomas Y. Crowell, 1966.

_____ (ed.). *The Politics of American Federalism.* Lexington, Mass.: D.C. Heath, 1969.

Fannin, Paul, Ernest W. McFarland, Leonard E. Goodall, and John P. White. *The Office of Governor in Arizona.* Phoenix: Bureau of Governmental Research, Arizona State University, 1964.

Fenton, John H. *Midwest Politics.* New York: Holt, Rinehart, and Winston, 1966.

_____. *Politics in the Border States.* New York: Russell and Russell, 1974.

Flinn, Thomas. *The Governor and the Minnesota Budget.* New York and Indianapolis: Bobbs-Merrill, 1961. (Inter-University Case Program, No. 60.)

Gantt, Fred, Jr. *The Chief Executive in Texas: A Study in Gubernatorial Leadership.* Austin: University of Texas Press, 1964.

Graves, W. Brooke. *American State Government,* 4th ed. Boston: Heath, 1953.

_____. *American Intergovernmental Relations: Their Origins, Historical Development and Current Status*. New York: Scribner's, 1964.

Greene, Evarts B. *The Provincial Governor in the English Colonies of North America*, Vol. 7, Harvard Historical Studies. New York: Longmans, Green, 1898.

Griffith, Ernest S. *The American System of Government*, 5th ed. London: Methuen, 1976.

Haider, D.H. *When Governments Come to Washington*. New York: The Free Press, 1974.

Harris, Joseph P. *California Politics*. San Francisco: Chandler, 1967.

Havard, William C. (ed.). *The Changing Politics of the South*. Baton Rouge: Louisiana State University Press, 1969.

Hodges, Luther H. *Businessman in the Statehouse: Six Years as Governor of North Carolina*. Chapel Hill: University of North Carolina Press, 1962.

Hunt, William Welch. *The Book of Governors*. Los Angeles: Washington Typographers, 1935.

Illinois Assembly on the Office of the Governor. *The Office of Governor: Final Report and Background Papers*. Urbana: Institute of Government and Public Affairs, University of Illinois, 1963.

Jacob, Herbert, and Kenneth Vines (eds.). *Politics in the American States: A Comparative Analysis*. Boston: Little, Brown, 1971.

James, Judson L. *American Political Parties in Transition*. New York: Harper & Row, 1974.

Jewell, Malcolm E. *The State Legislature: Politics and Practice*. New York: Random House, 1962.

_____. *Legislative Representation in the Contemporary South*. Durham, N.C.: Duke University Press, 1967.

Jewell, Malcolm E., and Samuel C. Patterson. *The Legislative Process in the United States*. New York: Random House, 1966.

Jonas, Frank H. (ed.). *Politics in the American West*. Salt Lake City: University of Utah Press, 1969.

Kallenbach, Joseph E. *The American Chief Executive: The Presidency and the Governorship*. New York: Harper & Row, 1966.

Kelley, Stanley, Jr. *Professional Public Relations and Political Power*. Baltimore: Johns Hopkins Press, 1956.

Key, V.O., Jr. *Southern Politics*. New York: Alfred A. Knopf, 1949.

_____. *American State Politics: An Introduction*. New York: Alfred A. Knopf, 1956.

_____. *Politics, Parties, and Pressure Groups*, 5th ed. New York: Thomas Y. Crowell, 1964.

_____. *The Responsible Electorate: Rationality in Presidential Voting 1936-1960*. New York: Vintage Books, 1966.

Kramer, Michael, and Sam Roberts. *"I Never Wanted to Be Vice-President of*

Anything!": An Investigative Biography of Nelson Rockefeller. New York: Basic Books, 1976.

Laski, Harold J. *The American Democracy: A Commentary and an Interpretation.* London: Allen and Unwin, 1949.

LeBlanc, Hugh, and Don T. Allensworth. *Politics of States and Urban Communities.* New York: Harper & Row, 1971.

Lees, John D. *The Political System of the United States.* London: Faber and Faber, 1969.

Levin, Murray B. and George Blackwood. *The Compleat Politician: Political Strategy in Massachusetts.* New York: Bobbs-Merrill, 1962.

Liebling, A.J. *The Earl of Louisiana, The Liberal Long.* New York: Simon and Schuster, 1961.

Lipset, Seymour Martin. *Political Man.* New York: Doubleday, 1960.

Lipson, Leslie. *The American Governor: From Figurehead to Leader.* Chicago: University of Chicago Press, 1949.

Liu, Ben-Chieh, with Robert Gustafson and Bruce Marcy. *The Quality of Life in the United States: 1970, Index, Rating, and Statistics.* Kansas City, Mo.: Midwest Research Institute, 1973.

Lockard, Duane. *New England State Politics.* Princeton, N.J.: Princeton University Press, 1959.

_____. *The Politics of State and Local Government.* New York: Macmillan, 1963.

_____. *The New Jersey Governor: A Study in Political Power.* New York: Van Nostrand & Reinhold, 1964.

Maddox, Russell W., Jr. (ed.). *Issues in State and Local Government.* Princeton, N.J.: D. Van Nostrand, 1965.

Marquis Who's Who, Inc. *Who's Who In America, 1950 [-1975].* Chicago: A.N. Marquis, 1950-1975.

Martin, James W. *An Executive Office of the Governor for Kentucky.* Lexington: College of Business and Economics, University of Kentucky, 1972.

Martin, Roscoe C. *The Cities and the Federal System.* New York: Atherton Press, 1965.

Matthews, Donald R. *U.S. Senators and Their World.* New York: Vintage Books, 1960.

Mayer, George H. *The Political Career of Floyd B. Olson.* Minneapolis: University of Minnesota Press, 1951.

Merriam, Charles E., and Harold F. Gosnell. *The American Party System.* New York: Macmillan, 1933.

Mitau, G. Theodore. *Politics in Minnesota.* Minneapolis: University of Minnesota Press, 1960.

Morris, Joe Alex. *Nelson Rockefeller.* New York: Harper and Brothers, 1960.

Morris, Thomas R. *Virginia's Lieutenant Governors: The Office and the Person.* Charlottesville: Institute of Government, University of Virginia, 1970.

Moscow, Warren. *Politics in the Empire State*. New York: Alfred A. Knopf, 1948.

Munger, Frank (ed.). *American State Politics: Readings for Comparative Analysis*. New York: Thomas Y. Crowell, 1966.

Murphy, William T., Jr., and Edward Schneier. *Vote Power*. New York: Anchor Press/Doubleday, 1974.

Napolitan, Joseph. *The Election Game and How to Win It*. New York: Doubleday, 1972.

Nathan, Richard P., Allen D. Manvell, Susannah E. Calkins et al. *Monitoring Revenue Sharing*. Washington, D.C.: The Brookings Institution, 1975.

Neustadt, Richard. *Presidential Power*. New York: John Wiley and Sons, 1960.

Nimmo, Dan. *The Political Persuaders: The Techniques of Modern Election Campaigns*. Englewood Cliffs, N.J.: Prentice-Hall, 1970.

Nispel, Benjamin. *Reform of the Office of Lieutenant Governor*. Washington, D.C.: Public Affairs Press, 1958.

Ogg, Frederic A., and P. Orman Ray. *Introduction to American Government*, 5th ed. London: D. Appleton-Century, 1931.

Patterson, R.F. *The Office of Lieutenant-Governor in the United States*. Vermillion: Governmental Research Bureau, University of South Dakota, 1944.

Patterson, Thomas E., and Robert D. McClure. *The Unseeing Eye: The Myth of Television Power in National Politics*. New York: Putnam, 1976.

Peirce, Neal R. *Megastates of America: People, Politics, and Power in the Ten Great States*. New York: W.W. Norton, 1972.

_____. *People, Politics, and Power in the American States*, 6 vols. New York: W.W. Norton, 1970-1976.

Plumb, Ralph G. *Our American Governors*. Manitowoc, Wisc.: Manitowoc Printing and Lithographing Corp., 1956.

Ransone, Coleman B., Jr. *The Office of Governor in the South*. University: University of Alabama Press, 1951.

_____. *The Office of Governor in the United States*. University: University of Alabama Press, 1956.

Reichley, A. James. *States in Crisis: Politics in Ten American States, 1950-1962*. Chapel Hill: University of North Carolina Press, 1964.

Ries, John C. *Executives in the American Political System*. Belmont, Calif.: Dickenson, 1969.

Riordon, William L. (ed.). *Plunkitt of Tammany Hall*. New York: E.P. Dutton, 1963.

Roberts, Nancy. *The Governor*. New York: McNally and Loftin, 1972.

Sabato, Larry. *Aftermath of 'Armageddon': An Analysis of the 1973 Virginia Gubernatorial Election*. Charlottesville: Institute of Government, University of Virginia, 1975.

_____. *Virginia Votes: 1969-1974*. Charlottesville: Institute of Government, University of Virginia, 1975.

_____. *The Democratic Party Primary: Tantamount to Election No Longer.* Charlottesville: University Press of Virginia, 1977.

Sanders, John L. *Report on the Office of the Governor of North Carolina.* Chapel Hill: Institute of Government, University of North Carolina, 1965.

Sanford, Terry. *But What About The People?* New York: Harper & Row, 1966.

_____. *Storm Over the States.* New York: McGraw-Hill, 1967.

Scace, Homer E. *The Organization of the Executive Office of the Governor.* New York: Institute of Public Administration, 1950.

Scammon, Richard M. (ed.). *America Votes*, Vols. 1-9. New York: The Macmillan Company, 1956 [-1970].

Schlesinger, Joseph. *How They Became Governor: A Study of Comparative State Politics, 1870-1950.* East Lansing: Michigan State University Press, 1957.

_____. *Ambition and Politics: Political Careers in the United States.* Chicago: Rand-McNally, 1966.

Scott, Andrew M., and Earle Wallace. *Politics USA: Cases on the American Democratic Process*, 4th ed. New York: Macmillan, 1974.

Sharkansky, Ira. *The Politics of Taxing and Spending.* Indianapolis: Bobbs-Merrill, 1969.

_____. *Regionalism in American Politics.* Indianapolis: Bobbs-Merrill, 1970.

_____. *The Maligned States: Policy Accomplishments, Problems, and Opportunities.* New York: McGraw-Hill, 1972.

Sindler, Allan P. *Huey Long's Louisiana.* Baltimore: Johns Hopkins Press, 1956.

Smallwood, Frank. *Free and Independent.* Brattleboro, Vt.: Stephen Greene Press, 1976.

Snider, Clyde F. *American State and Local Government*, 2nd ed. New York: Appleton-Century-Crofts, 1965.

Sorauf, Frank J. *Party Politics in America.* Boston: Little, Brown, 1968.

Spence, James R. *The Making of a Governor: The Moore-Preyer-Lake Primaries of 1964.* Winston-Salem, N.C.: John F. Blair Publisher, 1968.

Sprengel, Donald P. *Gubernatorial Staffs: Function and Political Profiles.* Iowa City: Institute of Public Affairs, University of Iowa, 1969.

_____ (ed.). *Comparative State Politics: A Reader.* New York: Charles E. Merrill Co., 1971.

Tarrance, Lance, and Walter DeVries. *The Ticket-Splitter: A New Force in American Politics.* Grand Rapids, Mich.: William B. Eerdmens, 1972.

_____. *The World Almanac and Book of Facts.* Published annually by Newspaper Enterprise Association, Inc., New York and Cleveland (by Doubleday, Inc.).

Thach, Charles C. *The Creation of the Presidency, 1775-1789*, Johns Hopkins University Studies in Historical and Political Science, Series 50, Number 4. Baltimore: Johns Hopkins Press, 1922.

Theis, Paul A., and Edmund L. Henshaw, Jr. (eds.). *Who's Who in American Politics* (various issues). New York: R.R. Bowker, 1967-1975.

Thorpe, Francis Newton. *The Federal and State Constitutions, Colonial Charters, and Other Organic Laws of the States, Territories, and Colonies*, 7 vols. Washington, D.C.: Government Printing Office, 1909.

de Tocqueville, Alexis. *Journey to America.* (J.P. Mayer, ed.) London: Faber and Faber, 1959.

Turnbull, George S. *Governors of Oregon.* Portland: Binfords and Mort, 1959.

Turner, Henry A. *American Democracy: State and Local Government.* New York: Harper & Row, 1968.

Van Riper, Paul. *Handbook of Practical Politics*, 3rd ed. New York: Harper & Row, 1967.

Walker, Harvey. *The Legislative Process.* New York: Ronald Press, 1948.

White, Leonard D. *The States and the Nation.* Baton Rouge: Louisiana State University Press, 1953.

Williams, G. Mennen. *A Governor's Notes.* Ann Arbor: Institute of Public Administration, University of Michigan, 1961.

Articles

"As Newsmen See the Conference." *State Government* 31 (Summer 1958):173-77.

Baker, Russell. "Best Road to the White House—Which?" *New York Times Magazine*, November 27, 1960.

Bane, Frank. "The Job of Being a Governor." *State Government* 31 (Summer 1958):184-89.

Bebout, John E. ' New Federalism—New State Politics." *National Civic Review* 62 (September 1973):408-11.

Beyle, Thad L. "State Executives." In Richard H. Leach (ed.), *Compacts of Antiquity: State Constitutions.* Atlanta: Southern Newspaper Publisher's Association's Foundation, 1969, pp. 27-34.

_____ and John E. Wickman. "Gubernatorial Transition in a One Party Setting." *Public Administration Review* 30 (January/February 1970):10-17.

Black, Earl. "Southern Governors and Political Change: Campaign Stances on Racial Segregation and Economic Development, 1950-69." *Journal of Politics* 33 (August 1971):703-34.

Broder, David S. "What's The Best Road to the White House?" *New York Times Magazine*, September 22, 1963.

_____. "The Unhappy State of the States." *The Washington Post*, January 25, 1976.

_____. "The Rise of the Governors." *The Washington Post*, June 12, 1976.

Brooks, Glen. "The Governors: Often Winners in Past Presidential Sweep-Stakes, Their Future is Now in Doubt." *Johns Hopkins Magazine* 14 (November 1962):5-9.

_____. "The Business of Being Governor." *State Government* 31 (Summer 1958):145-49.

Campbell, Angus, and Warren E. Miller. "The Motivational Bases of Straight and Split Ticket Voting." *American Political Science Review* 51 (June 1957):293-312.

Carleton, William G. "The Southern Politician 1900 and 1950." *Journal of Politics* 13 (May 1951):215-31.

Carley, David. "Legal and Extra-Legal Powers of Wisconsin Governors in Legislative Relations," Parts I and II. *Wisconsin Law Review* (January and March 1962):3-64; 280-341.

Cheatham, Richard. "An Overview of Contemporary Gubernatorial Inaugurals." *Southern Speech Communication Journal* 40 (1975):191-203.

Clem, Alan L. "Popular Representation and Senate Vacancies." *Midwest Journal of Political Science* 10 (February 1966):52-77.

_____ . "Comeback of the States." *U.S. News and World Report*, October 27, 1969, pp. 48-50.

Cowart, Andrew T. "Electoral Choice in the American States: Incumbency Effects, Partisan Forces, and Divergent Partisan Majorities," *American Political Science Review* 67 (September 1973):835-53.

Croy, James B. "Federal Supersession: The Road to Domination." *State Government* 58 (Winter 1975):32-36.

David, Paul T. "The Role of Governors at the National Party Conventions." *State Government* 33 (Spring 1960):103-10.

Dawson, Richard E., and James Robinson. "Inter-Party Competition, Economic Variables, and Welfare Policies in the American States." *Journal of Politics* 25 (1963):265-89.

Detchmendy, Judith Ann. "Competent State Governments: The Growth of Concern." *National Civic Review* 62 (September 1973):421-32.

Diamond, Martin. "The Ends of Federalism." *Publius* 3 (Fall 1973):129-52.

Dodd, W.F. "The First State Constitutional Conventions, 1776-1783." *American Political Science Review* 2 (November 1908):1545-61.

Dolliver, James. "State Planning and the Governor's Office." *State Planning Issues.* Lexington, Ky.: The Council of State Governments, May 1973, pp. 39-40.

Dye, T.R. "Executive Power and Public Policy in the States," *Western Political Quarterly* 22 (December 1969):926-39.

Egger, Rowland. "The Governorship of Virginia, 1776 and 1976." *University of Virginia Newsletter* 52 (August 1976):41-44.

Elazar, Daniel J. "The Resurgence of Federalism." *State Government* 53 (Summer 1970):166-73.

_____ . "The New Federalism: Can the States be Trusted?" *Public Interest* 11 (Spring 1974):89-102.

Epstein, Leon. "Electoral Decision and Policy Mandate: An Empirical Example." *Public Opinion Quarterly* 28 (Winter 1964):564-67.

Elau, Heinz, and David Koff. "Occupational Mobility and Political Career." *Western Political Quarterly* 15 (September 1962):507-21.

Ewing, Cortez A.M. "Southern Governors." *Journal of Politics* 10 (May 1948):385-409.

_____. "Five Former Governors Appraise the Governors' Conference." *State Government* 31 (Summer 1958):168-72.

Gibbons, Charles. "Transition of Government in Massachusetts," *State Government* 34 (Spring 1961):100-01.

Gilligan, John J. "Reappraising State Government: A Prelude to Action." Woodrow Wilson International Center for Scholars, May 21, 1975.

Gleason, Eugene J., Jr., and Joseph F. Zimmerman. "Executive Dominance in New York State." Paper presented to the Northeastern Political Science Association, Saratoga Springs, N.Y., November 9, 1974.

Gove, Samuel K. "Why Strong Governors?" *National Civic Review* 53 (March 1964):131-36.

Gravlin, Leslie M. "An Effective Chief Executive," *National Municipal Review* 36 (March 1947):137-41.

_____. "Gubernatorial Transition in the States." *State Government Administration* 3 (December 1968):18.

Hain, Paul L., and Terry B. Smith. "Congress: New Training Ground for Governors." *State Government* 48 (Spring 1975):114-15.

Halverson, Guy. "Can States Regain Power?" *The Christian Science Monitor*, January 7, 1970.

Harris, Joseph P. "The Governors' Conference: Retrospect and Prospect." *State Government* 31 (Summer 1958):190-96.

Harris, Lee. "Geographer Offers Plan to Redesign the U.S." *Los Angeles Times*, August 12, 1973.

Harris, Louis. "Why the Odds are Against a Governor's Becoming President." *Public Opinion Quarterly* 4 (July 1959):361-70.

_____. "The Harris Survey: More Trust for State Government." *The Chicago Tribune*, July 5, 1976. (Copyright *The Chicago Tribune*, 1976.)

Harwell, James. "The States' Growing International Role." *State Government* 48 (Winter 1975):2-5.

Havard, William C. "Notes on a Theory of Constitutional Change: The Florida Experience." *The Journal of Politics* 21 (February 1959):90-116.

Highsaw, Robert B. "The Southern Governor: Challenge to the Strong Executive Theme." *Public Administration Review* 19 (Winter 1959):7-11.

Hofferbert, Richard I. "The Lieutenant Governorship in Indiana," *Indiana Public Affairs Notes* 4 (January/February 1962):1-6.

Holcomb, Henry, and Bill Furlow. "Gilligan: Dark Horse with One Eye on the White House." *The Cincinnati Post*, February 9, 11, 12, 1976.

_____. "How States Handle Governor Succession." *Congressional Digest* 25 (March 1946):75 ff.

_____. "How the States Provide for Disability." *Congressional Digest* 37 (January 1958):4-5.

Hyneman, Charles S. "Administrative Reorganization: An Adventure into Science and Theology." *Journal of Politics* 1 (February 1939):66.

254

Jacob, Herbert, and Michael Lipsky. "Outputs, Structure, and Power: An Assessment of Changes in the Study of State and Local Politics." *Journal of Politics* 30 (May 1968):510-38.

Jennings, M. Kent, and Harmon Ziegler. "The Salience of American State Politics." *American Political Science Review* 64 (June 1970):532-35.

Jewell, Malcolm E. "State Decision Making: The Governor Revisited." In Aaron Wildavsky and Nelson Polsby (eds.), *American Governmental Institutions.* Chicago: Rand McNally, 1968, pp. 545-65.

Jonas, Frank H., and Garth Jones. "J. Bracken Lee and the Public Service in Utah." *Western Political Quarterly* 9 (September 1956):755-65.

Kallenbach, Joseph E. "Constitutional Limitations on Re-eligibility of National and State Chief Executives." *American Political Science Review* 46 (June 1952):438-54.

_____. "Governors and the Presidency." *Michigan Alumnus Quarterly Review* 60 (Spring 1954):234-42.

Kammerer, Gladys M. "The Governor as Chief Administrator in Kentucky." *Journal of Politics* 26 (May 1954):236-56.

_____. "Kentucky's All-Pervasive Spoils Politics." *Good Government* (July-August 1958):32-37.

Kelley, Stanley, Jr., Richard E. Ayres, and William G. Bowen. 'Registration and Voting: Putting First Things First." *American Political Science Review* 61 (June 1967):359-79.

Key, V.O., Jr., and Corinne Silverman. "Party and Separation of Powers: A Panorama of Practice in the States." *Public Policy* 5 (1954):382-412.

Kilian, Michael. "Gov. Patrick Lucey's Silent Lessons in Political Success." *The Chicago Tribune*, April 6, 1975.

Kraft, Joseph. "Governors: More Power to Them?" *The Washington Post*, March 1, 1973.

Lambert, Louis. "The Executive Article." In W. Brooke Graves (ed.), *Major Problems in Constitutional Revision*. Chicago: Public Administration Service, 1960, pp. 185-200.

Langlie, A.B. "Responsibility of the States and their Governors." *State Government* 29 (August 1956):144-45.

_____. " 'Lean Look' is the Latest Fashion in State Budgets." *U.S. News and World Report*, March 1, 1976, p. 75.

Lowance, Carter O. "The Governor of Virginia," *The University of Virginia News Letter* 36 (February 15, 1960):5-8.

McCally, Sarah P. "The Governor and his Legislative Party," *American Political Science Review* 60 (December 1966):923-42.

Mallan, John P., and George Blackwood. "The Tax That Beat a Governor: The Ordeal of Massachusetts." In Alan F. Westin (ed.), *The Uses of Power*. New York: Harcourt, Brace & Jovanovich, 1962, pp. 285-322.

Marando, Vincent L. "The Reemerging Role of States in Local Reorganization," *State Government* 58 (Summer 1975):177-82.

Matthews, John M. "The New Role of the Governor," *American Political Science Review* 6 (May 1912):217-30.

Michaelson, Ronald D. "An Analysis of the Chief Executive: How a Governor Uses His Time." *Public Affairs Bulletin* 4 (September/October 1971):1-6.

Morehouse, Sarah McCally. "The State Political Party and the Policy-Making Process." *American Political Science Review* 67 (March 1973):55-72.

Morgan, Murray. "The Most Powerful Governor in the U.S.A." *Harper's*, October 1965, pp. 98-107.

Oelsner, Lesley. "High Court Frees States and Cities from U.S. Pay Law." *The New York Times*, June 25, 1976.

Peirce, Neal R. "Structural Reform of Bureaucracy Grows Rapidly." *National Journal Reports* 7 (April 5, 1975):502-08.

_____. "The Politics of Austerity." *The Washington Post*, September 30, 1975.

_____. "The States: Innovative Solutions to the Recession." *The Washington Post*, February 27, 1976.

Pettigrew, Thomas F., and Ernest Q. Campbell. "Faubus and Segregation: An Analysis of Arkansas." *Public Opinion Quarterly* 24 (Fall 1960):436-47.

Pomper, Gerald M. "Governors, Money, and Votes." In Power (ed.), *Elections in America.* New York: Dodd, Mead, 1968, Chapter 6, pp. 126-48, 270-73.

Prescott, Frank W. "The Executive Veto in American States." *The Western Political Quarterly* 3 (March 1950):99-114.

Ransone, Coleman B., Jr. "Political Leadership in the Governor's Office." *Journal of Politics* 26 (February 1964):197-220.

_____ et al. "The American Governor in the 1970's." *Public Administration Review* 30 (January 1970):1-44.

Reichley, A. James. "The Statehouses Are Back in the Political Spotlight." *Fortune*, August 1975, pp. 138-40.

_____. "Revenue Sharing Bill Passes House." *Intergovernmental Perspective* (Advisory Commission on Intergovernmental Relations) 2 (Summer 1976):2.

Romney, George H. "A New Era of Federalism: Challenge for the U.S." *National Civic Review* 62 (January 1973):7-14, 58.

Schlesinger, Joseph A. "Stability in the Vote for Governor, 1900-1958." *Public Opinion Quarterly* 24 (Spring 1960):85-91.

_____. "The Structure of Competition for Office in the American States." *Behavioral Science* 5 (July 1960):197-211.

_____. "The Governor's Place in American Politics." *Public Administration Review* 30 (January 1970):2-10.

Simmons, Robert H. "American State Executive Studies: A Suggested New Departure." *Western Political Quarterly* 17 (December 1964):777-83.

Solomon, Samuel R. "United States Governors, 1940-1950." *National Municipal Review* 41 (April 1952):190-97.

_____. "Governors, 1950-1960." *National Civic Review* 49 (September 1960):410-16.

_____. "Governors: 1960-1970." *National Civic Review* 60 (March 1971):126-46.

Sorauf, Frank. "The Silent Revolution in Patronage." *Public Administration Review* 20 (1960):28-39.

Stanfield, Rochelle L. "The PIGS: Out of the Sty, Into Lobbying with Style." *National Journal* 8 (August 14, 1976):1134-39.

Stratton, William G. "The Governors' Conference Through Fifty Years—and Tomorrow." *State Government* 31 (Summer 1958):125-26.

Swinerton, E. Nelson. "Ambition and American State Executive." *Midwest Journal of Political Science* 12 (November 1968):538-49.

Symposium. "The Governor's Views on Federal State and State-Local Relations." *Public Administration Review* 30 (January/February 1970):27-42.

Titus, James E. "Kansas Governors: A Résumé of Political Leadership," *Western Political Quarterly* 17 (June 1964):356-70.

Treaster, Joseph B. "States Shore Up Governors' Role." *The New York Times*, January 25, 1970.

Turett, J. Stephen. "The Vulnerability of American Governors, 1900-1969." *Midwest Journal of Political Science* 15 (February 1971):108-32.

Walker, Jack L. "The Diffusion of Innovations among the American States." *American Political Science Review* 63 (September 1969):880-89.

Welsh, Matthew E. "The Role of the Governor in the 1970's." *Public Administration Review* 30 (January 1970):24-26.

Westmeyer, Troy R., and Wesley Westmeyer (eds.). "Cities v. States on Finance." *National Civic Review* 65 (July 1976):358-59.

Witcover, Jules. "Will a Governor Lead Them?" *The Washington Post*, May 19, 1973.

Wright, Deil S., and David E. Stephenson. "The States As Middlemen: Five Fiscal Dilemmas." *State Government* 57 (April 1974):101-07.

Wyner, Alan J. "Gubernatorial Relations with Legislators and Administrators." *State Government* 51 (Summer 1968):199-203.

Young, William H. "The Development of the Governorship." *State Government* 31 (Summer 1958):178-83.

Public Documents, State

Brown, Edmund G., Jr. "Report to the Legislature." Governor's Office, Sacramento, Calif., January 7, 1976.

_____. "Budget Message to the Legislature." Governor's Office, Sacramento, Calif., January 10, 1976.

Hughes, Richard J. "A Moral Recommitment for New Jersey: Special Message to the Legislature." Governor's Office, Trenton, N.J., April 25, 1968.

Iowa, State of. *The Governor's Office.* Office of the Governor, Des Moines, 1968.

Louisiana, State of. "Report of the Louisiana Governor's Committee to Consider Changes in the Powers, Duties, and Responsibilities of the Governor." Office of the Governor, Baton Rouge, May 11, 1966.

_____. "Acts 1 and 199 of 1975 Relating to Open Election System." Office of the Secretary of State, Baton Rouge, 1975.

Maine, State of. *The Governor's Office: A Manual of Operations.* Office of the Governor, Augusta, 1974.

Massachusetts, Commonwealth of. "Report Relative to Duties and Powers of the Lieutenant Governor." Massachusetts Legislative Research Council, Boston, December 29, 1971.

Massachusetts Legislative Research Council. "Report Relative to Joint Election of Governor and Lieutenant Governor (Proposed Constitutional Amendment)." Commonwealth of Massachusetts, Senate Document No. 949, March 3, 1965.

Minnesota, State of. "Study of the Organization and Functioning of the Governor's Office." Office of the Governor, St. Paul, June 1964.

Mississippi, State of. "Governor's Office Manual." Governor's Office, Jackson, 1970.

Nevada, State of. "Staff Study on the Role of the Lieutenant Governor." Legislative Commission of the Legislative Counsel Bureau, Carson City, September 1974.

New Jersey, State of. "First Annual Message of Woodrow Wilson, Governor of New Jersey, to the Legislature of New Jersey." *Legislative Documents* 1 (1911).

Ohio Legislative Service Commission. "Problems in the Transition of Government," Staff Research Report No. 57. Columbus, January 1963, pp. 18-56.

_____. "Staffing the Office of the Governor," Staff Research Report No. 57. Columbus, January 1963, pp. 4-17.

Pennsylvania Senate, Special Committee to Study Confirmation Procedure. *Senate Confirmation of the Governor's Appointment.* Harrisburg, 1973.

Wisconsin, State of. "The Executive Office Transition." Office of the Governor, Madison, November 1970.

Rockefeller, Nelson A. "The Future of Freedom." U.S. Government Printing Office, Washington, D.C., 1976.

Public Documents, National

Congressional Quarterly, Inc. *Congressional Quarterly Almanac.* Washington, D.C.: Congressional Quarterly, Inc., published annually.

_____. *Congressional Quarterly Weekly.* Washington, D.C.: Congressional Quarterly, Inc., published weekly.

_____. *Guide to U.S. Elections.* Washington, D.C.: Congressional Quarterly, Inc., 1975.

258

Office of the President. *Proceedings of a Conference of Governors in the White House.* Washington, D.C.: U.S. Government Printing Office, 1909.
U.S. Bureau of the Census. *State Government Finances.* Washington, D.C.: U.S. Government Printing Office, published annually.
_____. *County and City Data Books.* Washington, D.C.: U.S. Government Printing Office, published annually.
_____. *Statistical Abstracts of the United States.* Washington, D.C.: U.S. Government Printing Office, published annually.
_____. *Census of Population 1950 [1960, 1970].* Washington, D.C.: U.S. Government Printing Office 1951, 1961, 1971.
U.S. Department of the Treasury. "Federal Aid to States, Fiscal Year 1975." Washington, D.C.: Department of the Treasury, 1976.

Newspapers

The following newspapers were used for general reference:

The New York Times
The Washington Post
The Richmond Times-Dispatch

The Christian Science Monitor
The Los Angeles Times
The Chicago Tribune
The Cincinnati Post

Periodical Magazines

The following periodical magazines were used for general references:

Business Week
Newsweek
Time
U.S. News and World Report

Organization Reports

Advisory Commission on Intergovernmental Relations (ACIR). "Revenue Sharing and Taxes: A Survey of Public Attitudes." Washington, D.C.: ACIR, August 1973.
_____. *Federalism 1973: The System Under Stress.* Washington, D.C.: ACIR, January 1974.
_____. *State Actions 1973: Toward Full Partnership.* Washington, D.C.: ACIR, January 1974.

259

_____. *American Federalism: Into the Third Century.* Washington, D.C.: ACIR, May 1974.

_____. *State Actions 1974: Building on Innovation.* Washington, D.C.: ACIR, February 1975.

_____. *Trends in Fiscal Federalism, 1954-1974.* Washington, D.C.: ACIR, February 1975.

_____. *Federalism in 1974: The Tension of Interdependence.* Washington, D.C.: ACIR, February 1975.

_____. *American Federalism: Toward a More Effective Partnership.* Washington, D.C.: ACIR, August 1975.

_____. *Federal-State-Local Finances: Significant Features of Fiscal Federalism, 1974-75.* Washington, D.C.: ACIR, November 1975.

_____. *ACIR State Legislative Program.* Washington, D.C.: ACIR, November 1975.

_____. *The States and Intergovernmental Aids.* Washington, D.C.: ACIR, 1976.

_____. *Significant Features of Fiscal Federalism: 1976 Edition.* Washington, D.C.: ACIR, June 1976.

_____. *Changing Public Attitudes on Governments and Taxes, 1976.* Washington, D.C.: ACIR, July 1976.

_____. *Pragmatic Federalism: The Reassignment of Functional Responsibility.* Washington, D.C.: ACIR, July 1976.

_____. *State Actions in 1975.* Washington, D.C.: ACIR, July 1976.

_____. *Improving Urban America: A Challenge to Federalism.* Washington, D.C.: ACIR, September 1976.

_____. *Annual Reports.* Washington, D.C.: ACIR, published annually.

_____. *Intergovernmental Perspective.* Washington, D.C.: ACIR, published four times a year.

Alexander, Herbert E., and Kevin L. McKeough. *Financing Campaigns for Governor: New Jersey, 1965.* Princeton, N.J.: Citizens' Research Foundation (Study #16), 1966.

American Assembly, The. *The Forty-Eight States: Their Tasks as Policy Makers and Administrators.* New York: The American Assembly, Graduate School of Business, Columbia University, 1955.

_____. *State Legislatures in American Politics.* Englewood Cliffs, N.J.: Prentice-Hall, 1966.

Citizens' Conference on State Legislatures (now Legis 50). *The Sometime Governments: A Critical Study of the 50 American Legislatures.* New York: Bantam Books, 1971.

Council of State Governments. *The Book of the States.* Lexington, Ky.: Council of State Governments, published biennially.

_____. *Proceedings of the National Governors' Conference.* Lexington, Ky.: Council of State Governments, 1908-1974, published annually by the

Council of State Governments until the National Governors' Conference became an independent organization in 1975; since that time published annually by the National Governors' Conference.

_____. *The American Governors: Their Backgrounds, Occupations, and Governmental Experience.* Lexington, Ky.: Council of State Governments, published periodically.

_____. *The Governors of the American States, Commonwealths and Territories: Biographical Sketches and Portraits.* Lexington, Ky.: Council of State Governments, 1975. (Published periodically.)

_____. "Trends of State Government: As Indicated by the Governor's Messages." *State Government.* (Appear annually in the spring or summer issue.)

_____. *The Governor and Public Information: Selected Methods Employed by Governors' Offices in Communicating with the Public.* Lexington, Ky.: Council of State Governments, 1961.

_____. *Budgeting by the States.* Lexington, Ky.: The Council of State Governments, 1967.

_____. *National Governors' Conference, 1908-1968.* Lexington, Ky.: Council of State Governments, 1968.

_____. *Gubernatorial Transition in the States.* Lexington, Ky.: Council of State Governments, 1968 (revised 1972).

_____. *Issues in Gubernatorial Succession.* Lexington, Ky.: Council of State Governments, 1969.

_____. *Central Management in the States.* Lexington, Ky.: Council of State Governments, 1970.

_____. *The Governor: The Office and Its Powers.* Lexington, Ky.: Council of State Governments, 1972.

_____. *Cumulative Index to Suggested State Legislation, 1941-1973.* Lexington, Ky.: Council of State Governments, 1972.

_____. *Reorganization in the States.* Lexington, Ky.: Council of State Governments, 1972.

_____. *The Lieutenant Governor: The Office and Its Powers.* Lexington, Ky.: Council of State Governments, 1973.

_____. *The Governors of the States, 1900-1974.* Lexington, Ky.: Council of State Governments, 1974 (revised).

_____. *State Use of Electronic Data Processing.* Lexington, Ky.: Council of State Governments, 1974.

_____. *Budgetary Processes in the States (A Tabular Display).* Lexington, Ky.: Council of State Governments, 1975.

_____. "Innovations from the Laboratories of Democracy," *State Government News* (August 1976):2-3.

Gallup, George. *Gallup Opinion Index.: The Anatomy of Victory*, Report No. 42. Princeton, N.J.: Gallup International, December 1968.

Greenhill, H. Gaylon. *Labor Money in Wisconsin Politics, 1964.* Princeton, N.J.: Citizens' Research Foundation (Study #12), 1966.

Howard, S. Kenneth. *Changing State Budgeting.* Lexington, Ky.: Council of State Governments, 1973.

Keech, William R., and Donald R. Matthews. *The Party's Choice*, Studies in Presidential Selection #7. Washington, D.C.: The Brookings Institution, 1976.

Martin, James W. *Staffing the Office of the Governor.* Lexington, Ky.: Council of State Governments, 1971.

Moynihan, Daniel P. "The Future of Federalism," address given to the National Conference on Federalism in Action. Washington, D.C.: Advisory Commission on Intergovernmental Relations, February 22, 1975.

National Association of State Budget Officers. *Principles for State Executive Budget Offices.* Lexington, Ky.: Council of State Governments, 1975.

National Conference of Lieutenant Governors. *Biographical Sketches and Portraits.* Atlanta, Ga.: National Conference of Lieutenant Governors, issued annually.

National Education Association. *Rankings of the States.* Washington, D.C.: National Education Association, published annually.

National Governors' Conference (now National Governors' Association). *Meet the Governors.* Lexington, Ky.: Council of State Governments, 1973.

_____. *The State of the States.* Washington, D.C.: National Governors' Conference, 1974.

_____. *Innovations in State Government: Messages from the Governors.* Washington, D.C.: National Governors' Conference, June 1974.

_____. *States' Responsibilities to Local Governments: An Action Agenda.* Washington, D.C.: National Governors' Conference, August 1975.

_____. *The Critical Hundred Days: A Handbook for the New Governor.* Washington, D.C.: National Governors' Conference, 1975.

_____. *The States, Governors, and Policy Management.* Washington, D.C.: National Governors' Conference, Center for Policy Research and Analysis, 1975.

_____. *The National Economy and the Governors.* Washington, D.C.: National Governors' Conference, Center for Policy Research and Analysis, 1975.

_____. *Health Planning, Medical Care, and Medical Insurance.* Washington, D.C.: National Governors' Conference, Center for Policy Research and Analysis, 1975.

_____. *The Governors' Contribution to the Quest for National Energy Policy and Program.* Washington, D.C.: National Governors' Conference, Center for Policy Research and Analysis, 1975.

_____. *On Being Governor.* Washington, D.C.: National Governors' Conference, 1976.

_____. *Federal Roadblocks to Efficient State Government.* Washington, D.C.: National Governors' Conference, 1976.

_____. *The Proposed Fiscal '77 Federal Budget: Impact on the States.* Washington, D.C.: National Governors' Conference, February 1976.

_____. *Revenue Sharing and the States: An Impact Survey.* Washington, D.C.: National Governors' Conference, February 1976.

_____. *Fiscal Profile of the States.* Washington, D.C.: National Governors' Conference, June 1976.

_____. *Constraint and Concern: The Governors' State of the State Messages.* Washington, D.C.: National Governors' Conference, February 1976.

National Municipal League, Committee on State Government. *Model State Constitution with Explanatory Articles.* New York: National Municipal League, 1948.

Owens, John R. *Trends in Campaign Spending in California, 1958-1970: Tests of Factors Influencing Costs.* Princeton, N.J.: Citizens' Research Foundation (Study #22), 1973.

Rich, Bennett M. *State Constitutions: The Governor,* State Constitutional Studies Project, Series 11, No. 3. New York: National Municipal League, 1960.

Roady, Elston, and Carl D. McMurray. *Republican Campaign Financing in Florida, 1963-1967.* Princeton, N.J.: Citizens' Research Foundation (Study #15), 1969.

Sturm, Albert L. *Trends in State Constitution-Making, 1966-1972.* Lexington, Ky.: Council of State Governments, 1973.

Texas Research League. *Functions and Organization of the Office of Governor of Texas.* Austin, Tex.: Texas Research League, 1968.

Bibliographies

Beyle, Thad, and J. Oliver Williams (eds.). *The American Governor in Behavioral Perspective.* New York: Harper & Row, 1972. (Bibliography in appendix, 8 pp.)

Citizens' Conference on State Legislatures. "Selected Bibliography on State Legislatures." Kansas City, June 1968, 39 pp.

Council of State Governments. "Bibliography: Seminar for New Governors-Elect." Lexington, Ky.: The Council of State Governments, November 1970, 5 pp.

Herndon, James, Charles Press, and Oliver P. Williams (eds.). "A Selected Bibliography of Materials in State Government and Politics." Lexington: Bureau of Government Research, University of Kentucky, 1963, 143 pp.

Hoppes, Muriel. "State Government: An Annotated Bibliography." Chicago: Council of State Government, 1959, 46 pp.

Press, Charles. "Bibliography Introduction to American State Government and Politics'" East Lansing: Institute for Community Development and Services, Michigan State University, 1964, 34 pp.

Unpublished Materials

Botner, Stanley B. "The Office of Governor of Missouri." Unpublished Ph.D. dissertation, Department of Political Science, University of Missouri, Columbia, 1963.

Bradley, Leonard Keelon, Jr. "Gubernatorial Transition in Tennessee: The 1970-71 Experience." Unpublished M.A. thesis, University of Tennessee, Knoxville, 1973.

Coor, Lattie Finch, Jr. "The Increasing Vulnerability of the American Governor." Unpublished Ph.D. dissertation, Department of Political Science, Washington University, Seattle, 1964.

Gibson, Juanita M. "The Office of Governor in Florida." Unpublished Ph.D. dissertation, Department of Political Science, University of Michigan, Ann Arbor, 1958.

Guida, Joseph F. "Prisoner or Keeper?—The Management Styles of Two Virginia Governors." Unpublished undergraduate Honors Thesis, University of Virginia, Charlottesville, 1976.

Harvey, Richard B. "The Political Approach of Earl Warren, Governor of California." Unpublished Ph.D. dissertation, Department of Political Science, University of California at Los Angeles, 1959.

Holmes, Jack E. "Party, Legislation and Governor in the Politics of New Mexico, 1911-1963." Unpublished Ph.D. dissertation, Department of Political Science, University of Chicago, 1964.

Kessell, John H. "Road to the Mansion: A Study of the 1956 Gubernatorial Campaign in Ohio." Unpublished Ph.D. dissertation, Department of Political Science, Columbia University, New York, 1958.

Larson, Robert N. "The Governor's Council in New England." Unpublished Ph.D. dissertation, Department of Political Science, Boston University, 1960.

Lieberman, Carl. "The 1966 Gubernatorial Campaign in Pennsylvania: A Study of the Strategies and Techniques of the Democratic Candidate." Unpublished Ph.D. dissertation, Department of Political Science, University of Pittsburgh, 1969.

Mills, Warner, Jr. "Ross Sterling, Governor of Texas." Unpublished Ph.D. dissertation, Department of Political Science, Johns Hopkins University, Baltimore 1956.

Parker, Daisy. "An Examination of the Florida Executive." Unpublished Ph.D. dissertation, Department of Political Science, University of Virginia, Charlottesville, 1959.

Rollins, Overman R. "The Power to Persuade: A Study of the Governor of North Carolina." Unpublished undergraduate thesis, Department of Political Science, Duke University, Durham, N.C., 1965.

Schlesinger, Joseph A. "Emergence of Political Leadership: A Case Study of American Governors." Unpublished Ph.D. dissertation, Department of Political Science, Yale University, New Haven, Conn., 1955.

Young, Wayne F. "Oklahoma Politics: With Special Reference to the Election of Oklahoma's First Republican Governor." Unpublished Ph.D. dissertation, Department of Political Science, University of Oklahoma, Norman, 1964.

Zimmerman, James L. "The Office of Governor of New York: Its Development Under Nelson A. Rockefeller." Unpublished M.P.A. thesis, Baruch College of the City University of New York, 1972.

Index

Note: All those who have served at some point as governor appear in bold type.

nors, 21, 59(fn. 24), 77-78; as state legislators, 21

Blair, C. Stanley, 158(table)

block grants, federal, 174-177, 179, 188; organization and significance of, 177

Boggs, Caleb, 233(fn. g)

Bolack, Tom, 233(fn. g)

Bond, Christopher "Kit," 52(table), 79, 85, 141

Bonner, John, 113(table)

Border states, 25(table), 26, 27(table), 29, 30(table), 32(table), 33, 40(table), 43-44, 54, 103, 106(table), 117(table), 120, 123, 126-129, 141, 154, 163

Boren, David, 155

borrowing, state, 65, 108, 178

Boston (Massachusetts), 44

Breathitt, Edward, 52(table)

Brennan, William J., 72

Brewer, Albert P., 111(table)

Briscoe, Dolph, 161

Broder, David, 1, 89, 202, 204

Broderick, Raymond J., 158(table)

Brookings Institution, The, 177

Brooks, Darlene, 22

Brooks, Ralph, 22

Brown, Edmund G., Jr. (Jerry), 19, 29, 31, 33, 52(table), 61, 169(fn. 82), 203-205

Brown, Edmund G., Sr. (Pat), 19, 52(table), 108, 111(table), 155

Brown, John W., 233(fn. g)

Brown, Joseph, 14

Browning, Gordon, 52(table), 104, 114-115(table)

Bryan, Charles W., 197

Bryce, James (Lord), 5, 79

Brzezinski, Zbigniew, 204

Buckley v. Valeo, 161

Buckson, David P., 233(fn. g)

budget, executive, 63, 65, 70, 76, 78-79, 82, 84-86, 90, 98; legislative control of, 85; methods of, 85; selection of director of, 85

Budget and Accounting Act, 84

Bumpers, Dale, 52(table), 156, 157(table), 160, 233(fn. g)

Burch, Palmer, 50

Burney, Dwight W., 48

Burns, Haydon, 112(table)

Burns, John A., 52(table), 157(table), 160

Burroughs, John, 114(table)

Busbee, George, 161

business, 19; government as, 73; as occupation of governors, 23-24, 43, 55, 59(fn. 33, 34)

Byrd, Harry F., Jr., 154

Byrd, Harry F., Sr., 66, 99

Byrne, Brendan, 109

Byrnes, James F., 32, 39, 41, 42

cabinet, governor's, 67, 76

cabinet, U.S., 49, 174, 187; as post-gubernatorial career, 45-46, 55; as pre-gubernatorial career, 42; as pre-presidential office, 195, 200

Cahill, William T., 41, 52(table), 114(table)

California, 5, 19, 21, 24, 29, 33, 41, 43, 44, 47, 50, 52(table), 54, 66, 67, 80, 88, 100(table), 108, 109, 111(table), 122, 124-125(fig.), 132, 134(table), 138-139(table), 142, 155, 157(table), 160, 161, 167(fn. 54), 169 (fn. 82), 181, 187, 196, 197, 198, 203-205; lieutenant governor in, 76

Calloway, Howard "Bo," 15, 49-50

campaign finance. *See* finance, campaign

campaign gimmicks, 155

campaign management, 155-156

campaigns. *See* elections

campaign technology, 155-156, 162

candidate(s), 88; absence of black gubernatorial, 20-23, 59(fn. 24); campaign finance affecting, 154-162, 157-159(table); constitutional and statutory requirements for gubernatorial, 17-19; in contested elections, 15-17; election issues and, 107-122, 111-115(table), 116(table), 117(table); independent, 14, 15, 58(fn. 5), 97, 127(fig. fn.), 130(table, fn. a), 142, 153-154, 197, 199; informal requirements for gubernatorial, 17-19; presidential, 28, 140-141, 149, 181, 195-206; qualified voter requirement for, 18(table); ticket splitting affecting, 145-154; unsuccessful gubernatorial, 43-44, 49-50. *See also* elections, gubernatorial; party, Democratic; party, political; party, Republican

canvassing, 155

Carey, Hugh, 52(table), 54

Careys (of Wyoming), 19

Cargo, David F., 52(table)

Carlson, Frank, 52(table), 233(fn. g)

careers: correlating with education, 25; frequency trees of gubernatorial, 36-37(fig.), 38-39(fig.); of outstanding governors, 55-56, 57(table); post-gubernatorial, 44-50, 55-56, 57(table); pre-gubernatorial, 13, 23-24, 33-44, 36-37(fig.), 38-39(fig.), 40(table), 55, 56(table). *See also* occupations

Carter, Jimmy, 181; and Georgia reorganization, 68, 103; governorship of, 52(table), 103, 119, 204; 1970 election

106(table), 117(table), 119, 120, 123,
126-127, 128(table), 129, 141, 142,
144, 154, 155, 181
Notte, John, 110, 114(table)
Nunn, Louie, 110

oaths, religious, 17
O'Brien, Leo, Jr., 159(table)
O'Callaghan, Mike, 42, 52(table), 158(table)
occupations: of candidates, 19, 44; correlating with education, 25; of governors,
23-24, 55; of outstanding governors, 55.
See also careers
Ogilvie, Richard, 49, 52(table), 108,
112(table)
Ohio, 42, 48, 52(table), 74, 78, 84, 88, 98,
100(table), 104, 108, 114(table), 117,
124-125(fig.), 133, 136(table), 138-
139(table), 141, 158(table), 160, 187,
196, 198, 233(fn. g)
Oklahoma, 47, 49, 52(table), 69, 79,
100(table), 114(table), 124-125(fig.),
129, 130(table), 138-139(table), 141,
155, 158(table), 233(fn. g)
Olson, Jack B., 159(table)
ombudsman, 75
O'Neill, C. William, 114(table)
one-party states, 122, 129-132, 137,
138(table), 140, 143(fig.), 144(fig.), 145
Oregon, 19, 26, 46, 47, 51, 52(table), 54,
70, 74, 90, 100(table), 109, 114(table),
124-125(fig.), 132, 135(table), 138-
139(table), 140, 153, 154, 155,
158(table), 167(fn. 54), 181, 184, 203
outstanding governors, xiv, 42, 50-56,
57(table), 61(fn. 80), 155; definition of,
51, 53; party competition and, 145;
qualifications on list of, xiv, 51, 53-54;
tax issue and, 108-109; tenure and, 107

Paine, Thomas, 2
pardoning power, gubernatorial, 2-4
participation, voter. *See* turnout, voter
parties, third, 50, 132, 135(table, fn. a),
154, 197
party, American (Independent), 50, 197
party, American ("Know Nothing"), 154
party, anti-Masonic, 154
party competition, 97, 118-120, 122-145,
123(table), 124-125(fig.), 126(fig.),
127(fig.), 128(table), 130(table),
131(table), 134-135(table), 136(table),
138-139(table), 143(fig.), 144(fig.), 154,
156, 173, 186; causes of increased, 143-
145; in evenly-divided states, 133, 137,
139(table), 142-143, 144(fig.), 145;

modern classification of, 137-143,
144(fig.); in the normally Democratic or
Republican states, 132, 134-135(table),
137, 138(table), 140, 143(fig.),
144(fig.), 145; in the one-party states,
122, 129-132, 130(table), 131(table),
137, 138(table), 140, 143(fig.), 145;
qualifications concerning classification
of, 137; and ticket splitting paradox,
153; in two-party states, 133,
136(table), 137, 138-139(table), 141-
143, 143(fig.), 144(fig.), 145
party, Conservative, 146(table, fn. b)
party, Democratic, 19, 21, 22, 24, 30-31,
48, 49, 58(fn. 5) 77, 79, 109, 175, 184;
age of governors in, 32-33; and campaign
finances, 154-162; and election issues,
117(table), 120; elections won by, 14;
full participation rules of, 198; and independent voting, 145-154; in National
Governors' Association, 181; occupations of governors belonging to,
25(table), 26; outstanding governors in,
52-53(table), 54; and party competition,
122-145; and presidential politics, 195-
206; pre-gubernatorial careers of governors in, 40(table), 43; proportion of governors belonging to, 14, 16, 124-125(fig.);
religion of governors in, 28-29. *See also*
elections; party competition; party, political
party, Democratic-Farmer-Labor, 154
party, Dixiecrats, 197
party, Farmer-Labor, 135(table, fn. a), 154
party, Free Soil, 154
party, Greenback, 154
party, People's Independent, 154
party, political, 19, 24, 34, 102, 119, 172;
and campaign financing, 154-162; and
election issues, 109, 117(table), 120; and
gubernatorial patronage, 71-74; lack of
allegiance by young to, 164; loosening of
ties to, 145-154, 156; in National Governors' Association, 180-181; and party
competition, 122-145; as postgubernatorial activity, 49; as pre-
gubernatorial activity, 42-43; pre-
gubernatorial occupational difference
by, 24; and presidential politics, 195-
206; as source of friction in executive
branch, 70, 76; third, 50, 132,
135(table, fn. a), 154, 197; turnover in
governorships by, 127, 128(table). *See
also* candidates; elections; nomination,
party; party competition; party, Democratic; party, Republican

278

Proxmire, William, 50
Pryor, David, 52(table)
public financing (of campaigns), 162. *See also* finance, campaign
public service commission, state, 39
Pyle, Howard, 22, 111(table), 140

qualifications for gubernatorial candidacy. *See* requirements for gubernatorial candidacy
Quinn, William F., 52(table), 112(table), 233(fn. f)

race: of candidates, 19-21; of governors, 20-24
race issue, 15, 43, 48, 59(fn. 24), 104; and defeats of governors, 110, 111-115(table), 116(table), 117(table), 117-120, 140
Rampton, Calvin, 52(table), 73, 109, 132, 133, 137
ranching: as pre-gubernatorial career, 24
Rand Corporation, 85
Ranney, Austin, 137
Ransone, Coleman B., Jr., 6, 68, 86-87, 104, 123, 132, 155
Ravenel, Charles "Pug," 18
Ray, Dixy Lee, 22
Ray, Robert, 52(table), 73
Reagan, Ronald, 24, 31, 43, 109, 157 (table), 160, 181, 196, 198, 203, 205
reapportionment, 48, 64-65, 79-84, 90, 152, 185-186
recall, popular, 106-107
recognition, name. *See* name recognition
red tape, federal, 174-175
Reed, John, 113(table)
reelection eligibility of governors, 64, 86, 97-107, 108, 120, 202-203; affecting success of governors, 97, 118; arguments for and against, 99, 101-104; and political machines, 99; two-term limit on, 103-104, 118. *See also* term of office
referenda, 88, 109, 117, 165(fn. 12)
reform, penal, 8
reform, tax. *See* taxes
regions, U.S., xiii, 12(fig.), 24, 25(table), 26, 27(table), 29, 30(table), 32(table), 33, 40(table), 43-44, 46, 48, 54, 72, 73, 103, 104, 106, 117(table), 118-120, 122-123, 126-127, 128(table), 129, 140, 141, 142, 144, 154, 155, 156, 163-164, 180-181, 197, 203
registered electorate, 169(fn. 89)
registration, voter, 155, 164, 169(fn. 89)
religion, 59(fn. 42); of candidates, 19; of governors, 26-29, 30(table), 55; of out-

standing governors, 55, 61(fn. 80); restrictions on, of gubernatorial candidates, 17
reorganization, state, 63-65, 103, 173; modern sweep of, 66-68, 90, 186; need for, 6, 185
representatives, U.S., 20, 22, 164, 169(fn. 85), 206; former governors as, 45(table), 48, 57(table); as gubernatorial candidates, 41-42, 44. *See also* Congress, U.S.; House of Representatives, U.S.; Senate, U.S.
Republican party. *See* party, Republican
requirements for gubernatorial candidacy, 17-19; age, 17, 18(table), 32; ban on simultaneous office, 19; citizenship, 17, 18(table); criminal conviction ban, 18-19; nativity, 17; qualified voter, 18 (table); property, 17; religious, 17; residency, 18
residency requirements, 18
resignation, gubernatorial, 106-107, 233 (fn. a). *See also* lieutenant governor; vacancies
Reston, James, 1
revenue-sharing, federal, 122, 174-177, 179, 188; development of, 175-176; faults of, 176-177; National Governors' Association and, 181, 184; operation of, 176-177
reverse "coattail" effect, 149
Reynolds, John, 115(table), 116
Rhode Island, 17, 42, 46, 52(table), 65, 66, 98, 101(table), 109, 110, 114(table), 117, 124-125(fig.), 132, 134(table), 138-139(table), 141, 159(table), 160, 233(fn. g); contested election in, 16
Rhodes, James, 104
Ribicoff, Abraham, 45-46, 52(table)
Rich, Bennett, 64
right-to-work law, 117
Riley, Bob, 233(fn. g)
Roberts, Dennis J., 16, 52(table), 114 (table), 117
Roberts, Sam, 156
Rockefeller, Nelson A., 19, 31, 42, 45(table, fn. e), 52(table), 54, 109, 133, 156, 158 (table), 173, 176, 181, 197, 199, 206
Rockefeller, Winthrop, 19, 42, 52(table), 54, 65, 111(table), 140, 145, 156, 157 (table), 160
Rolvaag, Karl F., 16, 113(table)
Roman Catholic church: governors belonging to, 26-29; outstanding governors and, 55
Romney, George, 13, 43, 46, 52(table), 67, 68, 109, 149, 181; and his lieutenant

About the Author

Larry Sabato is a Rhodes Scholar and Danforth Fellow at Oxford University. He is a 1974 Phi Beta Kappa graduate of the University of Virginia. After graduate study at Princeton University's Woodrow Wilson School of Public and International Affairs, he received the Ph.D. degree in 1977 from Oxford University where he is now a lecturer in politics at New College. Dr. Sabato has written several books and monographs on his native state of Virginia and has served as a consultant for numerous governorship and congressional campaigns. He is the recipient of more than two dozen major scholarships and academic prizes and has lectured throughout Great Britain on American politics.